MICROSOFT® PROFESSIONAL EDITIONS

W9-AVH-637

Exclusively for Owners of the
Microsoft Windows NT Server Resource Kit
Version 4.0

Microsoft®
WindowsNT®
Server
ResourceKit
Version 4.0, Supplement One

Microsoft Press

PUBLISHED BY
Microsoft Press
A Division of Microsoft Corporation
One Microsoft Way
Redmond, Washington 98052-6399

Copyright © 1997 by Microsoft Corporation

All rights reserved. No part of the contents of this book may be reproduced or transmitted in any form or by any means without the written permission of the publisher.

Library of Congress Cataloging-in-Publication Data pending.

Printed and bound in the United States of America.

1 2 3 4 5 6 7 8 9   QMQM   2 1 0 9 8 7 6

Distributed to the book trade in Canada by Macmillan of Canada, a division of Canada Publishing Corporation.

A CIP catalogue record for this book is available from the British Library.

Microsoft Press books are available through booksellers and distributors worldwide. For further information about international editions, contact your local Microsoft Corporation office. Or contact Microsoft Press International directly at fax (206) 936-7329.

Microsoft, the Microsoft logo, Microsoft Press, the Microsoft Press logo, MS-DOS, Visual Basic, Win32, and Windows NT are registered trademarks and ActiveX and BackOffice are trademarks of Microsoft Corporation in the United States and/or other countries.

Other product and company names herein may be the trademarks of their respective owners.

Acquisitions Editor: Casey Doyle
Project Editor: Stuart J. Stuple

This book is dedicated to all who use and support Windows NT Server version 4.0.

Contributors to this book include the following:

Documentation Manager
Ken Western

Writing Manager
Peggy Etchevers

Technical Writers
June Blender Cahn, Maureen Carmichael, Peter Costantini, Jeff Howard, Jan Jolan James, Mitch Kief, Edward Lafferty, Cary Reinstein, Kate Robinson, Maureen Sullivan

Managing Editor
Sonia Marie Moore

Editing Lead
Shelly Hawkins

Technical Editors
Stephanie Briner, Miriam Harline, Kate Robinson, Sharon Schenck

Production Manager
Karye Cattrell

Production Lead
Nikole Faith

Production Team
Jay French, Cathy Pfarr, Jane Dow

Lead Graphic Designer
Chris Blanton

Design Support Team
Gabriel Varela, Sue Wyble, Jan Yeager

Software Program Manager
Ryan Marshall

Lead Software Developer
Martin Holladay

Software Tester
Cliff Hudson

Product Support Liaison
Todd Hafer

Technical Consultants
Reza Baghai, Bill Blomgren, Carl Calvello, Arren Conner, Lance Craig, Denise Y. Deng, Jerry Gallagher, James Gilroy, Scott Harrison, Chris Hawkins, Vic Horne, Joseph Hughes, Neel Jain, Murali Krishnan, Stuart Kwan, Edward Lafferty, Richard Lerz, David MacDonald, Rachid Ouchou, Cary Reinstein, Bob Ripley, Christophe Roberts, Bart Robertson, Craig Robicheaux, Rodger Seabourne, Nk Srinivas, Scott Suhy, David Treadwell, Brad Waters, Lester Waters, David Wohlferd, and numerous other hardworking Windows NT Developers, Program Managers, and Product Support Specialists

Contents

Part II   Optimizing IIS Server Performance

Figures and Tables

Tables

Introduction

Welcome to the *Microsoft® Windows NT® Server Resource Kit Supplement 1* book. The *Supplement 1* book supports use of Windows NT Server with a network and the Internet, and provides answers about issues Microsoft product support people consider timely and important. The in-depth, technical information in this book builds on information in the documentation for the Windows NT Server version 4.0 operating system and in the *Microsoft Windows NT Server Resource Kit version 4.0.* Some *Supplement 1* information also pertains to the *Microsoft Windows NT Workstation Resource Kit version 4.0.*

Supplement 1 includes a compact disc (CD) containing utilities for both Windows NT Workstation and Windows NT Server. The CD also provides an online version of the *Windows NT Workstation Resource Kit: Windows NT Workstation Resource Guide.*

About the Windows NT Server Supplement 1 Book

This book includes the following chapters and appendixes:

- Chapter 1, "Securing Your Web Site," discusses how features of Microsoft Internet Information Server (IIS) version 2.0 and Microsoft Windows NT Server 4.0 can combine to protect your World Wide Web site against intruders.

- Chapter 2, "Locating Network Resources," provides information about using a Microsoft Domain Name System (DNS) server to connect to the Internet and to identify your IIS sites for remote users.

- Chapter 3, "Adding Bandwidth for Internet Connectivity," introduces the new Internet telecommunications infrastructure, describes how to estimate your network's bandwidth requirements, and explains how to evaluate different options for providing an IIS connection to the Internet.

- Chapter 4, "Using ISDN," discusses how Windows NT Server provides built-in support for Integrated Services Digital Network (ISDN), a high-speed, fully digital telephone service you can use to connect to the Internet.

- Chapter 5, "Monitoring Virtual Memory," describes how Internet Information Server uses the Windows NT virtual memory system and suggests techniques for determining whether your server has enough physical memory to operate efficiently.

- Chapter 6, "Preventing Processor Bottlenecks," discusses some common causes of computer processor overload and several monitoring methods to avoid bottlenecks.

- Chapter 7, "Monitoring Bandwidth and Network Capacity," examines bandwidth and network capacity on an Internet Information Server and suggests methods to measure and improve transmission rates and connection handling.

- Chapter 8, "Effects of IIS Security Features on Performance," describes techniques to measure the performance overhead required by security features and ways to accommodate security requirements without impairing server performance.

- Chapter 9, "Monitoring Dynamic Page Generation," covers techniques for monitoring the Common Gateway Interface (CGI) and Internet Server Application Programming Interface (ISAPI), which are used to generate dynamic Web pages on Internet Information Server.

- Chapter 10, "Additional Network Services: Enterprise Level," describes the business reasons for selecting Directory Service Manager for NetWare and Web Administration for Windows NT Server at the fictitious Terra Flora Corporation, described in *Windows NT Server Resource Kit: Windows NT Server Networking Guide*.

- Appendix A, "Major Revisions to Existing Resource Kit Books," supplements and corrects errors in the *Windows NT Workstation Resource Guide* and *Windows NT Server Networking Guide*, covering major changes that will not be incorporated into reprinted editions of these books.

- Appendix B, "Minor Revisions to Existing Resource Kit Books," lists the changes to be incorporated into reprints of *Windows NT Server Resource Kit* and *Windows NT Workstation Resource Kit* books.

The *Supplement 1* book also provides a glossary that consolidates several earlier *Windows NT Resource Kit* glossaries.

Resource Kit Compact Disc

The *Supplement 1* CD contains information resources, tools, and utilities that make networking and working with Windows NT even easier than before. This new CD replaces all previous ones.

Note The utilities on this CD are designed and tested for the U.S. version of Windows NT 4.0. Use of these utilities with any other version of Windows NT may cause unpredictable results.

Two major items included on the *Supplement 1* CD are a Help file of Performance Monitor counter descriptions and a Help file with explanations and suggested user actions for the majority of the messages included in Windows NT 4.0. This Windows NT Messages Help file also includes new messages from various Windows NT components, including Internet Information Server and DNS.

Updates to these files and others will be provided, when available, on the Microsoft Web site for the Windows NT Resource Kits. For the exact site address, as well as the addresses of other Microsoft information sites, see the Rktools.hlp file.

After installing the *Windows NT Server Resource Kit*, please refer first to the following three files:

- The Readme.wri file, which contains a complete list of all the tools and utilities on the *Supplement 1* CD and additional setup instructions for some of them.

- The Rkdocs.hlp file, which provides a single entry point for all of the major components of the Resource Kit's online documentation.

- The Rktools.hlp file, which provides an overview of the Resource Kit tools and utilities and basic instructions on how to use many of them, along with links to additional documentation and, in some cases, to the program files.

The most current corrections to these tools and utilities and their documentation, as well as the POSIX and Perl source code files, are available on the Internet at the following Microsoft FTP site:

ftp://ftp.microsoft.com/bussys/winnt/winnt-public/reskit/nt40/

The following notes describe some of the enhancements made to the existing tools and utilities, and introduce new tools and utilities added for this *Supplement 1* release:

- The Network Connections tool, Netcons.exe, enables you to click on a taskbar icon to view a list of all mapped network connections. You can double-click a listed connection to start an instance of a command prompt window or Windows Explorer.

- The LinkCheck tool, Linkck.exe, tests all the hypertext markup language (HTML) links in a page, directory, or Web site. LinkCheck features a graphical user interface.

- Microsoft Desktops, Desktops.exe, now includes an improved user interface along with a desktop creation wizard and other new features.

- The second beta version of our Telnet Server, Telnetd.exe, provides major enhancements including an easier installation process, greater manageability, and improved performance.

- The CACLS tool, Cacls.exe, now enables you to set from the command line all options offered through File Manager or Windows Explorer.

- The telephony application programming interface (TAPI) Heartbeat Monitor tool, Tapihart.exe, monitors telephony servers. It checks to ensure the telephony server is functioning and provides basic usage information.

- The Microsoft Index Server works with Windows NT Server 4.0 and Internet Information Server 2.0 to provide your organization with access to all documents stored on your intranet or Internet site. Using Index Server, you can perform full-text searches and retrieve all types of information from any Web browser in just about any format. You can also use Index Server to create customized query forms and search-results pages, optimize your query service, query in seven different languages, and write content filters. In addition, Index Server performs automatic self-maintenance.

- The Windows NT Registry Entry Help file, Regentry.hlp, has been updated with new entries; see especially the entries for Internet Information Server.

Resource Kit Support Policy

The SOFTWARE supplied in the *Windows NT Server Resource Kit* is not officially supported. Microsoft does not guarantee the performance of the *Windows NT Server Resource Kit* tools, response times for answering questions, or bug fixes to the tools. However, we do provide a way for customers who purchase the *Windows NT Server Resource Kit* to report bugs and receive possible fixes for their issues. You can do this either by sending Internet mail to Rkinput@Microsoft.com or by referring to one of the options listed in the *Windows NT Server Start Here* book, which is included with your Windows NT Server product. This electronic mail address is only for *Windows NT Server Resource Kit* related issues.

The SOFTWARE (including instructions for its use and all printed and online documentation) is provided "AS IS" without warranty of any kind. Microsoft further disclaims all implied warranties, including, without limitation, any implied warranties of merchantability or of fitness for a particular purpose. The entire risk arising out of the use or performance of the SOFTWARE and documentation remains with you.

In no event shall Microsoft, its authors, or anyone else involved in the creation, production, or delivery of the SOFTWARE be liable for any damages whatsoever (including, without limitation, damages for loss of business profits, business interruption, loss of business information, or other pecuniary loss) arising out of the use of or inability to use the SOFTWARE or documentation, even if Microsoft has been advised of the possibility of such damages.

PART I

Connecting to the Internet with IIS Server

C H A P T E R   1

Securing Your Web Site

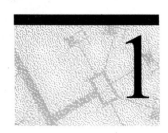

A home page on the World Wide Web represents an open invitation to every Internet user. With the increase in numbers of corporate Web sites (a twofold increase from 1995 to 1996, according to International Data Corporation), technology professionals must learn to guard their networks against Internet-borne intruders.

A vigilant system administrator might feel safe in providing Gopher and File Transfer Protocol (FTP) services. But when implementing the World Wide Web (WWW) service, the system administrator has to confront several questions:

- How secure is a corporate network that has a Web site?
- Can someone on the Internet intercept and copy a user's ID and password?
- Is a site that allows anonymous users truly secure?

This chapter answers these questions and describes how Windows NT Server and Internet Information Server (IIS) combine to provide a thoroughly integrated security solution for their Internet services.

This chapter focuses on Internet Information Server version 2.0 and Windows NT Server version 4.0 and includes the following sections:

- "Using Built-in Windows NT Server Security"
- "How Internet Information Server Security Works"
- "Using Internet Service Manager Security Features"
- "Using SSL to Safeguard Transmitted Data"
- "Using Internet Services Application Program Interface (ISAPI) Security Functions"
- "Guarding Against SYN Attacks"

Using Built-in Windows NT Server Security

Windows NT Server has powerful security features that protect server files against external attack. However, before setting up Internet Information Server, the Windows NT Server administrator should take these security steps:

- Disable floppy disk booting.
- Stipulate that users cannot share logons and passwords.
- Follow proper password creation guidelines.
- Rename the Administrator account and use the account lockout feature.
- Keep the Guest account disabled.
- Review user permission levels.
- Implement a logon screen with a notice prohibiting unauthorized access and use.

You always need to explain to your users that they have security responsibilities. Users must have passwords and renew them at a set interval. You must make it known that users are not permitted to share user IDs and passwords. At the same time, you must also state that your network is meant for your company to conduct its business, and that any other use of its software and hardware is discouraged. Users should then acknowledge their responsibilities, either in a written or an electronic form. By doing this, you clearly demonstrate that your company is protecting its information assets. This acknowledgment helps you protect your company's right to legal recourse against anyone who causes malicious damage to its data resources. Legal notices on logon screens are a way that you can gain this important acknowledgment from external users. You should also post legal notices for Internet users on your Web page.

For more information on displaying legal notices for a user of Windows NT, see the section "Displaying a Legal Notice Before Logon" in Chapter 6, "Windows NT Security," in the *Windows NT Workstation Resource Kit: Windows NT Workstation Resource Guide.*

Windows NT Server Security Features

Windows NT Server incorporates the features found in the Department of Defense *Trusted Computer System Evaluation Criteria (TCSEC)* Division C Controlled Access Protection, called C2 for short.

Table 1.1 compares C2 criteria with Windows NT Server features.

Table 1.1   C2 Criteria and Windows NT Server Equivalent

C2 Criteria	Windows NT Server feature
Discretionary Access Control	Access Control List.
Object Reuse	NTFS-deleted files cannot be undeleted.
	Data in memory is not left behind to be reused.
Auditing	Windows NT Server logs identify users and actions.
User Identification and Authentication	Logon and password.
Protection	Memory and files are protected by NTFS; they cannot be accessed directly.
	Kernel runs in 32-bit protected mode.

For more information on how to set up your computer according to the TCSEC C2 requirements, see the *Microsoft Windows NT Administrator's Security Guide*.

Windows NT Server gives you comprehensive protection against Internet intruders at the file level with an Access Control List (ACL) and a user ID and password requirement. Other security features work behind the scenes to keep the data in your server's memory secure. Finally, you always have the ability to track users.

Access Control Lists (ACLs)

Windows NT Server protects information resources by requiring assigned user accounts and password authentication. A system administrator can control access to these resources by defining a user's access level. Perhaps the greatest advantage of integrating the Internet Information Server with Windows NT Server is that there is no need to duplicate a directory of user accounts. Internet Information Server uses the Windows NT Server directory database of user accounts.

In the Windows NT Server File System (NTFS), the system administrator adds a user to an Access Control List. The ACL allows the user to access a file, and at the same time, the ACL can prevent the user from copying or executing a file.

Note Internet Information Server always uses the identity of the WWW or FTP client before attempting to access a file or program. (If anonymous access is being used, then the WWW server uses the IUSR_*computername* account.) For better security and flexibility than you can get with FAT partitions, use an NTFS partition for all Internet services — WWW, FTP, and Gopher — and for all virtual directories.

Because client applications need access to server directories to load dynamic-link libraries (DLLs), an incorrectly configured Access Control List can result in unavailable files and resources. Therefore, when designing your IIS services, always keep in mind the full range of data files and DLLs that a user might need. If you set up directories that contain the necessary files for your users and assign the directory and folders the correct level of NTFS permissions, you can guarantee security while providing uninterrupted service to your users.

Access Control Entries (ACEs)

Each Access Control List is made up of Access Control Entries (ACEs). An ACE specifies that a user or group of users has access or auditing permissions for a file or resource. There are three ACE types—two for discretionary access control and one for system security.

The discretionary ACEs are AccessAllowed and AccessDenied. These explicitly grant and deny access to a user or group of users. NTFS always processes an AccessDenied ACE before an AccessAllowed ACE. The first AccessDenied ACE that denies a user access to a resource causes the ACEs to cease further processing.

The Windows NT Server operating system reserves system security ACEs for its own use. For example, SystemAudit is a system security ACE that Windows NT Server uses to log security events. These events range from identifying users who access particular files to generating and logging security audit messages.

How Internet Information Server Security Works

Internet Information Server security builds on the security available with Windows NT Server 4.0. Every connection request that Internet Information Server receives must undergo a rigorous, step-by-step validation process. The Internet Information Server security process is responsible for:

1. Checking the source IP address.

2. Identifying and authenticating Internet users.

3. Assigning logon modes.

4. Allowing access by using NTFS.

Figure 1.1 illustrates how this process works.

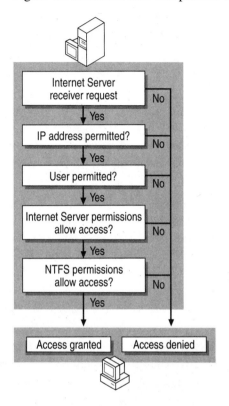

Figure 1.1   How Internet Information Server verifies each Internet connection request

In addition, Windows NT Server applications can have Common Gateway Interface (CGI) and ISAPI extensions that require additional logon and password requirements. (For more information on CGI and ISAPI, see "Using ISAPI Security Functions," later in this chapter.)

It is also important to note that each Internet service — WWW, Gopher, and FTP — has different security requirements. When you set up an Internet server, it is best to review which services you plan to provide and to install only those services.

For more installation and configuration information, see the *Microsoft Internet Information Server Installation and Administration Guide*. For a detailed discussion on Internet security, see Chapter 3, "Server Security on the Internet," in the *Microsoft Windows NT Server Resource Kit: Windows NT Server Internet Guide*.

Checking the Source IP Address

You can configure Internet Information Server to grant access to specific IP addresses and subnet masks. In this way, you allow only specific users to access your Internet server. At the same time, by specifying IP addresses, you can prevent entire networks or an individual site from accessing your server. This technique is especially useful to block an address from which you have logged a volume of suspicious activity.

Internet Information Server checks the source IP address of every received packet against the settings you specified on the **Advanced** tab of the **WWW Service Properties** dialog box. You can use that dialog box to set separate IP address access restrictions for each Internet Information Server service.

Note If your Internet server is attached to a proxy server or firewall, your source IP address emanates from the proxy server or firewall. In such cases, your filter must distinguish an external source IP address from the source IP address of your firewall or proxy server. Set your system to log and restrict any incoming packet with an external source IP address that exactly matches your internal proxy server and firewall source address. Such packets usually indicate that an Internet user is "spoofing" (mimicking) your source IP address in an attempt to gain access to your network.

Configuring Internet Information Server IP Settings

Configuring your Internet server to grant or deny access to a specific source IP address or subnet mask is a simple procedure in Internet Information Server. And it provides a very effective first-level barrier against unauthorized users.

▶ **To configure the Internet Information Server IP settings**

1. In the Internet Service Manager, choose the service. From the **Properties** menu, click **Properties**, and then click **Service Properties**. Click the **Advanced** tab. (For an example, see Figure 1.2.)

2. In the **IP Address** box, type the IP address or subnet mask to which you want to grant or deny access, then click **Add**.

3. Select **Denied Access** or **Granted Access**, then click **OK**.

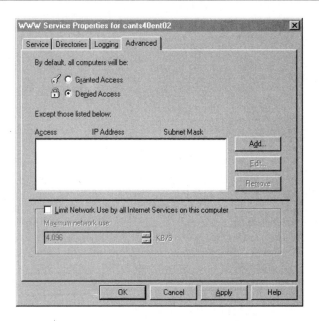

Figure 1.2   Using the Advanced tab of the WWW Service Properties dialog box to grant or deny access

Although you can set access control for each Internet service by specifying an IP address, you cannot do so for individual virtual directories. If you need to set IP address restrictions on an individual virtual directory, you must either design an ISAPI filter or purchase one from a third party. An ISAPI filter can examine the request source's Uniform Resource Locator (URL), mapped directory path, or source IP address, and then grant or deny access to the virtual directory. For more information, see "Using ISAPI Security Functions," later in this chapter.

Identifying and Authenticating Internet Users

For successful user identification, authentication, and logon, Internet Information Server goes through a five-step process. During this process, Internet Information Server checks that:

1. The supplied user name and password are valid.

2. There are no specific account restrictions in place.

3. The account is not disabled or locked out.

4. The account password has not expired.

5. The user is following the correct logon protocol, either local or network.

Of the five situations listed above, the last — using an incorrect logon protocol — is the most common reason that a user cannot access the WWW or FTP service. (The Gopher service only requires anonymous authentication.) For more information on authentication, see Chapter 3, "Server Security on the Internet," in the *Windows NT Server Internet Guide*.

Assigning Logon Modes

On a computer running Windows NT Server, users who do not belong to the Administrators group also do not, by default, have the Log on Locally user right. In the case of FTP or WWW basic authentication, Internet Information Server attempts by default to log the user on as a local user. With Internet Information Server 2.0 or later, you can change the default logon method by changing the Registry setting, unless the **Windows NT Challenge / Response** option is checked in the **Service Properties** dialog box. (Although you should change system configuration by using administrative tools whenever you can, some logon mode settings can be changed only by modifying Registry values.)

Warning   To add or modify a Registry value entry, use administrative tools such as Control Panel or System Policy Editor whenever possible. Using a Registry editor (Regedit or Regedt32) to change a value can have unforeseen effects, including changes that can prevent you from starting your system.

Logon Modes in Internet Information Server

Registry value entries for the WWW service are located in the following Registry path:

HKEY_LOCAL_MACHINE\System
    \CurrentControlSet
        \Services
            \W3SVC
                \Parameters

That value entry that controls logon is **LogonMethod**:

LogonMethod   REG_DWORD   0 | 1 | 2

Table 1.2 explains what the numerical values for **LogonMethod** represent. (For more information on how logon modes work with authentication and user accounts in the IIS services, see Table 1.3, "Services, Authentication, Logon Mode, and Accounts," later in this section.)

Table 1.2   Logon Mode Registry Values

Value	Logon Mode	Definition
0 (default)	Log on Locally	A local user: logon password required.
1	Log on as Batch	Similar to local, except the user is logged off after a process or thread completes.
2	Log on as Network	Remote, network, user: accepts cryptographic verification.

Registry value entries for the FTP service are located in the following Registry path:

HKEY_LOCAL_MACHINE\System
   \CurrentControlSet
      \Services
         \MSFTPSVC
            \Parameters

Registry value entries for the Gopher service are located in the following Registry path:

HKEY_LOCAL_MACHINE\System
   \CurrentControlSet
      \Services
         \GOPHERSVC
            \Parameters

Allowing Access by Using NTFS

After a user logs on, Windows NT Server associates the user with a set of credentials. These credentials are used to create the user's Security Context. The Security Context defines the user's logon mode. The logon mode then determines how NTFS allows the user access to files. Windows NT Server supplies a special user account that corresponds to each Internet service.

Table 1.3 lists the default authentication methods and logon modes and their corresponding Windows NT Server user accounts.

Table 1.3   Services, Authentication, Logon Mode, and Accounts

Service	Authentication Method	Default Logon Mode	Windows NT User Account
WWW	None (Anonymous)	Local	WWW anonymous account (typically IUSR_*computername*)
WWW	HTTP Basic	Local	Specified by Web user
WWW	Windows NT Server challenge / response	Always network	Specified by Web user
WWW	Windows NT Server challenge / response (as a Guest account)	Local	WWW anonymous account if Guest access is enabled (typically IUSR_*computername*)
FTP	Anonymous	Local (Change to network recommended)*	FTP anonymous account (typically IUSR_*computername*)
FTP	FTP user name / password	Local (Change to network recommended)*	Specified by FTP user
Gopher	None (always Anonymous)	Local (Change to network recommended)*	FTP anonymous account (typically IUSR_*computername*)

* Preferred because Windows NT Server accepts cryptographic validation.

In the local and batch logon modes, Windows NT Server requires the user's actual password, except for anonymous accounts. In the network logon mode, Windows NT Server accepts cryptographic validation. To make sure that users with local and batch logon modes are configured correctly, you can create a new user group, such as Web Users, and grant the local and batch rights to that group.

Anonymous User Account

Anonymous authentication handles client requests that do not contain a user name and password. Each Internet Information Server service maintains a Windows NT Server user name and password for these anonymous requests. You can view and set an anonymous logon user account in the Internet Service Manager **Service Properties** dialog box.

During setup, Internet Information Server creates the IUSR_*computername* account for anonymous connections. For example, if the server name is SERVER1, the default anonymous user name is IUSR_SERVER1.

Internet Information Server Setup creates the same anonymous logon user account for all Internet services. But Internet services can use either the same anonymous account or different accounts.

In the Windows NT Server security model, every user account has a unique security ID (SID). Windows NT Server tracks permissions through the SIDs. Permissions are recorded within an Access Control List.

For anonymous requests, NTFS grants permission based on the request's Access Control List. If the ACL does not assign these permissions to the anonymous logon user, then the request fails. If the server file does not grant permissions to an anonymous user account, you can eliminate the chance that an intruder might access a server file by selecting only the **Allow Anonymous** option in the **WWW Service Properties** dialog box.

You can set the Internet Information Server WWW service to respond to failed anonymous requests by selecting the **Windows NT Server Challenge / Response** option in the **Service Properties** dialog box. In this case, the server asks for a Windows NT Server user name and password. An intruder can take advantage of this to gain access to a server.

Because the Gopher service offers a published menu, it requires only anonymous authentication. You should configure FTP and Gopher users for the network logon mode. However, the FTP and WWW services also provide file and data transfer, which requires a higher level of anonymous security.

Note   Do not use the network logon mode if you are using a remote SQL Server with Integrated Security, or any other second-level server that requires authentication. Although the network logon mode allows a user to access the primary Internet server, the primary Internet server is unable to authenticate the user for a remote or second-level server.

WWW Service Security

Servers that host Web sites allow Internet users to launch server applications and extract data. For the system administrator, the interaction between the client browser and the Web site presents the most challenging security problem.

Several scenarios can occur:

- The WWW service receives a user name and password.

    When the WWW service receives a client request with a user name and password, it does not use the anonymous logon user account. Instead, the WWW service first processes the user name and password. Then, if the service does not grant permission to access the requested resource, the service generates a message and sends it back to the client.

- The WWW service receives an anonymous request that does not have specific permissions.

    An anonymous WWW service request fails when the anonymous logon user account does not have permission to access the desired resource. The WWW service response to the client indicates which authentication scheme the WWW service supports. If the response indicates that the WWW service supports hypertext transfer protocol (HTTP) Basic authentication, most Web browsers display a dialog box in which the user can enter a name and password. The Web browser then reissues the request with credentials that include the user name and password.

- The Web browser connecting to the WWW service supports Windows NT Server challenge/response.

    The scenario is different when a Web browser supports the Windows NT challenge/response authentication protocol and the WWW service also supports this protocol. In this case, if an anonymous request to the WWW service fails because it lacks adequate permissions, the Web browser then automatically uses the Windows NT challenge/response authentication protocol. The browser sends a user name and encrypted password from the client to the service. The WWW service reprocesses this client request with the user name and encrypted password.

- The WWW service supports basic authentication and Windows NT Server challenge/response.

A more complicated security process can occur when the WWW service supports basic authentication and Windows NT challenge/response. When this happens, the WWW service returns both authentication methods to the browser in a hypertext markup language (HTML) header. The browser reads the HTML header to choose an authentication method. If the header lists the Windows NT challenge/response protocol first and the browser supports this protocol, the browser uses it. A browser that does not support the challenge/response protocol uses basic authentication. Currently, Windows NT Server challenge/response authentication is supported only by Internet Explorer version 2.0 or later.

Using Internet Service Manager Security Features

You use the Internet Service Manager interface (shown in Figure 1.3) to administer WWW, Gopher, and FTP services.

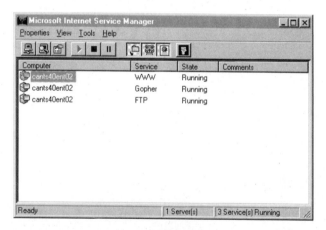

Figure 1.3   Internet Service Manager

You can use the Internet Service Manager to administer security, and also to configure Secure Sockets Layer (SSL) keys and initiate secure communication through a WWW service connection.

Setting Security Properties

You can select an Internet service and change its properties; these properties include security options. The section "Checking the Source Address," earlier in this chapter, described how to configure Internet Information Server to check source IP addresses. In addition, you can specify in the Internet Service Manager **Service Properties** dialog box that passwords are encrypted before they are transmitted. Because the Windows NT security model is built into the Internet Service Manager, you can authorize users to administer your Internet services and you can authorize users to grant read and write permissions to directories.

Note To keep others from viewing your directory structure and naming convention, leave the **Directory Browsing Allowed** box in the **WWW Service Properties** dialog box in its default, unselected mode.

The **Service Properties** dialog box contains a **Logging** property sheet that controls important aspects of your Internet server's log. You can set your log's format, either in a standard or National Center for Supercomputing Applications (NCSA) format. You can also set new logs to open automatically at specified intervals or when the log reaches a certain size. The log records valuable information about your Internet server, which includes a client's user name, IP address, and what operation the client performed on which computer. The log even records which files the client accessed.

Authentication Options

For the WWW service, you can choose any or all of these Internet Service Manager authentication options in the **Service Properties** dialog box:

- **Allow Anonymous**

  When you select this box, the WWW service processes anonymous connections and uses the anonymous logon user name and password for these connections. When you clear this box, the WWW service rejects all anonymous connections. In this case, the WWW service uses the basic or Windows NT challenge/response authentication protocol to access the resource.

- **Basic (clear text)**

  When you select this box, the WWW service processes requests by using basic authentication.

  Warning This check box is cleared by default for security reasons. Basic authentication sends Windows NT Server user names and passwords across the network without encryption.

- **Windows NT Challenge/Response**

  This box is selected by default. It sets the WWW service to use the Windows NT challenge/response protocol to honor requests by clients to send user account information. This protocol uses encrypted passwords for secure transmission. Windows NT challenge/response authentication works only with version 2.0 and later of Internet Explorer for Windows NT and Windows 95. For more details on when the server automatically uses challenge/response, see the "WWW Service Security" section earlier in this chapter.

The FTP service options include:

- **Allow Anonymous Connections**

  When you select this box, the user enters the user name "Anonymous." The FTP service processes these connections for the Windows NT user account specified in the FTP **Service Properties** dialog box. When you clear this box, users must enter valid Windows NT user names and passwords to log on to the FTP service.

- **Allow only anonymous connections**

  When you select this box, the FTP service rejects user logons with a user name other than Anonymous.

Warning   The FTP service sends Windows NT Server user names and passwords across the network without encryption. For security, this box is cleared by default.

The Gopher service allows only anonymous connections.

Using SSL to Safeguard Transmitted Data

Digital packets transmitted between Web browser and Web server by using Transmission Control Protocol/Internet Protocol (TCP/IP) are susceptible to unauthorized interception. In the case of anonymous access, such as in most Gopher or FTP service requests, this is not an issue. However, you usually secure your data transmission when you are conducting confidential business transactions that involve sensitive financial information or electronic correspondence.

There is no standard way to secure the FTP or Gopher service. You can use the Secure Sockets Layer protocol in Internet Information Server to transmit your encrypted information through the WWW service. This gain in security will cost processor performance, however.

The Secure Sockets Layer protocol provides data privacy, integrity, and authentication in a point-to-point connection between a Web browser and a Web server. Internet Information Server can send and receive private communication across the Internet with a browser that supports SSL. (SSL is based on a combination of public key and symmetric key cryptography, in addition to digital signature and certificate technology.)

Browser and server, although they have never before communicated with each other, can transmit encrypted data by using an agreed-upon method, a cryptographic key pair. By using digital signatures, each party can positively identify the other.

For international communications, you must limit your SSL key to 512 bits. The 1024-bit and 768-bit key options cannot be used internationally. For more information on SSL, see Chapter 3, "Server Security on the Internet," in the *Windows NT Server Internet Guide*, and the online *Windows NT Server Microsoft Internet Information Server Installation and Administration Guide*.

Both the browser and the server use an SSL security handshake to initiate a secure TCP/IP connection. The client and server agree on the level of security they will use and how to fulfill authentication requirements for their connection. After the handshake, the only role of SSL is to encrypt and decrypt the WWW service byte stream. The WWW service and the Web browser encrypt all the information in both request and response, including:

- The URL the client is requesting.
- Any submitted form contents, such as credit card numbers.
- Any WWW service user names and passwords.
- All data the server sends back to the client.

To maintain the performance level of your computer running Windows NT Server, consider using SSL only for highly sensitive information such as credit card transactions. Presently, SSL-encrypted transmissions are slower than unencrypted transmissions. As a consequence, Web server performance levels drop because of the encryption.

During the SSL session setup, browsers usually generate multiple threads reading from the server. This means that a client can initiate three or four session setups simultaneously that amount to nearly a quarter of a second of real processor time (3sessions x 85 milliseconds). During the SSL session setup, the initial private-key process takes approximately 85 milliseconds of real processor time for a 1024-bit key. Adding to this processor time are the interrupts for new packets and the input/output completion.

Once the server starts encrypting the stream back to the client, the overhead is 14 to 18 instructions per byte, depending on the architecture. Also, the maximum window size of an SSL encapsulated message is only 16K. The server cannot send larger, more efficient streams of data back to the client. Also, this SSL activity takes place in user mode, thus preventing the server from using TransmitFile or other fast APIs to send the data.

For more information on maximizing server performance, see Chapter 6, "Preventing Processor Bottlenecks," later in this book.

Using ISAPI Security Functions

The Internet Server Application Programming Interface (ISAPI) provides security functions for Windows NT Server and the Internet Information Server Database Connector. Because ISAPI figures prominently in Windows NT Server, this section discusses the advantages of ISAPI over the Common Gateway Interface (CGI), the differences between an ISAPI application and filter, and how to install an ISAPI filter in Windows NT Server.

CGI and ISAPI

The Common Gateway Interface is one method that a Web browser can use to run an application on your server. You can write a CGI application in a script and run it through a Perl interpreter; or you can compile the application in C/C++.

Windows NT Server relies on ISAPI instead of CGI as a method to efficiently request information from other applications. Unlike CGI, an ISAPI application exists as a dynamic-link library rather than an executable program. The ISAPI DLL is a communication pipe between Internet Information Server and an Internet service. The WWW service loads ISAPI DLLs when needed.

An ISAPI application can also take advantage of the Win32 API and the Open Database Connectivity (ODBC) standard. An ISAPI application provides better performance because it takes advantage of memory pointers and does not have to be restarted to process new data requests.

If multiple clients request dynamic content that can be supplied by one ISAPI DLL, then the WWW service loads the DLL only once. It unloads the DLL from memory if it goes unused for a long period. The advantage to loading an ISAPI DLL once is that the DLL is loaded in the WWW service process, and the Web server's performance improves when it does not have to switch among multiple processes. The Web server also does not need to create and destroy new processes.

When loaded, the ISAPI DLL code is part of the WWW service and the ISAPI application then acts as an extension.

The Internet Information Server works with two types of ISAPI DLLs:

- ISAPI applications are add-ons that permit dynamic content generation and, when requested, explicit content generation. Explicit pages reside on a Web server; dynamic pages are not assembled until the client requests them. For more information, see Chapter 9, "Monitoring Dynamic Page Generation."
- ISAPI filters add themselves to the path between the client and the server. An ISAPI filter modifies or monitors all input and output and is able to change the behavior of the server. (See Figure 1.4.)

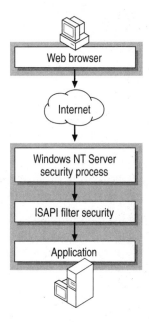

Figure 1.4   The ISAPI filter can provide an additional security barrier

Installing an ISAPI Filter

Internet Information Server uses ISAPI filters to monitor HTTP transactions and to authenticate users. Before Internet Information Server can load these filters, they must be added to the W3SVC key in the Registry. After they are added, Internet Information Server loads these ISAPI filters automatically when the WWW service starts.

▶ **To install an ISAPI filter**

1. Copy the filter DLL to an appropriate subdirectory, such as Scripts or Cgi-Bin.

2. Run **Regedt32.exe**.

3. Add the full path of the filter DLL to this Registry path:

   HKEY_LOCAL_MACHINE\System
     \CurrentControlSet
       \Services
         \W3SVC
           \Parameters
             \Filter DLLs

Note If there is more than one filter DLL file, separate them with commas. For example:

```
c:\Inetsrv\Server\Sspifilt.dll,c:\Inetsrv\Scripts\Myfilter.dll
```

The security precautions you must take for ISAPI Scripts subdirectories are similar to the permissions you have in place for Cgi-Bin subdirectories. Always review who has write permission to the ISAPI Scripts and Cgi-Bin subdirectories.

Guarding Against SYN Attacks

A *SYN attack* refers to an intruder proliferating SYN (synchronizing character) messages in a malicious attempt to deny users access to a server by generating an overwhelming amount of half-open Transmission Control Protocol (TCP) port connections.

You can prevent Internet "mail bombings" — unwanted incoming mass electronic messages — by judicious use of IP address settings and permissions. However, protecting your Web site against SYN attacks is not so simple.

How SYN Attacks Happen

In a normal message exchange, a client initiates access to your server by contacting your system. The client first sends a SYN message; your server responds to the client with a SYN-ACK message. Your server retains this half-open TCP port connection until the client returns an ACK (acknowledgment) message and establishes a connection.

A SYN attack (also called "SYN flooding") occurs when your server receives a SYN message with an incorrect source IP address. Your system responds with a SYN-ACK message and waits for an ACK reply that never arrives.

In the meantime, the intruder sends more SYN messages with incorrect IP addresses. Your server sets up a queue for each of these half-open connections.

Although your server can eventually become hindered in responding to legitimate users, these queues are small and do not necessarily place extraordinary demands on your server's processing capacity. But during a SYN attack, a given TCP port reaches its limit of half-open connections and, until resources are freed up, responds to further connection requests with a port reset. Thus, the intentional proliferation of half-open connections can prevent legitimate users from gaining access to the attacked server. This can shut down operations for an organization dependent on access by Internet, such as an Internet service provider.

How to Prevent SYN Attacks

SYN attacks take advantage of the Transmission Control Protocol and do not exploit any inherent weakness in Windows NT Server. SYN attacks are not harmful to your information resources, but they can tie up your Internet service in a destructive way.

To prevent SYN attacks, first you must ensure that your network is not a source of SYN attacks. To do this, set the filter attached to your proxy server or firewall to examine packets and prevent them from going out if their source address is not the same as your network address.

At the same time, make sure your Internet service provider has appropriate filters in place to discourage SYN attacks.

As part of system maintenance, it is a good idea to log activity on TCP ports. Then, if the volume of SYN requests dramatically increases, the administrator can deal with the problem before users report difficulty gaining access to resources.

If you suspect that your server is experiencing a SYN attack, at the command prompt type:

netstat -n -p tcp

An Active Connections report appears, which shows instances of SYN_RECEIVED connections. An abnormal amount of SYN_RECEIVED connections can indicate a SYN attack.

For the latest information on how you can use Windows NT Server to protect your Internet services against SYN attacks, search the Knowledge Base by using the keywords "SYN attack."

C H A P T E R   2

Locating Network Resources

The Internet is a collection of networks that use the Transmission Control Protocol/Internet Protocol (TCP/IP) suite of protocols to communicate with other computers on the Internet. The Domain Name System (DNS) is used in TCP/IP networks to identify and locate shared network resources such as World Wide Web or e-mail servers by using host and domain names and IP addresses. You must use DNS if you connect your private intranet to the Internet, so remote users can access your Web, File Transfer Protocol (FTP), or Gopher server running under Internet Information Server and Windows NT Server version 4.0.

Microsoft DNS server is one of the TCP/IP networking services included in Windows NT Server. It enables you to provide and manage DNS services for intranets and the Internet. Microsoft DNS server is based on a client/server architecture using data records referred to as *resource records* to locate computers and other resources on TCP/IP networks.

This chapter is provided for network administrators and support personnel who need to administer Microsoft DNS servers to support networks that connect to the Internet. This chapter contains the following sections:

- "Uniform Resource Locators, Names, and IP Addresses." This section describes how Internet computer addresses are formed.

- "DNS Name Servers." This section describes DNS name servers, how DNS name servers manage domain name space, and the naming conventions Internet service providers (ISPs) offer.

- "Using Microsoft DNS Server." This section provides some introductory information on Microsoft DNS server.

- "Using DNS Manager to Configure Zones and Create DNS Resource Records." This section briefly describes DNS Manager, how to configure primary and secondary zones for Microsoft DNS server, and the different types of resource records and how to create them by using DNS Manager.

- "Troubleshooting Microsoft DNS Server." This section offers some suggestions for solving problems with Microsoft DNS server.

This chapter supplements Chapter 9, "Managing Microsoft DNS Servers," in *Microsoft Windows NT Server Resource Kit: Windows NT Server Networking Guide.* If you need more information about DNS, the management of Microsoft DNS servers, or the integration of Microsoft DNS servers with Windows Internet Name Service (WINS) servers and Dynamic Host Configuration Protocol (DHCP) servers, see that chapter or the *Windows NT Server Networking Supplement.*

Uniform Resource Locators, Names, and IP Addresses

To allow remote users on the Internet to connect to computers on your intranet, for example a Web server running under Internet Information Server, you must use DNS, the name resolution service used on the Internet. While NetBIOS computer names and Windows Internet Name Service (WINS) are the name resolution service traditionally used in Windows-based TCP/IP networks, DNS is used on the Internet.

Uniform Resource Locators

Every resource available to remote users over the Internet must have a location identifier referred to as a Uniform Resource Locator (URL). The URL is a naming convention that uniquely identifies the location of a computer, directory, file, or document on the Internet. A basic URL identifies a computer that contains directories, documents, or files. For example, the URL for a Web server at Microsoft looks like this: **http://www.microsoft.com**.

A URL is composed of several pieces of information. The first part of the URL indicates the TCP/IP-based protocol used to access the remote computer. For Web servers, the URL starts with **http:**, because hypertext transfer protocol (HTTP) is the protocol used to access Web servers. For FTP servers, the URL starts with **ftp:**, because FTP is the protocol used to access FTP servers.

The second part of the URL is composed of the DNS host name, enterprise or organization domain name, and an Internet domain name. The second part of the URL looks like this: **www.microsoft.com**, where *www* is the host name or host alias,*microsoft* is the enterprise domain name, and *com* is the top-level Internet domain name.

A complex URL that connects your computer to a specific document or file has more than these two parts and includes directory and document names. For example, the URL used to connect to an article published for small businesses on the Microsoft Web server looks like this:

http://www.microsoft.com/technet/analpln/smallbiz/sbnisp.htm#What's_an_I SP?2

Host and Domain Names

As previously described, the second part of a basic URL used to connect to a specific computer includes the DNS host name, the name of the enterprise or organization domain in which the intranet server is located, and the name of the top-level Internet domain in which the enterprise is registered.

DNS is based on a conceptual hierarchical structure called the domain name space. The root or topmost level of the domain name space is managed by the Internet Network Information Center (InterNIC). In the United States, there are seven domain name servers providing name resolution services at the root level. When you install Microsoft DNS server, the Internet Protocol (IP) addresses of these root name servers are made available in a file named cache.dns.

Under the top-level domains are additional groupings referred to as second-level domains. Second-level domains can also be divided into other, lower levels with additional domains, which themselves can be subdivided into more lower-level domains, and so on.

One of the top-level domains of the Internet is the .com domain, a commercial domain used mainly within the United States. Contained within the .com domain are second-level domains that contain the enterprises registered with InterNIC as part of the .com domain. The names of each of these second-level domains identify the enterprise connected with that particular domain; for example, the domain name microsoft.com identifies the domain containing all computers that exist within Microsoft Corporation.

Individual computers exist within a domain. Each computer in the domain must have its own name, referred to as the host name. The combination of a host name, the enterprise domain name, and the Internet top-level domain name creates a name that is unique across the Internet. This unique name is referred to as the *fully qualified domain name* (FQDN). Each part of the FQDN is joined to the others by using the . character (the PERIOD, also referred to as a dot), creating a name that looks like this: www.microsoft.com.

IP Addresses

To participate on the Internet, every workstation and server computer must have a unique FQDN, and this FQDN must be mapped to a unique IP address. If a computer is *multihomed,* meaning that it is associated with more one IP address, each of the computer's IP addresses also must be unique.

TCP/IP, the protocol used throughout the Internet, is a *routeable* protocol, meaning that data can be passed, or routed, from one TCP/IP network to another. The intermediary devices that connect networks, referred to as *routers*, use IP addresses, rather than friendly names such as www.microsoft.com. The IP addresses provide routers an efficient method for locating computers and for addressing messages (in the form of IP packets) between computers. Therefore every device attached to a TCP/IP network must be identified by a unique IP address.

An IP address is a structured 32-bit number divided into four numeric fields separated by the . character (the PERIOD, also referred to as a dot), for example 172.46.8.34. Each of the four numeric fields is a byte (8 bits) in length. Each field can represent some number between 0 and 255; 255 is the maximum value that can be expressed by using 8 bits.

The four fields of an IP address represent two pieces of information, the network ID and the host ID of a computer. The *network ID* identifies a physical network. All computers on the same physical network must have the same network ID, and the network ID must be unique throughout the Internet. The *host ID* identifies a workstation, server, router, or other TCP/IP device. Each computer connected to a TCP/IP network must have a host ID.

Your intranet network administrator or Internet service provider (ISP) must provide a host ID and network ID for each computer that connects to the network. This IP address can either be manually configured or dynamically assigned by using Dynamic Host Configuration Protocol (DHCP) servers.

To connect your intranet to the Internet, you can obtain an allocation of network IDs for your enterprise computers by contacting either your ISP or the following regional Internet Registries:

- InterNIC, the regional Internet Registry for the United States. Contact InterNIC at **http://www.internic.net/**.

- Reseaux IP Europeene (RIPE) NCC, the regional Internet Registry for Europe. Contact RIPE NCC at **http://www.ripe.net/**.

- Asia-Pacific Network Information Center (AP-NIC), the regional Internet Registry for Asia-Pacific. Contact AP-NIC at **http://www.apnic.net/**.

DNS Name Servers

In Internet terminology, computers referred to as *name servers* provide services that maintain name-to-IP address mappings. These DNS name servers provide this information to client computers and programs that need to connect to other computers on a network.

When a user types a URL into an Internet browser, the browser first contacts a DNS name server to resolve the host and domain name portion of the URL to an IP address. After the DNS name server returns the name-to-IP address mapping, the browser can connect to the remote computer by using the IP address.

The Internet implementation of DNS distributes the responsibility for maintaining name-to-IP address mapping to DNS name servers located throughout the Internet. Each DNS name server on the Internet manages only a portion of the domain name space and is said to be *authoritative* for only that portion it manages. In other words, each DNS name server only maintains DNS data for the domain for which it is authoritative and no other.

When other name servers on the Internet need name-to-IP address mappings, they contact the authoritative name server for names of any computers contained within the domain for which the server is authoritative. This process allows the DNS data and management of that data to be distributed across the Internet.

A DNS name server can manage an entire domain or one or more subdomains by using administrative groupings referred to as zones. A *zone* is an administrative and DNS server database grouping used to manage all or part of an enterprise domain. If the domain is large (containing many subdomains and computers) the domain authoritative name server can delegate management of parts of the domain to one or more other DNS name servers.

Primary and Secondary DNS Name Servers

Each zone must be managed by using at least one primary and one secondary DNS name server. A *primary* name server contains the original name-to-IP address mappings in a zone file located on the local computer. A *secondary* name server contains a copy of the zone's name-to-IP address mappings. It receives this copy from a master name server, either the primary server or some other secondary DNS server.

Note Although a secondary name server can receive its zone data from another secondary name server, this configuration is not recommended. It is recommended that a secondary name server receive the zone data from a primary zone server. For more information, see Request for Comments (RFC) 1912, "Common DNS Operational and Configuration Errors." *RFCs* are the official documents of the Internet Engineering Task Force (IETF) specifying the details for TCP/IP protocols.

Using both a primary and a secondary server is required to provide database redundancy and a degree of fault tolerance. Providing a primary and a secondary DNS name server is also a requirement for domain registration with InterNIC.

If you establish a site on the Internet and register your enterprise with InterNIC, you must provide information about both your primary and secondary name servers. InterNIC established this requirement to ensure registered domains can always provide the name-to-IP address mappings needed for Internet connectivity. For more information about primary and secondary DNS servers, see later sections of this chapter.

Note For more information about InterNIC registration requirements, contact the InterNIC registration site at: **http://www.internic.net/**.

Using a DNS Name Server Provided by an Internet Service Provider

If you connect your enterprise to the Internet, you are using an Internet service provider (ISP). ISPs can be large corporations, such as telephone companies, or small businesses that provide specialized services. In any case, ISPs can provide more than the telecommunication link to the Internet.

The services ISPs can provide include DNS servers and databases. You can choose to use only DNS servers and services provided by your ISP, only your own enterprise DNS name servers, or some combination.

If yours is a small enterprise, perhaps using a single computer running Windows NT Server with Internet Information Server, you may want to use only the DNS services and technical experience provided by your ISP. An ISP can help you choose and register your enterprise domain with InterNIC and maintain DNS servers and resource records with your enterprise computers' name-to-IP address mappings.

The domain name options that an ISP can offer your company's Internet site include the following:

- *yourcompany.ISPname*.com. This form means your enterprise is a subdomain in the ISP enterprise domain.
- *yourcompany*.com. This form means your enterprise is its own domain and is not a subdomain of any other enterprise.

Many enterprises prefer the second option because such a name identifies an enterprise as a second-level enterprise. The second option also allows flexibility in choosing an ISP. If you use the second option, you do not need to change and reregister the enterprise domain if you later switch to a different ISP.

If you choose to provide your own DNS server and services and use your ISP only for a telecommunications link, you are responsible for administering the DNS server and database files that contain the name-to-IP address mappings for computers in your intranet domain. You must create name-to-IP address mappings for any computer that has a static IP address (that is, a permanent IP address). Such computers include any Windows NT Server computer configured with Internet Information Server with services that will be accessed by users on the Internet.

Note If you are using dial-up networking to connect to your ISP, see the section "Configuring Dial-Up Networking for ISP DNS," later in this chapter.

Using Microsoft DNS Server

Microsoft DNS server for Windows NT Server version 4.0 is an RFC-compliant DNS name server based on a client/server architecture. Because Microsoft DNS server is an RFC-compliant name server, it can be used with other DNS name servers such as UNIX-based DNS name servers as either a primary or secondary name server.

You can install Microsoft DNS server on a computer running Internet Information Server or on any computer running Microsoft Windows NT Server 4.0.

Note If you choose to use some combination of your intranet and your ISP's DNS name servers to provide the primary and secondary name servers required by InterNIC, you must correctly add and configure the ISP DNS servers and zones in Microsoft DNS server using DNS Manager. For more information on how to do so, see "Configuring Primary and Secondary Servers and Zones," later in this chapter.

A computer configured with Microsoft DNS server can manage one or more zones and zone databases. You also can create up to a maximum of 15 virtual DNS servers on a multihomed computer configured with Microsoft DNS server. The Microsoft DNS server support for zones and virtual DNS servers enables you to configure your computers in the fashion that best supports your business and networking requirements.

DNS name server zone files contain name-to-IP address mappings and other identifying information (such as a host alias name) in data records referred to as *resource records*. These resource records must be created for any computer in a zone that has a static IP address and that is a resource for users on the Internet.

Note Resources that are frequently used by remote users on the Internet are manually assigned static IP addresses. However, the interoperability of Microsoft DNS server and Microsoft WINS servers enables you to dynamically create IP addresses for your intranet computers by using Microsoft DNS, Microsoft WINS, and DHCP servers. For more information, see Chapter 9, "Managing Microsoft DNS Servers," in *Windows NT Server Networking Guide.*

To help you create and edit resource records and perform other DNS server management tasks, Microsoft DNS server provides DNS Manager. DNS Manager is automatically installed when you install Microsoft DNS server. DNS Manager eliminates the need to manually edit text files and enables you to create a full range of DNS resource records.

Using DNS Manager to Configure Zones and Create DNS Resource Records

DNS Manager is automatically added to **Administrative Tools** on the **Program** menu when you install Microsoft DNS server on a computer running Windows NT Server 4.0. You use DNS Manager to administer local and remote Microsoft DNS servers and to create the resource records that provide name resolution information and support connectivity for remote users on the Internet and TCP/IP intranets.

▶ **To start DNS Manager**

1. Click the **Start** button.

2. Point to **Programs.**

3. Point to **Administrative Tools.**

4. Click **DNS Manager**.

The tasks you can perform using DNS Manager include the following:

- Adding DNS servers for local server, remote server, and virtual server management.
- Configuring server properties.
- Configuring primary and secondary zones.
- Configuring transfer of data between primary and secondary zones. Such transfer of data is referred to as a *zone transfer*.
- Adding A (address) records with host name-to-IP address mappings for computers in the zone that are assigned static IP addresses. For more information on different resource record types, see Table 2.1, "DNS Resource Record Types," later in this chapter.
- Adding PTR (pointer) records with IP address-to-host name mappings. (Each PTR record must have a corresponding A record and vice versa.)
- Adding CNAME (alias), MX (mail exchange), and other resource records as needed.
- Monitoring usage of DNS servers by using DNS Manager statistics.
- Editing and maintaining zone configurations and resource records as needed.

For a more complete list of the tasks and procedures you can perform by using DNS Manager, see the "How To" topic in Microsoft DNS Manager Help.

Note You cannot administer or create resource records on non-Microsoft DNS servers by using DNS Manager. To administer such records, use a text editor or the tool provided by the non-Microsoft DNS server.

Configuring Primary and Secondary Zones

With DNS Manager, you can add or change Microsoft DNS servers and the zones managed by those servers. It is important to note that when creating the primary and secondary servers required for Internet connectivity, you must first define and configure a server by using DNS Manager. You then define one or more zones managed by that server.

The generally used reference to primary and secondary DNS servers is actually misleading when applied to the actual configuration and operation of DNS name servers. Because each DNS server manages its portion of the domain name space using the administrative grouping of a zone, data on the server is stored in zone files.

When data is transferred between primary and secondary servers, it is the zone files that are transferred. Microsoft DNS server is designed to incorporate this operational characteristic by assigning the primary or secondary characteristic to the zone file. In other words, the designation of primary or secondary data source is configured on a zone-by-zone basis and not a server-by-server basis. You configure zone properties to create the primary or secondary data files.

An Example Configuration of Primary and Secondary Zones

The following procedures provide an example of how to add a Microsoft DNS server and primary and secondary zones. This example assumes that the server managing the primary zone is configured on the local computer and that the server managing the secondary zone is located on a remote computer in the same network that is configured with Microsoft DNS server. In addition to illustrating zone concepts, this example also illustrates that you can manage multiple computers configured with Microsoft DNS server from one central computer configured with Microsoft DNS server.

▶   **To add the Microsoft DNS server that will manage the primary zone**

1. In DNS Manager, double-click the Server List icon.

2. On the **DNS** menu, click **New Server**, and in the **Add DNS Server** dialog box enter either the DNS server host name or the IP address.

3. Click **OK**.

DNS Manager automatically creates the new server icon in the right pane of the DNS Manager window.

▶   **To configure server properties**

1. Right-click the server icon, and click **Properties**.

2. Click the **Interfaces** tab.

3. Type an IP address, and click **Add**.

4. Repeat until all IP addresses configured on the server are entered. You can enter only a maximum of 15 IP addresses, even if the computer is a multihomed computer configured to support more than 15 IP addresses.

   If you do not specify IP addresses on the **Interfaces** tab and the computer is a multihomed computer configured with more than 15 IP addresses, you might encounter Event 410 or 520 errors. These errors occur in part because if no IP addresses are specified, by default Microsoft DNS Manager attempts to monitor all IP addresses configured on the server computer.

5. If you are using a DNS forwarder to control access to the Internet, click the **Forwarders** tab, and enter the IP address of the Microsoft DNS server that is designated as the forwarder.

6. Click **OK**.

▶ **To add a server on the local computer that represents a remote computer configured with Microsoft DNS server**

1. In DNS Manager, double-click the Server List icon.

2. Click **New Server**, and in the **Add DNS Server** dialog box enter either the DNS server host name for the remote computer or its IP address.

3. Click **OK**.

DNS Manager automatically adds a new server icon that represents the remote server in the right pane of the DNS Manager window.

If you follow the preceding procedures for a local and a remote server, the servers are added to DNS Manager on the local computer. For the sake of brevity in this example, configuration of the remote server properties is not presented. The next procedures in this example show the creation of primary and secondary zones.

Note Before creating a zone, make sure you have correctly configured TCP/IP Properties by entering the correct host name and domain name for the local computer on the **DNS** page in the **Microsoft TCP/IP Properties** dialog box. To reach this dialog box, click the **Start** button, point to **Settings**, and click **Control Panel**. Double-click the Network icon, click the **Protocols** tab, click **TCP/IP Protocol** in the **Network Protocols** list, and then click **Properties**.

▶ **To add a primary zone**

1. Right-click the local server icon, and click **New Zone** to start the zone wizard.

2. Click **Primary**, and then click **Next**.

   The zone wizard prompts you for additional information and then automatically creates the zone and zone file and adds SOA, NS, and A data records to the zone file.

Tip To create a reverse-lookup zone, use this same procedure and use a zone name that complies with the reverse-lookup name format (*nnn.nnn.nnn.in-addr.arpa*). For example, the reverse-lookup zone to contain PTR records for IP addresses 172.16.16.1 through 172.16.224.254 would be named .16.172.in-addr.arpa.

Whenever possible, create a reverse-lookup zone for each zone before adding A records for computers contained in that zone, so that you can use the automatic **Create PTR Record** option in the **Add Host** dialog box.

▶ **To add a secondary zone**

1. Right-click the remote server icon, and click **New Zone** to start the zone wizard.

2. Click **Secondary**, and enter the requested information.

3. Click **Next**.

   The zone wizard prompts you for additional information and then automatically creates the zone and zone file and adds the SOA, NS, and server A records to the zone file.

After you have successfully added a zone, you can perform additional configuration by changing the zone properties as described in the following list:

- Change the zone from a primary to secondary, or vice versa, by using the **General** tab.

- Modify the default server time-to-live (TTL) values, by using the **SOA Record** tab.

- Modify the refresh and zone transfer rates, by using the **SOA Record** tab.

- Configure the primary zone server to automatically notify the secondary zone server when changes are made to the primary zone files, by using the **Notify** tab.

- Configure the zone server to use WINS for host name resolution, by using the **WINS Lookup** tab. On a reverse-lookup zone, this tab is labeled **WINS Reverse Lookup**.

The following figure illustrates the **Zone Properties** dialog box for a normal zone.

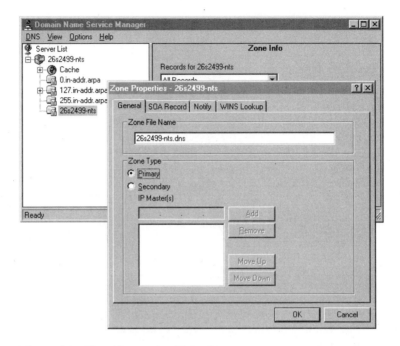

Figure 2.1   Zone Properties dialog box

The only difference in the **Zone Properties** dialog box for a reverse-lookup zone is the text on the **WINS Lookup** tab, as illustrated in the following figure.

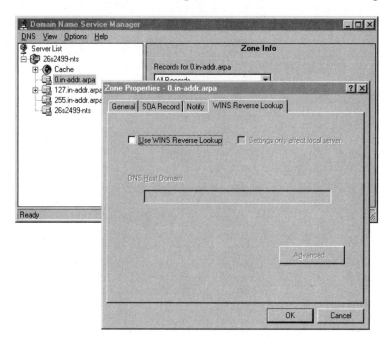

Figure 2.2   Zone Properties dialog box for reverse-lookup zone

Adding Resource Records

After you create a zone, you can add A, PTR, and other resource records for computers logically contained within the zone. To display a menu of actions that you can perform on the zone, point to the zone folder and right-click.

The two menu commands you can use to add information about the computers in the zone are **New Host** and **New Record**.

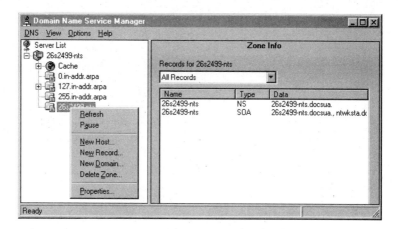

Figure 2.3   Zone Menu

You must use the **New Host** command to add A and PTR records for the zone computers that have statically assigned IP addresses. The A resource record provides the name-to-IP address mapping used in name resolution. The PTR resource record contains the reverse look-up (IP address-to-name) mapping that is needed by some programs.

The following figure illustrates the **New Host** dialog box.

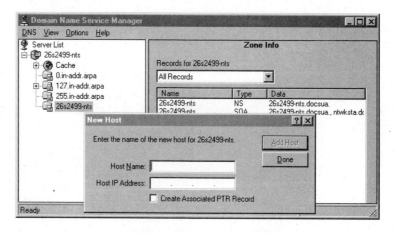

Figure 2.4   New Host dialog box

You use the **New Record** command to add other types of DNS resource records such as CNAME (alias), MX (mail exchange) or ISDN records.

The following figure illustrates the **New Resource Record** dialog box.

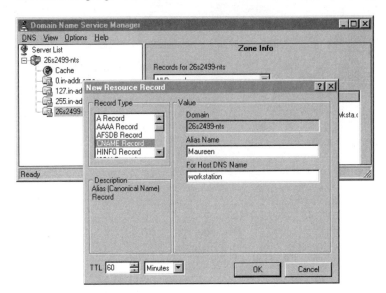

Figure 2.5   New Resource Record dialog box

The following table lists the types of resource records you can create and edit by using DNS Manager.

Table 2.2   DNS Resource Record Types

Record type	Description
A	An address record that maps a host name to an IP address in a DNS zone. Its counterpart the PTR resource record is used to map an IP address to a host name in a DNS reverse lookup zone (those in the in-addr.arpa. DNS domain). It's important you add an A record for every computer in the zone that has a static IP address, including the local DNS name server and any computer running Internet Information Server.
AFSDB	An address record that gives the location of either an Andrew File System (AFS) cell database server or a Distributed Computing Environment (DCE) cell's authenticated name server. The AFS system uses DNS to map a DNS domain name to the name of an AFS cell database server. The Open Software Foundation's DCE Naming service uses DNS for a similar function.

Table 2.2   DNS Resource Record Types *(Continued)*

Record type	Description
CNAME	A canonical name resource record, which creates an alias for the specified host name (that is, a name synonymous with the host name). You can use CNAME records to hide the implementation details of your network from the clients that connect to it. For example, in the Terra Flora case study used in the *Windows NT Server Resource Kit,* ftp.terraflora.com is an alias (that is, a CNAME) for the real name of the computer that runs the Terra Flora FTP server. A CNAME or alias also allows the FTP server to be moved easily to a different computer if necessary. If such a move is required, only the CNAME record need change, not the actual computer name.
HINFO	The host information resource record, which identifies a host's hardware type and operating system. The CPU type and operating system identifiers used in an HINFO record should come from the list of computer and system names in RFC 1700.
ISDN	The Integrated Services Digital Network (ISDN) resource record, a variation of the A resource record. Rather than mapping a hostname to an IP address, the ISDN record maps the host name to an ISDN address. An ISDN address is a phone number that consists of a country code, an area code, a local phone number, and optionally a subaddress. Use the ISDN resource record in conjunction with the RT resource record, described following.
MB	The mailbox resource record. This record, which is experimental, specifies a DNS host with the specified mailbox. Other related experimental records are the MG resource record, the MR resource record, and the MINFO resource record, all described following.
MG	The mail group resource record. This record, which is experimental, specifies a mailbox that is a member of the mail group (that is, mailing list) specified by the DNS domain name. Other related experimental records are the MB resource record, the MR resource record, and the MINFO resource record.
MINFO	The mailbox information resource record. This record, which is experimental, specifies the mailbox that is responsible for a specified mailing list or mailbox. Other related experimental records are the MB resource record, the MG resource record, and the MR resource record.
MR	The mailbox rename resource record. This record, which is experimental record, specifies a mailbox that is the proper rename of the other specified mailbox. Other related experimental records are the MB resource record, the MG resource record, and the MINFO resource record.

Table 2.2   DNS Resource Record Types *(Continued)*

Record type	Description
MX	The mail exchange resource record, which specifies a mail exchange server for a DNS domain name. A *mail exchange server* is a host that will either process or forward mail for the named DNS domain. Processing mail means either delivering it to the addressee or passing it to a different type of mail transport. Forwarding the mail means sending it to its final destination server, sending it by using Simple Message Transfer Protocol (SMTP) to another mail exchange server closer to its final destination, or queuing it for a specified amount of time.
NS	The name server resource record, which identifies the DNS server or servers for the DNS domain. NS resource records appear in all DNS zones and reverse zones (those in the in-addr.arpa DNS domain).
PTR	The pointer resource record, which maps an IP address to a host name in a DNS reverse zone (those in the in-addr.arpa DNS domain). Its counterpart, the A (address) resource record, is used to map a host name to an IP address in a DNS zone.
RP	The responsible person resource record, which indicates who is responsible for the specified DNS domain or host. You can specify multiple RP records for a given DNS domain or host. The record has two parts: an e-mail address in the same DNS format as the one in the SOA resource record, and a DNS domain name that points to additional information about the contact.
RT	The route through resource record, which specifies an intermediate host that routes packets to a destination host. The RT record is used in conjunction with the ISDN and X.25 resource records. It is syntactically and semantically similar to the MX record type and is used in much the same way.
SOA	The start of authority resource record, which indicates that this DNS server is the authoritative source of information for the data within this DNS domain. The SOA resource record is the first record in each of the DNS database files. It is created automatically by DNS Manager when you create a new DNS zone.
TXT	The text resource record, which associates general textual information with an item in the DNS database. A typical use is for identifying a host's location (for example, "Location: Building 26S, Room 2499"). The text string must be less than 256 characters, but you can associate multiple TXT resource records with one item.
WINS	A record that contains the IP address of the WINS server configured on this DNS Server for WINS name resolution. A WINS record is automatically created by configuring a zone property for WINS lookup. In other words, it is not created by using the **Add Record** command in DNS Manager.

Table 2.2   DNS Resource Record Types *(Continued)*

Record type	Description
WINS_R	A record that instructs Microsoft DNS server to use a NetBIOS node adapter status (**nbtstat**) command to resolve a DNS client reverse-lookup query. The *reverse-lookup query* requests the name of a computer identified only by an IP address. A WINS_R record is automatically created by configuring a zone property for WINS reverse lookup. In other words, it is not created by using the **Add Record** command in DNS Manager.
WKS	The well-known service resource record, which describes the services provided by a particular protocol for a particular interface. The protocol is usually TCP or User Datagram Protocol (UDP) but can be any of the entries listed in the Protocols file (*Systemroot*\System32\Drivers\...\Protocol on the drive where your Windows NT Server system files reside). The services described are the services listed below port number 256 in the Services file (*Systemroot*\System32\Drivers\...\Services).
X.25	The X.25 resource record is a variation of the A resource record. Rather than mapping a host name to an IP address, the X.25 record maps the name to an X.121 address. X.121 is the International Standards Organization (ISO) standard that specifies the format of addresses used in X.25 networks. The X.25 resource record is designed for use in conjunction with the RT resource record.

All of the resource records listed in the preceding table are commonly used by DNS name servers on the Internet *except* for the WINS and WINS_R resource records. These records are specifically implemented for interoperability between Microsoft DNS servers and Microsoft WINS servers.

Because these records are unique to Microsoft DNS servers, when transferring primary zone files to a secondary zone, these records should not be copied to a DNS name server running non-Microsoft DNS server software.

If you are using WINS lookup or WINS reverse lookup with a non-Microsoft DNS server, use the following procedure.

▶ **To prevent copying WINS or WINS_R records to a non-Microsoft DNS server**

1. Start DNS Manager.
2. Right-click the folder for the appropriate zone.
3. Click **Properties.**
4. Click the **WINS Lookup** or **WINS Reverse Lookup** tab.
5. Select the **Settings only affect local server** check box.
6. Click **OK**.

The remaining sections of this chapter provide information about using the **New Host** and **New Record** commands to provide the information that allows remote users to locate your Internet Information Server and Web, FTP, and Gopher services.

Resource Records for Web, FTP, and Gopher Services

As noted in the online *Windows NT Server Microsoft Internet Information Server Installation and Administration Guide,* to allow remote Internet users to access information on a computer configured with Internet Information Server (IIS), you must use a static IP address for that computer.

After you install and configure Internet Information server, A and PTR records must be added to the DNS primary zone in which your Internet Information Server computer is located. If this primary zone is managed by Microsoft DNS server, you can use the **New Host** option to add the A and PTR resource records. For information about adding A and PTR records, see DNS Manager Help or the *Windows NT Server Networking Guide.*

The A and PTR resource records contain the name-to-IP address mappings and IP address-to-name mappings that allow users on the Internet to connect to a remote computer. However, additional types of resource records can be used to help balance the load of traffic on a computer configured with Internet Information Server or to mask the actual configuration of your Internet Information Server. The remainder of this section describes these additional types of resource records.

Creating an Alias

The host name portion of a URL may actually be an alias, also referred to as a *canonical name.* In the address **http://www.microsoft.com**, www is an alias commonly used for World Wide Web servers, Microsoft is the domain name, and .com indicates the commercial branch of the DNS hierarchy of names for the Internet.

The CNAME resource record is used to establish an alias name in DNS server zone files. CNAMEs are frequently used in conjunction with Web, FTP, and Gopher servers and when a host name is changed. The following figure illustrates the **New Resource Record** dialog box used to create CNAME records.

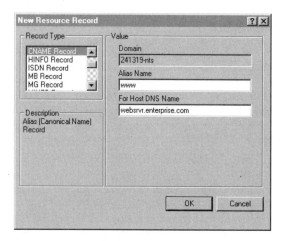

Figure 2.6   Adding a CNAME record

In the preceding illustration, an alias of **www** is being associated to a host name. The use of CNAMEs is accepted on the Internet for generalized names for servers such as www to indicate a Web server. However, other uses of the CNAME records can create problems for DNS name resolution throughout the Internet.

RFC 1912, which describes common errors in the creation of DNS resource records, states: "Don't use CNAMEs in combination with RRs (that is, resource records) which point to other names like MX, CNAME, PTR and NS." For more information on these resource record types, see Table 2.1, "DNS Resource Record Types," earlier in this chapter.

Using Round-Robin to Distribute Traffic Among Your Servers

Microsoft DNS server supports a process referred to as *round-robin*, which balances the number of clients connecting to Internet sites supported by multiple servers. Round-robin is specified by RFC 1794. To make use of round-robin, you use an alias such as the generalized server name www.

To understand how round-robin works, consider the following example. Suppose a user types the URL **http:\\www.microsoft.com** into an Internet browser. Doing so causes a name resolution query for www.microsoft.com to be sent to a DNS name server. The DNS name server returns a list of name-to-IP address mappings for each CNAME resource record that maps a host name to the alias www.microsoft.com.

The next time the DNS server receives a name resolution query for www.microsoft.com, the order of the list CNAME records is changed in a round-robin fashion. The address mapping that was first in the previous list is last in the new list. Because the process on the client computer generally uses the first name-to-IP address mapping in the list, the client connects to a server different from the server connected to on the previous request. In this manner, client connections to the Internet site are distributed among the supporting servers.

To enable round-robin when you use multiple servers to support a Web, FTP, or Gopher site, create CNAME records for each server as described in the preceding section, "Using An Alias."

Configuring Resource Records for Virtual Servers

You can configure a single computer running under Windows NT Server and Internet Information Server with multiple IP addresses and FQDNs so that it appears to remote users that there are additional servers, referred to as *virtual servers*. This feature makes it possible to service Web requests for two or more domain names (for example, company1.com and company2.com) by using a single computer configured with Internet Information Server. For example, an ISP can use this feature to service multiple companies by using a single computer running Windows NT Server and Internet Information Server. However, virtual servers require a special resource record treatment.

First, configure your virtual IIS servers as described in the online *Windows NT Server Microsoft Internet Information Server Installation and Administration Guide*. After you have done so, use DNS Manager to add new primary and secondary zones for the domain represented by the virtual server.

These primary and secondary zones must be configured on the DNS name servers identified in the InterNIC domain registration. After you have created the zones, map the IP address of the virtual server to the virtual domain name by using DNS Manager to add a new host A record. Add a second new host A record that maps the virtual server IP address to the host name of the computer on which the virtual server exists. Finally, if you want to use alias names, add new CNAME records that map aliases (such as WWW and FTP) to the host name (that is, the name of the computer on which the virtual server exists) and the virtual domain name.

Troubleshooting Microsoft DNS Server

Establishing a DNS name server and creating a database of resource records is not a trivial task. Errors are common; many of these errors are described in RFC 1912, "Common DNS Operational and Configuration Errors."

As previously discussed, DNS is used in TCP/IP networks. You can use the TCP/IP utilities provided with Microsoft Windows NT Server version 4.0 to troubleshoot problems you may encounter when using Microsoft DNS server. Most useful are the following TCP/IP utilities:

- nslookup. A diagnostic tool for DNS servers.
- ipconfig. A utility used to display information about the TCP/IP configuration of local and remote computers.
- ping. A utility used to test network connectivity of local and remote hosts.

If you encounter problems with DNS servers, see the topic "TCP/IP Procedures Help" in Control Panel Help and the *Windows NT Server Networking Guide*. The remaining sections of this chapter provide additional information you can use to troubleshoot Microsoft DNS server.

Examining Microsoft DNS Files and Resource Records

RFC 1912 highly recommends verifying all data entered into DNS name server zone files. One common error with DNS name server data is incorrect formatting of DNS resource records. By using DNS Manager to automatically create and maintain resource records, potential resource record formatting errors are prevented.

Incorrect usage of resource records and entry of invalid data, however, is not precluded by using DNS Manager. Common data errors include inconsistent IP addresses in A and PTR records, alias names in PTR records, and invalid characters within host names. Common usage errors include invalid CNAME records, missing MX records, and incomplete or invalid zone delegation, also referred to as lame zone delegation.

It is not possible to address all possible data or usage errors in this chapter, but information is provided following to help you examine your Microsoft DNS server data files to identify data errors or incorrect usage of resource records for your own specific implementation of Microsoft DNS server.

The following database files are important in troubleshooting Microsoft DNS server. These files are located in the *Systemroot*\System32\DNS\ directory.

Table 2.3   Microsoft DNS Server Database Files

Name of file	Description
Cache.dns	This file is essentially the same on all DNS name servers connected to the Internet and must be present. It contains the names and addresses for the top-level name servers.
Zonename.dns	This file contains the name-to-IP address mappings for a specific zone. A zone file is created for each zone managed by the local Microsoft DNS server.
NetworkID.in-addr.arpa.dns	This file contains the IP address-to-name mappings for a reverse lookup zone. The *NetworkID* portion of a reverse lookup zone name is the network and subnet numbers that InterNIC or your ISP has allocated to your enterprise and for which your server is therefore authoritative.

Cache File

When you install Microsoft DNS server, the cache file is automatically installed from the product disk. The data in this file contains name-to-IP address mappings for the InterNIC root domain name servers. Microsoft DNS server uses this information when name resolution queries must be resolved by getting information from name servers outside the local enterprise by contacting name servers on the Internet. You should not change this file unless the name-to-IP address mappings of the Internet root servers change.

If the computer on which you install Microsoft DNS server does not connect to the Internet, you should delete all the entries in this file and replace them with NS and A records for your intranet root name servers.

Zone File

The zone file is automatically created when you configure a zone on a computer running Microsoft DNS server. The zone file is named with the same name as the zone. Resource records are added to this file when you configure zone properties and add new records by using DNS Manager. If your computer running Microsoft DNS server is configured with multiple zones, you will have multiple zone files in the DNS directory on that computer.

Reverse Lookup File

A reverse lookup zone file is automatically created when you create a reverse lookup zone.

Format of Resource Records

As stated previously, when you use DNS Manager to create your zone files the data for each resource record is automatically formatted. In general, you do not need to worry about the format of resource records. However, if you manually examine the DNS data files, you must understand the record format.

The standard format of a resource record as specified by RFCs 1034 and 1035 is shown following:

```
<name> [<ttl>] [<class>] <type> <data>
```

The following table describes the fields in a resource record.

Table 2.4   Resource Record Format

Field	Description
Name	A host name.
TTL	The time-to-live (TTL) value is an optional entry. It is a 32-bit integer that represents, in seconds, the length of time the record is valid, after which it should be discarded.
Class	The class identifies the protocol and is generally IN, for Internet. Microsoft DNS server uses only IN class.
Type	The type specifies a resource record type. The most commonly used types are SOA, NS, A, CNAME, MX, and PTR.
Data	The data field is variable and is different for each record type. This field contains the information that is defined by the record type. The data in this field is specific to a particular host.

Most resource records are represented as single-line text entries. Records can use multiple lines by using a right parenthesis character at the end of the first line and a left parenthesis character at the end of the last line.

Under Microsoft DNS server, each resource record is entered into the zone file with preceding and following blank lines to improve readability. All blank and comment lines begin with a semicolon (;) and end with a carriage return. The semicolon character instructs Microsoft DNS server to ignore the line.

Consider the following example, which is taken from the sample DNS zone file place.dns, located in the *root*\system32\dns\examples directory.

```
;    START OF AUTHORITY
;
@    IN   SOA     nameserver.place.dom.   postmaster.place.dom. (
                                  1         ; serial number
                                  36000     ; refresh    [1h]
                                  600       ; retry      [10m]
                                  86400     ; expire     [1d]
                                  3600 )    ; min TTL    [1h]


;
;    NAME SERVERS
;
;
place.dom
@               IN   NS      nameserver.place.dom.
@               IN   NS      nameserver2.place.dom.
nameserver      IN   A       192.5.29.7
nameserver2     IN   A       192.5.29.8
;
;    WINS LOOKUP
;
;    The WINS LOOKUP is specific to the Microsoft DNS server
;    implementation of DNS resource records and may be attached ONLY
;    to the zone root. Presence of a WINS record at the zone root
;    instructs the name server to use WINS to lookup any requests for A
;    (address) records for names which are DIRECT children of zone root,
;    and which do NOT have A records in the zone file.
;
@    IN   WINS    LOCAL    192.5.29.2 192.5.29.3
;
;    E-MAIL SERVERS
;
@               IN   MX      10        mailserver1
@               IN   MX      15        mailserver2
mailserver1     IN   A       192.5.29.17
                                192.5.29.19
;
;    CNAME RECORDS
;
;    The following records are sometimes called "aliases" but are
;    technically referred to as "Canonical Names (CNAME)" entries.
;    These records allow you to use more than one name to point to
;    a single host.
;
;    For example, the entries below mean that:
;
;    ftp.place.dom. is really host.place.dom.
```

```
;     www.place.dom. is really other-host.place.dom.
;
;     By using CNAME records, you avoid typing duplicate information
;     in your database files.
;
ftp               IN   CNAME    host
www               IN   CNAME    other-host
```

Note that some line entries contain the @ character in the name field (that is, the first field). When the @ character exists in a name field, Microsoft DNS server assumes the name value is the same as the name of the zone. When the name field is blank, Microsoft DNS server assumes the name value is the same as that for the preceding record.

The name field is followed by the optional TTL field. If this field is blank, Microsoft DNS server assumes that TTL value is the same as the TTL value that was specified in the SOA record by using DNS Manager to configure zone properties. The default TTL value is 60 minutes. You can change this default value by using DNS Manager to edit the SOA value.

▶ **To change the default TTL value**

1. Start DNS Manager.

2. Right-click the folder for the zone whose default TTL value you want to change.

3. Click **Properties**.

4. Click the **SOA Record** tab.

5. Increase or decrease the value in the **Minimum Default TTL** box.

6. Increase by 1 the value in the **Serial Number** box. The serial number is the number used to identify the version of the file.

7. Click **OK**, then click **OK** again.

Configuring Dial-up Networking for ISP DNS

Dial-up networking enables you to connect to remote networks by using a modem or adapter such as an ISDN adapter. If you connect to an ISP by using dial-up networking and do not correctly configure TCP/IP or DNS name server information in dial-up networking, you can experience connectivity or name resolution errors.

To configure a computer with a dial-up network connection to an ISP, use the configuration procedure described in this section. Before you start, you must have completed the following:

- You must have installed and configured your modem or adapter.
- You must have installed TCP/IP on your computer.
- You must have installed and configured Windows NT Server Remote Access Service (RAS), which provides the dial-up networking feature.

You will also need the following information before you start:

- Your user name.
- Your password.
- Your ISP domain name.
- Telephone number to dial up the ISP network.
- Your default gateway address—the IP address of the ISP computer to which you connect.
- The IP addresses of your DNS name server and the DNS name server used by your ISP. The installation by default configures dial-up networking to use the ISP DNS name server. However, if your ISP does not provide a DNS name server or if you to want to specify a combination of your intranet and the ISP DNS name servers, you must configure the IP addresses.
- Any telephony options you must use, for example PBX or long-distance dialing.
- Your logon procedure. Providing this information is necessary only if your ISP uses a special logon procedure.

▶ **To create a phone book entry for a dial-up connection to an ISP**

1. Click the **Start** button, point to **Programs**, point to **Accessories**, and then click **Dial-Up Networking**.

   If this is the first time dial-up networking is started, the Dial-Up Networking Wizard starts. If this happens, click **OK.** Otherwise, click **New**.

2. Type the name of your ISP in the **Name the new phonebook entry** box, and then click **Next**.

3. Select the check boxes for any options that apply, and click **Next**.

4. Point to the modem or adapter that you will use, and click **Next**.

5. Type the ISP telephone number in **Phone Number**, and click **Next**.

6. Click **Finish**.

▶ **To configure TCP/IP and DNS name server information for an ISP phone book**

1. Start Dial-Up Networking, and in the **Dial-Up Networking** dialog box click **More**.

2. Click **Edit entry and modem properties**.

3. Click the **Server** tab.

4. Verify that the selected dial-up server type is PPP.

5. Under **Network Protocols**, clear the check boxes to disable IPX/SPX compatible and NetBEUI.

6. Click **TCP/IP Settings**.

7. Click **Server assigned IP address**.

   –Or–

   If the computer you are dialing from is your public Web, FTP, or Gopher server or the computer is assigned a static IP address for another reason, click **Specify an IP address**, and type the IP address in the **IP address** box.

   –Or–

   To configure name server information, click **Specify name server addresses**, type the IP address of your primary name server in the **Primary DNS** box, and type the IP address of your secondary name server in the **Secondary DNS** box.

8. Click **OK**, and close Dial-Up Networking.

Deleting Invalid Characters from a NetBIOS Computer Name

Name errors are common in the operation of DNS name servers. Name errors can occur because of the differences between what is acceptable in NetBIOS computer names and what is acceptable in DNS host names. NetBIOS computer names support a different character set than DNS host names, and by installation default, Windows NT Server and Windows NT Workstation are configured with a host name by using the NetBIOS computer name. In other words, the installation default for Windows NT Server and Windows NT Workstation is to configure the NetBIOS computer name as the DNS host name.

If the NetBIOS computer name contains invalid host name characters, Microsoft Windows NT Server and Windows NT Workstation attempt to correct the name by changing the invalid character in the host name to the - (HYPHEN) character. However, this change generates name resolution errors. For example, if your Web server NetBIOS computer name is Server#1, all attempts by remote TCP/IP network users to connect to the Web server by using the URL **http://Server#1** will fail. They do so because the invalid # character is changed in the DNS host name to Server-1.

If computers in the zone managed by your Microsoft DNS server use NetBIOS names containing characters not supported in DNS host names, you must manually configure a valid host name on those computers.

▶ **To change a host name to a valid string of characters**

1. Click the **Start** button, point to **Settings**, and click **Control Panel.**
2. Double-click the Network icon.
3. Click the **Protocols tab.**
4. In the **Network Protocols** list, click **TCP/IP Protocol**, and then click **Properties**.
5. Click the **DNS** tab**.**
6. In the **Host Name** box, type the corrected host name.
7. Click **OK**, click **OK** again, and then close Control Panel.

RFC 1912 defines the characters valid for DNS host names as: "Allowable characters in a label for a host name are only ASCII letters, digits, and the "-" character. Labels may not be all numbers, but may have a leading digit (e.g., 3com.com). Labels must end and begin only with a letter or digit. See RFC 1035 and RFC 1123.... The presence of underscores in a label is allowed in RFC 1033, except [RFC 1033] is informational only and was not defining a standard."

For more information about rules for creating valid host names, see RFC 1912, RFC 1035, and RFC 1123.

Enabling DNS to Correctly Locate Multihomed Computers

A *multihomed computer* is a single computer associated with multiple IP addresses. When a DNS name server is queried for a single host name-to-IP address mapping for a multihomed computer, it responds with a list of the host name-to-IP address mappings for that computer.

Because of the round-robin feature of Microsoft DNS server, described earlier in this chapter, the order of the listed mappings for a multihomed computer changes with each new name query. The round-robin feature enables DNS to respond with the list of mappings in a different order each time it receives a name query for the multihomed computer. This feature is used to balance the load of connections made to each IP address. If one or more of the listed mappings is incorrect, for example if there is an incorrect or nonexistent IP address, errors can occur as described following.

TCP/IP utility programs, NetBT programs, and Microsoft Internet Explorer all process the list of mappings for a multihomed computer differently.Some TCP/IP utility programs, such as FTP and Telnet, send a separate name resolution request to the DNS server each time an attempt is made to resolve a name to an IP address. These utilities use the first IP address in the list returned for each new request by the DNS server. If that first IP address is incorrect, the program fails to connect to the multihomed computer, even though it may have previously connected by using a previous name resolution query.

Programs that use NetBT to connect to remote computers process the list provided by the DNS server in a different manner. The first time a DNS client program using NetBT sends a name query to DNS server, it saves only the first mapping in the list in local cache on the DNS client computer. If the first mapping is incorrect, the program fails to connect to the multihomed computer.

The list is saved for a period of time defined as the CacheTimeout, which has a default value of 10 minutes. Any subsequent name resolution queries made within the CacheTimeout period are resolved by using the mapping saved in the local cache. Name queries made after the CacheTimeout period is expired require a new request for host name-to-IP address mapping. If the subsequent mapping is correct, the client program connects to the multihomed computer. If the subsequent mapping is incorrect, the client program fails to connect.

Microsoft Internet Explorer processes the list received from the DNS server differently than either the TCP/IP utilities or NetBT. Microsoft Internet Explorer tries to connect to the multihomed computer by using each name-to-IP address mapping until it succeeds or until all IP addresses in the list are attempted.

The responsibility of performing in this manner lies with the application. It is the responsibility of the resolver to return the addresses from DNS, not to define the manner in which the application uses the addresses.

▶ **To prevent failure to connect to a multihomed computer**

- Use DNS Manager to select the zone in which the multihomed computer exists and create A and PTR records for each IP address associated with multihomed computer.

  Do not create A and PTR resource records for IP addresses that are nonexistent on the multihomed computer.

- Use DNS Manager or a text editor to examine the data in the A and PTR records for the computer. Delete any A or PTR records that contain invalid IP address mappings.

Configuring to Avoid Error 2140 When Starting an Exchange Server

You might receive the following error message when starting the Internet Mail Connector service on the computer configured with Microsoft Exchange Server:

```
Stop  "Could not start the Microsoft Exchange Internet Mail Connector
         service on ..."
Error 2140: An internal Windows NT error occurred.
```

If so, the following event will be logged in the event viewer:

```
EventID 4058
Category: Initialization/Termination
```

This error occurs when the TCP/IP protocol properties for DNS name resolution are not properly configured, for example when there is a blank entry for the DNS domain name.

▶ **To configure a DNS domain name**

1. Click the **Start** button, point to **Settings**, and then click **Control Panel**.
2. Double-click the Network icon, click the **Protocols** tab, in the **Network Protocols** list click **TCP/IP Protocol**, and then click **Properties**.
3. To display the DNS information configured on the computer, click the **DNS** tab.
4. In the **Domain** box, type the DNS domain name (that is, the name of the enterprise in which the Microsoft Exchange server exists).
5. Click **OK**, click **OK** again, and then close Control Panel.

C H A P T E R   3

Adding Bandwidth for Internet Connectivity

Bandwidth refers to the amount of data that is transferred and received within a given interval of time over a communication link between a computer and the network. When using the Internet as a wide area network (WAN) to connect remote users and computers, you need to understand your WAN bandwidth requirements. This need holds true whether you are the network administrator of a business running a private Transmission Control Protocol/Internet Protocol (TCP/IP) network (that is, an intranet), a small World Wide Web content provider, or an Internet service provider (ISP).

This chapter provides information about optimizing your bandwidth requirements using the telecommunication and networking features of Microsoft Windows NT Server and Internet Information Server (IIS). Specifically, this chapter provides information about the configuration options on a computer running Windows NT Server and Internet Information Server that support your choice of Internet telephony service. This chapter includes the following sections:

- "What is the Bandwidth Problem?" This section presents information on the current U.S. and worldwide Internet infrastructure and describes the type of connectivity bandwidth problems that Internet site administrators usually face.

- "Estimating Connectivity Bandwidth Requirements." This section provides information on methods to estimate connectivity bandwidth requirements for an Internet site running Windows NT Server and Internet Information Server.

- "Evaluating the Bandwidth Capability of Connectivity Services." This section compares different types of telephone lines and data transmission technologies and provides information on evaluating your telecommunications hardware requirements.

- "Troubleshooting Bandwidth for Internet Connections." This section provides information on resolving problems on your intranet connections to the Internet.

What Is the Bandwidth Problem?

The bandwidth of a telecommunications link is measured by the number of data bits per second (bps) that can be transferred on that link. Typically, the capacity of a telecommunications link is measured in kilobits per second (Kbps). One kilobit per second is equal to 1024 bits per second; one megabit per second (Mbps) is equal to 1024 kilobits per second.

Users require more from the Internet than they did previously. Users now transfer everything from formatted text to graphics to audio to full-motion video data content over the Internet. Such transfers require increasing amounts of bandwidth from the Internet telecommunications infrastructure and also increasing bandwidth from the computers and devices that connect to the Internet.

WAN Connections to the Internet

The number of options that can be used to connect to the Internet is rapidly changing. Satellite connections are a reality for some enterprises, although a large number of WANs still use public common-carrier telephone lines to provide connectivity to remote users. Because of their established availability for many users, WAN connections to the Internet over public common-carrier telephone lines are the focus of this chapter.

These public common-carrier telephone lines used by remote users for connection are also referred to as *public switched telephone networks (PSTNs)*. PSTNs route users' connection requests to the desired Internet or private intranet server.

To provide access to your Internet Information Server (IIS), you need to provide a link to these telephone networks, by which remote users connect to your Internet Information Server site. This telephone link can terminate at a computer running Internet Information Server, at a computer configured with Windows NT Server and Remote Access Service (RAS) that routes remote clients to an Internet Information Server, or at some other network computer. A typical setup might include a firewall computer, a RAS server, and an Internet Information Server.

U.S. Internet Telecommunications Infrastructure

In 1995, the telecommunication infrastructure of the Internet in the United States changed from a publicly supported infrastructure to an evolving infrastructure of cooperating commercial enterprises. The infrastructure now consists of public telephone networks, network access points (NAPs), and Internet service providers (ISPs).

Figure 3.1   U.S. Network Access Points

The new commercial U.S. backbone infrastructure includes the NAPs shown in the preceding figure, which provide interconnection for commercial ISPs. It also includes a Routing Arbiter, which manages routing tables and databases that route the traffic between ISPs across the national backbone.

High-speed digital communications over the Internet infrastructure can provide transmission speeds between 45 and 155 megabits per second. Telecommunications at such speeds is referred to as *midband telecommunications*. National service providers (NSPs) provide backbone services for the Internet infrastructure using transmission technologies that range from midband telecommunications to fully switched broadband networks based on Asynchronous Transfer Mode (ATM) technology. ATM technology provides transmission speeds up to hundreds of megabits per second.

Demand exists for transmission technologies with even higher bandwidth on the Internet infrastructure. However, the bandwidth problem of primary concern to most administrators of Internet sites is the bandwidth from their sites to the Internet.

Connections to the Internet telecommunications infrastructure are often compared to a highway on-and-off ramp. The speed at which you enter and exit the highway (that is, the speed at which you send and receive data) depends on the road (the technology) that connects you to the Internet, rather than the maximum speed attained on the highway itself. In other words, the WAN bandwidth problems you can reasonably manage are most likely to occur over the connection between your server and your gateway to the Internet.

Using an Internet Service Provider

You connect to the Internet telecommunications infrastructure by using the services of an Internet service provider (ISP). ISPs can provide both dial-up connectivity for occasional connection to the Internet or dedicated digital lines for high-speed continuous 24-hour connectivity.

As discussed previously, there are a number of different types of organizations that make up the Internet telecommunications infrastructure. These range from telephone companies to specialized commercial enterprises. The Internet infrastructure is layered, with traffic from the ISPs in the lower layers funneled up to the national backbone service providers referred to as NSPs.

The separation between the backbone and regional network layers of the current infrastructure is blurring, as more regional areas connect directly to each other through the increasing number of ISPs in each region of the United States.

Connecting Directly to the Internet

Before the restructuring of the Internet telecommunications infrastructure in the United States during 1995, connecting directly to the Internet generally meant acquiring a dedicated, rather than dial-up, connection to the Internet. Today, this term may also refer to obtaining Internet connectivity services directly from an NSP at the backbone layer of the Internet telecommunications infrastructure.

Worldwide Internet Connectivity

There are also a number of backbone and midlevel networks in other countries. Most western European countries have national networks that are attached to Ebone, the European Internet backbone. The infrastructure is still inefficient in some places, and connections between countries are often slow or of low quality. It is common for Internet traffic between countries in Europe to be routed through the U.S. backbone.

The availability of full Internet service varies by location. In this chapter, discussion of WAN connectivity is limited to telecommunication services available in the United States. For example, Integrated Services Digital Network (ISDN) service, which is a preferred service for Internet connectivity for small to medium-sized enterprises connecting to the Internet in the United States, can be prohibitively expensive for sites in other parts of the world.

For information about worldwide Internet connectivity, available telecommunication services, and ISPs, search the International Telecommunications Union Web server at: **http://www.itu.ch**. You can also contact public telecommunication carriers in your area for additional information.

Estimating Connectivity Bandwidth Requirements

Before establishing an Internet site running Windows NT Server and Internet Information Server, be sure to evaluate your bandwidth requirements. Identifying bandwidth requirements helps you choose the telecommunication line service and related computer hardware configuration that best fit your needs.

First, identify the following information about the service you want to provide at your Internet Information Server site:

- Type of programs and content—for example, static or dynamic hypertext markup language (HTML) pages
- Desired response time—for example, 30 seconds or less to load an HTML page
- Expected number of simultaneously connected users

The bandwidth requirements of an intranet, or Internet, Web server that may support 1 to 10 simultaneously connected users are much smaller than the bandwidth requirements of a large business that handles thousands of simultaneously connected users.

The type of programs and content usually provided by your Internet Information Server also affect bandwidth requirements. For example, an Internet Information Server should accommodate more users when they are running programs that are small in data content and non-CPU-intensive, such as electronic mail (e-mail), Telnet, and File Transfer Protocol (FTP). Processes that are CPU-intensive include Common Gateway Interface (CGI) scripts, database queries, downloading of HTML files, and video and audio programs.

Note The number of simultaneously connected users should also be considered when selecting the computer on which to install Internet Information Server. For example, a Microsoft Web site that handles 3 million requests a day (an average of about 2,000 connections per minute) consists of two computers running Internet Information Server. Each computer has 66 megahertz Intel Pentium processors, 8 gigabytes of usable hard disk space, and 128 megabytes random access memory (RAM). One computer uses four Pentium processors; the other uses two.

Methods for Estimating Bandwidth Requirements

To help you identify your bandwidth requirements, two different methods are described in this section. For information on other methods, you can search Internet sites, as discussed later in this section.

The first method you can use to estimate bandwidth requirements is based on historical data from existing Internet sites. The number of bytes transferred is a commonly recorded statistic about Internet sites, and typical transfer statistics are available by searching the Internet. Many organizations publish statistics about data transferred and user connections on the World Wide Web, and the World Wide Web consortium at **http://www.w3.org** provides information about tools for gathering Web server statistics.

The following example illustrates this first estimation method. It calculates the kilobits per second (Kbps) of bandwidth required for a Web site that transfers approximately 250,000,000 bytes in an average 12-hour period:

```
250,000,000 × (8 bits data + 4 bits overhead) / ((12 hours × 60 minutes
× 60 seconds) × 1024) = 67.8 Kbps
```

This example site requires a minimum of two 56 kilobits per second dedicated lines or one ISDN line.

When examining data from historical sites, remember to correctly convert different units of measure to bits (the unit of measurement for bandwidth). To obtain the number of bits contained in one transferred byte, multiply the number of bytes by 12; there are 8 bits per byte, plus 4 bits of overhead data. You also need to express the results in terms of seconds. If your data is recorded as bytes per hour, multiply the number of hours by 3,600 (60 minutes per hour × 60 seconds per minute).

The second method you can use to estimate bandwidth requirements is based on the estimated number of simultaneous user connections and the average size of documents transferred. The following example illustrates this method:

```
(Average connections per day / Number of seconds per day) × (Average
document size in kilobytes × (8 bits data + 4 bits overhead))
```

Because there are 86,400 seconds in one day, 8 bits in a byte, and 4 bits overhead per byte of data, the formula can also be written as:

```
(Average connections per day / 86,400) × (Average document size in
kilobytes × 12)
```

For example, if you predict 3,000 connections per day and the average file size accessed by remote users to be 85K, your bandwidth requirements can be estimated as follows:

```
(3,000 / 86,400) × (85 × 1,024 × (8+4)) = 36.3 Kbps
```

You can search sites on the Internet to find discussions of bandwidth estimation methods used, or recommended, by other users with experience in establishing Internet and Web server sites. Considerations other than those discussed previously might arise. For example, bandwidth requirements should also account for a minimum acceptable transfer rate per user, based on a projected load per remote user accessing the Internet Information Server. In other words, you should consider whether your server will be able to transfer data to all users at a rate that is acceptable to remote users.

To predict a peak load on your Internet Information Server, you need to estimate the number of users who will simultaneously connect to your server and consider the type of service they will access. If your users will primarily access your Web service for HTML documents with audio and graphics, you need a much higher bandwidth connection than if your users will primarily access the Web server to browse text documents.

Do You Need Additional Bandwidth?

Bandwidth requirements can change monthly, weekly, daily, and even hourly. Use the estimation methods described in the preceding section whether you are planning a future Internet Information Server site or evaluating the bandwidth requirements of an existing site. You can tune and adjust your bandwidth estimates if the number of remote users connecting to your site exceeds your estimates, if connection response time increases, or if the number of rejected connections increases.

If your bandwidth estimates exceed the bandwidth provided by your connection to the Internet, you can do any of the following:

- Increase the connection bandwidth with improved line services from your ISP or telephone company.

- Reduce the services provided by the Internet Information Server.

- Reduce the number of remote clients that simultaneously connect to the Internet Information Server services, by modifying the value of the **MaxConnections** parameter as described in "Troubleshooting Bandwidth for Internet Connections," later in this chapter.

- Reduce the amount of network bandwidth that the Internet Information Server can use, by modifying the value of the **BandwidthLevel** parameter as described in "Troubleshooting Bandwidth for Internet Connections," later in this chapter.

If your bandwidth estimates indicate that you have adequate bandwidth on your Internet connection, but remote users are experiencing connectivity problems, examine the configuration of your Internet Information Server. Connectivity problems can be caused by computer configuration problems including inadequate processor or memory capacity.

If you are experiencing connectivity problems, use Performance Monitor to identify the cause of the symptoms. For information about using Performance Monitor with Internet Information Server, see Chapter 7, "Monitoring Bandwidth and Network Capacity." See also "Troubleshooting Bandwidth for Internet Connections," later in this chapter.

Evaluating the Bandwidth Capability of Connectivity Services

As previously stated, this chapter focuses on Internet communications that use the PSTN networks to provide connectivity between remote users. PSTNs are based on circuit-switching with dedicated capacity to transfer and route traffic throughout the PSTN.

Data communication on the Internet, however, is based on packet switching, designed for high throughput of all communications, including data, audio, and video. Packet-switching networks provide the highest rates of data transfer available; however, the Internet relies on PSTNs to deploy the packet-switching technologies. You can select different PSTN line services that will support data communications on Internet, and to support WANs and local area networks (LANs).

The next two sections describe the transmission technologies and telephone connections that you can choose to connect to the Internet. After you select a telephone line service that provides the amount of bandwidth you need, use the *Windows NT Hardware Compatibility List* to identify the hardware devices that you can select that will support the line service you chose.

Dial-Up vs. Dedicated Leased Telephone Lines

The types of telephone lines you can choose from are described in the following table.

Table 3.1   Classification of Telephone Line Types

Line type	Description	When to use	Line speed
Public dial-up network lines	These are common telephone lines. They require users to manually make a connection for each communication session.	This connection type is slow and not totally reliable for transferring data. However, for some companies it may be practical to dial up a temporary link between sites daily to transfer files or update databases.	Carriers are continually improving their dial-up line service. Some digital lines claim data transmission speeds of up to 56 kilobits per second by using error correction, data compression, and synchronous modems.
Leased, or dedicated, lines	These provide full-time dedicated connections that do not use a series of switches to complete the connection.	The quality of the line is often higher than that of a line designed only for voice transmissions.	Lines typically range in speed from 56 kilobits per second to 45 megabits per second or more.

If your Internet Information Server is used infrequently by a small number of users, dial-up line connectivity that provides limited connection and access to the Internet may be appropriate. However, if your Internet Information Server is accessed by a large number of simultaneous users or provides 24-hour continuous availability, you should choose a dedicated connection and line technology that provides adequate bandwidth and availability.

Dial-up telephone lines, even with a fast modem and data compression, can create a large telephone bill for even a temporary connection. Leased lines, which offer more continuous connections, are in the long run more economical for companies that want to provide continuous availability to remote users.

Transmission Technologies

Dial-up and dedicated leased lines can be connected to a telephone network by using line services based on different transmission technologies. The following table describes these transmission technologies.

Table 3.2   Description of Transmission Technologies

Technology	Description
X.25	X.25 is a set of protocols incorporated in a packet-switching network. An X.25 packet-switching network uses switches, circuits, and routes as available to provide the best routing and transmission of your data at any particular time.
Frame Relay	Frame Relay is a packet-switching technology that evolved from X.25. It performs much faster than X.25, due to reduced overhead. It requires a Frame Relay–capable router that can route and transfer data from your server to remote users.
Asynchronous Transfer Mode (ATM)	ATM is also an advanced form of packet-switching. It is a broadband method that transfers data in 53-byte cells rather than variable-length frames. It produces uniform frames that network equipment can switch, route, and move more quickly than frames of different sizes. ATM can be used with any media that include the necessary physical interfaces.
ISDN–Basic Rate Interface (BRI)	ISDN-BRI employs digital transmission that divides its available bandwidth into two 64-Kbps B channels and one 16-Kbps D channel, using existing regular telephone lines.
ISDN–Primary Rate Interface (PRI)	ISDN-PRI has a larger bandwidth capacity than ISDN-BRI. Primary Rate ISDN provides 23 64-Kbps B channels and one 64-Kbps D channel.
Fiber Distributed Data Interface (FDDI)	FDDI is a high-speed token-passing ring network that uses fiber-optic media and that was developed for high-end computers. It is used for environments that connect components such as mainframe and minicomputers in a traditional computer room, for backbone networks, for networks that require high data rates and fairly large bandwidth, and for high-speed office networks in general.
Synchronous optical network (SONET)	SONET is an emerging fiber-optic technology that can transfer data at more than one gigabit per second. Networks based on this technology are capable of delivering voice, data, and video.

Table 3.2   Description of Transmission Technologies *(Continued)*

Technology	Description
Switched Multimegabit Digital Service (SMDS)	SMDS is a switching service provided by some local exchange telephone networks. SMDS uses the same fixed-length cell relay technology as ATM and provides high-speed communication for multicast programs (that is, programs transmitted from one point to many simultaneous remote users, such as video broadcasts).
T1	T1 is an AT&T term for a digital carrier facility used to transmit a Digital Service 1 (DS-1) formatted digital signal at 1.544 megabits per second.
T3	T3 is a digital carrier facility used to transmit a Digital Service 3 (DS-3) formatted digital signal at 44.746 megabits per second.

The preceding table provides some information you can use to choose what technology best supports your Internet Information Server bandwidth requirements. In some cases, an enterprise might need to use a mix of available services. For example, the 1995 data communications WAN at Microsoft is a mix of services, primarily composed of point-to-point leased circuits of 64-kilobit per second or higher bandwidths, with smaller sites using X.25 services, ISDN-BRI, or analog dial-up.

The following table compares a few of the transmission technologies, listing different technologies' connection options, send and receive speeds, and number of simultaneous connections.

Table 3.3   Comparison of Transmission Technologies

Transmission method	Continuous connection	Send speed	Receive speed	Readily available	Simultaneous users
Analog modem	No	Up to 28.8 Kbps	Up to 28.8 Kbps	Yes	1–10
ISDN	No	128 Kbps	128 Kbps	Yes	10–500
T1 and fractional T1	Yes	1.5 Mbps	1.5 Mbps	Yes	50–500
T3	Yes	24–43.5 Mbps	24–43.5 Mbps	Yes	5,000 +

Dial-Up Internet Accounts

A connection to the Internet using a telephone line and modem can serve up to 10 simultaneous users. Modem connections are often called slow links because data is transferred at the speed of the modem, typically from 9,600 to 28,800 bits per second.

Dial-up connections require the TCP/IP suite of protocols, as do all connections to the Internet. Specifically, dial-up connections require the Internet Protocol (IP). ISPs generally refer to dial-up connections as IP accounts. Variations of IP accounts are based on the TCP/IP line protocol used by the IP account. The following list describes the three variations of IP accounts:

- PPP, which stands for Point-to-Point Protocol
- SLIP, which stands for Serial Line Internet Protocol
- CSLIP, which is a compressed version of SLIP

PPP is the current standard for encapsulating IP data and other network layer protocol information over point-to-point links. It also provides ways to test and configure lines and the upper level protocols of the Open Systems Interconnectivity (OSI) network architecture. PPP is an improvement over SLIP, which does not provide error correction.

To connect an Internet Information Server computer to the Internet, request a PPP account from your ISP. The PPP account is faster and more reliable than the other line protocols and is fully supported by the TCP/IP implementation under Windows NT Server and Windows NT Workstation.

Note Point-to-Point Tunneling Protocol (PPTP), which is a feature provided by Windows NT Server and Windows NT Workstation version 4.0, essentially converts PPP information into point-to-point packets transmitted by TCP to provide a secure "tunnel" through the Internet. For more information, see the *Windows NT Server Networking Supplement*.

Dedicated Digital Lines

When you lease a dedicated line for Internet connectivity, a network cable to your site is installed by your ISP (or your local telephone company if the telephone company is your ISP). Dedicated digital lines can provide speeds in the United States ranging from 56 kilobits per second by using Frame Relay technology to 43.5 megabits per second by using T3 technology.

Telecommunications Hardware Requirements

The computer that is connected to a telephone network is physically connected by using a hardware device such as a network adapter (also known as a network interface card, or NIC), modem, or ISDN card attached to the computer and a telephone line. The hardware device and device driver that you install on the computer that is connecting to the Internet must support the type of telephone line service and ISP account provided by your telephone company and ISP.

The telephone line connection to the local telephone central office is sometimes referred to as the last mile, at the maximum 18,000 feet of wiring that physically connects a private enterprise telephone line to the public telephone network. The distance between your telephone connection to a PSTN central office can affect your ability to get the PSTN service you need to support your bandwidth requirements.

You may need additional hardware to support your choice of telephone line service. Dedicated digital lines require additional networking equipment to attach a server or workstation to the Internet. For example, some configurations require a Channel Service Unit/Data Service Unit (CSU/DSU) that takes the digital data from the telephone network and processes it for the computer that is connected to the Internet on the digital line.

The additional CSU/DSU networking hardware is installed to physically connect your computer and modem to a dedicated digital line, for example, as shown in the following figure.

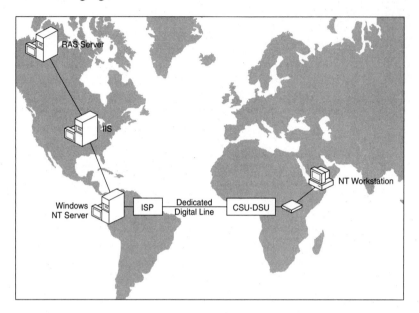

Figure 3.2   Hardware needed for digital line connectivity

Because the Internet continues evolving, other possible configurations of hardware and software may replace the typical CSU/DSU unit illustrated in the preceding figure. You also need additional equipment on the computer that is connected to the digital line. For more information on this additional equipment, see Chapter 4, "Using ISDN."

The output from the CSU/DSU goes to a router located at your site. A cable is run from the router to the LAN adapter card on the computer that is connecting to the Internet. Before purchasing your CSU/DSU equipment, consider these factors:

- CSU/DSU equipment bandwidth. Some CSU/DSU units operate at 56 kilobits per second, some work at T1 speeds, and some have a range of frequencies at which they operate.

- Router bandwidth. Routers have similar bandwidth capabilities, and your router must match your CSU/DSU unit bandwidth.

- ISP equipment compatibility. Your CSU/DSU and router must be compatible with the hardware used by your ISP.

Troubleshooting Bandwidth for Internet Connections

To prevent degraded or interrupted service to your Internet site running Windows NT Server and Internet Information Server, estimate your bandwidth requirements and acquire an Internet connection that provides adequate bandwidth with capacity for growth. You can also help prevent or troubleshoot performance and connectivity problems by using the information provided in Chapter 7, "Monitoring Bandwidth and Network Capacity."

Additionally, the following topics provide information about resolving specific problems that can occur when providing services with Internet Information Server to remote users on the Internet.

Changing IIS Parameters to Address Connection Problems

If your estimates indicate the bandwidth of your Internet connection is inadequate to service your remote users, you can change specific parameters in the Registry in response. Internet Information Server contains four Registry subkeys, one subkey for each IIS service. The IIS services are the following:

- FTP
- Gopher
- WWW (World Wide Web)
- Inetsrv (Internet Information Server)

The parameters for each service are located in the key:

HKEY_LOCAL_MACHINE\System
    \CurrentControlSet
        \Services
            \ServiceName
                \Parameters

In the previous key, *ServiceName* refers to the name of the particular IIS service whose parameters you want to change.

The value of the Registry parameter **MaxConnections** specifies a maximum number of simultaneous connections with an installation default value of 1,000 simultaneous connections. One **MaxConnections** parameter is located under each *ServiceName* key. To optimize the available bandwidth on your Internet Information Server, you can change this parameter to allow more or fewer simultaneous connections.

The value of the Registry parameter **BandwidthLevel** specifies the amount of network bandwidth that can be used by IIS services. Internet Information Server includes an automatic bandwidth service that monitors client connections and adjusts up or down depending on the amount of network bandwidth the services use. Such adjustment prevents IIS services from overwhelming the network bandwidth.

By default, the **BandwidthLevel** parameter is not started. To start the bandwidth throttler, which **BandwidthLevel** controls, you must change the installation default behavior. This is done by changing the value of the **BandwidthLevel** parameter.

Use the Internet Service Manager to change the value of the **BandwidthLevel** parameter without having to stop and start the server. You can also use a Registry editor (Regedit or Regedt32) to manually change the value of this parameter. The server should be stopped and restarted if you use a Registry editor. For additional information, see Chapter 7, "Monitoring Bandwidth and Network Capacity," and the online *Microsoft Windows NT Server Resource Kit: Windows NT Server Internet Guide*.

Warning To add or modify a Registry value entry, use admininstrative tools such as Control Panel or System Policy Editor whenever possible. Using a Registry editor (Regedit or Regedt32) to change a value can have unforeseen effects, including changes that can prevent you from starting your system.

Using the Idle Disconnect Feature

Idle disconnect reduces the cost of remote access carrier service and can be used to reduce the total capacity of dial-in communications links, based on the reduction of wasted remote connect time. This feature can be configured on remote clients that use Windows NT–based dial-up networking.

This new feature automatically terminates a RAS connection to your server after a certain period of time if there has been no activity over the remote dial-up communications link. The user or administrator can specify the amount of time before this feature is activated.

Troubleshooting Client Connections over Slow WAN Links

If remote clients that connect directly to your Internet Information Server over a slow dial-up connection experience connectivity problems, you can change specific Internet Information Server properties and Windows NT–based Registry parameters to resolve connection time-out problems. You can also change Registry parameters on remote Windows NT–based clients to adjust connection time-out problems.

You can change the behavior of TCP/IP, the protocol used for Internet communications, by changing the Registry parameters located in the following subkeys:

HKEY_LOCAL_MACHINE\System
\CurrentControlSet
   \Services
      \Tcpip
         \Parameters

HKEY_LOCAL_MACHINE\System
\CurrentControlSet
   \Services
      \AdapterName
         \Parameters
            \Tcpip

In the previous subkey, *AdapterName* refers to the name of the network adapter to which TCP/IP is bound. Most adapters are named to indicate the name of the card. However, some are not. For example, a DEC adapter is named Lance1.

Changing TCP/IP Parameters on the Remote Client

As previously mentioned, TCP/IP is the protocol used on the Internet. You may consider changing the following TCP/IP Registry parameters if remote clients are experiencing connectivity problems.

TcpMaxConnectRetransmissions

The Registry parameter **TcpMaxConnectRetransmissions** determines the number of times TCP retransmits a connect request (a SYN) before aborting the attempt. The retransmission time-out is doubled with each successive retransmission in a given connect attempt. The initial time-out value is 3 seconds.

Increasing the default value may allow a client to connect over a slow WAN. However, the value should only be changed in very small increments because the time-out value doubles after each transmission retry. Too large a value could ensure that a connection attempt never times out.

TcpWindowSize

The Registry parameter **TcpWindowSize** determines the maximum TCP receive window size offered by the computer. The receive window specifies the number of bytes a sender can transmit without receiving an acknowledgment (an ACK); in other words, it indicates the amount of receive data (in bytes) that can be buffered at one time on a connection. The sending host can send only the amount of data indicated by the receive window before waiting for an acknowledgment and window update from the receiving host.

In general, larger receive windows improve performance over high delay, high bandwidth networks. For greatest efficiency, the receive window should be an even multiple of the TCP maximum segment size (MSS).

However, if your clients experience connectivity problems because they time out before data transmission reaches them, you can change the value of the **TcpWindowSize** parameter. Reducing the value of **TcpWindowSize** causes an acknowledgment for data received to be sent to the sender sooner. Earlier acknowledgment lowers the possibility that the sender will time out while waiting for an acknowledgment. However, it also increases the amount of network traffic and causes slower throughput.

The TCP/IP stack is designed to self-tune in most environments. Instead of using a hard-coded default receive window size, TCP adjusts the window size to even increments of the MSS negotiated during connection setup.

Matching the receive window to even increments of the MSS increases the percentage of full-sized TCP segments used during bulk data transmission. By default, **TcpWindowSize** is set to 8 kilobytes (K) rounded up to the nearest MSS increment for the connection. If that increment is not at least four times the MSS, then it is adjusted to four times the MSS, with a maximum size of 64K.

The maximum window size is 64K because the field in the TCP header is 16 bits in length. Request for Comments (RFC) 1323 describes a TCP window scale option that can be used to obtain larger receive windows; however, Windows NT –based TCP/IP does not yet implement that option.

For Ethernet, the receive window is usually set to 8760 bytes (that is, 8192 rounded up to six 1460-byte segments). For 16/4 Token Ring or FDDI, it is set to around 16K. These are default values, and it is not generally advisable to alter them. However, if necessary you can either change **TcpWindowSize** to globally change the setting for the computer, or use the **setsockopt** Windows Sockets call to change the setting on a per-socket basis. For more information on Windows Sockets, see the Windows Sockets Software Development Kit (SDK).

C H A P T E R   4

Using ISDN

Integrated Services Digital Network (ISDN) is a high-speed, fully digital telephone service that can be used over the existing analog telephone network. A standard analog telephone line and modem connection typically transfers data at a maximum of 28.8 kilobits per second. ISDN can dramatically speed up transfer of information over the Internet or over a remote wide area network (WAN) link, because ISDN transfers data at rates of 64 to 128 kilobits per second.

ISDN is a powerful and complex telecommunication service that can be used to support many different types of telecommunication needs. It can provide connections to the Internet that support World Wide Web browsing, multimedia, and video presentation applications.

This chapter is limited to information about using ISDN to connect to the Internet with a computer running Windows NT Server version 4.0 with Internet Information Server. The information in this chapter is intended for network administrators and support personnel who need information about ISDN and how ISDN can be used to connect to the Internet. This chapter includes the following sections:

- "Introduction to ISDN." This section covers ISDN basics, including its data transfer rate, channel configuration, availability, and quality of connection. The section discusses two ISDN services, Basic Rate Interface and Primary Rate Interface, and describes hardware required for ISDN. It also briefly describes Microsoft support for ordering ISDN.

- "Windows NT Architecture Supporting ISDN." This section describes the Windows NT services and the application programming interfaces that support ISDN. It also discusses the Point-to-Point Protocol (PPP), Remote Access Service, and PPP Multilink as they relate to ISDN.

- "Configuring Windows NT Server for ISDN." This section tells you how to configure your Windows NT Server to work with ISDN and describes equipment and protocols required.

- "Alternatives to ISDN." This section briefly discusses some alternatives to ISDN.

Introduction to ISDN

ISDN is an international digital telephony standard defined by the International Telecommunications Union, formerly known as the Consultative Committee for International Telephony and Telegraphy (CCITT). ISDN protocols are mapped to Open Systems Interconnectivity (OSI) standards: to OSI layer 2 for call setup, maintenance, and disconnect and to OSI layer 3 for basic call control.

The ISDN standards provide an open architecture for digital telephony, enabling manufacturers to design and produce networking devices that can operate over any ISDN telephone line, regardless of the local telephone network.

ISDN provides end-to-end digital connectivity between a remote computer and another computer by using a local telephone line for network connection. Prior to ISDN, digital data communications were available only on proprietary networks, and Internet connections over telephone networks had to convert from digital to analog transmission. This conversion reduces quality of service, speed of transmission, and available bandwidth.

ISDN is typically supplied by the same company that supplies analog service, also referred to as plain old telephone (POTS) service. However, ISDN differs from analog telephone service in several ways, including:

- Data transfer rate
- Available channels per call
- Availability of service
- Cost of service
- Quality of connection

Data Transfer Rate

ISDN can provide data transfer rates of up to 128 kilobits per second. These speeds are slower than those of local area networks (LANs) supported by high-speed data communications technology. However, they are faster than those of analog telephone lines, which provide transfer rates of up to 28.8 kilobits per second.

In addition to the difference in data transfer rates, ISDN calls can be set up much faster than analog phone calls. While an analog modem can take up to a minute to set up a connection, you usually can start transmitting data in about two seconds with ISDN. Because ISDN is fully digital, the lengthy handshaking process of analog modems (those piercing, screeching noises) is not required.

Channels

POTS service provides a single channel, which can carry voice or digital communications but not both at the same time. ISDN service is available in several configurations of multiple channels that provide simultaneous voice and digital communications. In addition to increasing data throughput, multiple channels eliminate the need for separate voice and data phone lines.

Availability

POTS service is generally available throughout the United States. Although increasing in availability, ISDN service is not as widely available as POTS service.

Cost

The cost of ISDN hardware and service fees is generally higher than POTS modems and service fees.

Connection Quality

ISDN transmits data digitally and, as a result, is less susceptible to static and noise than analog transmissions are. Analog modem connections must dedicate some bandwidth to error correction and retransmission. This overhead reduces the actual throughput. In contrast, an ISDN line can dedicate all its bandwidth to data transmission.

Because ISDN is a digital service, it is sensitive to outside interference, and certain factors affect the quality of ISDN connections to the telephone network and the Internet. The computer connecting to the ISDN line must be within a given distance of the telephone company's central office equipment that serves the computer for the ISDN connection to work. The maximum distance allowed between the computer and the central telephone office is typically 18,000 feet. Additionally, ISDN connections can be adversely affected by telephone lines that are not wired using twisted-pair wiring.

Two types of ISDN service are currently available:

- Basic Rate Interface (BRI)
- Primary Rate Interface (PRI)

The most appropriate type of service for small Internet Information Server sites is ISDN-BRI. The most appropriate type of service for medium to large Internet Information Server sites is ISDN-PRI. The next two sections describe the two types of service in further detail.

ISDN-Basic Rate Interface

ISDN-BRI divides the telephone line into three digital channels: two bearer channels, commonly referred to as B channels, and one D channel. All three channels can be used simultaneously.

The B channels can be used to send voice, circuit-switched data, or packet-switched data at rates of 56 to 64 kilobits per second. The maximum available transfer rate is determined by your local telephone company. The B channels function independently of one another. They can be used simultaneously for separate calls or combined to provide a total bandwidth of 128 kilobits per second.

The D channel can transfer data at 16 kilobits per second and is used for signaling and control information sent between the computer and the telephone office. D channel signaling provides functions such as call setup, call monitoring, call termination, and enhanced telephony features.

When using ISDN-BRI, it is possible to perform several types of connections. For example, it is possible to have a voice conversation on one B channel, a circuit-switched data call on the second B channel, and a packet-switched data call on the D channel. The D channel can simultaneously complete all necessary signaling and call control functions.

ISDN-Primary Rate Interface

The U.S. standard for ISDN-PRI consists of 24 digital channels: 23 B channels and 1 D channel, commonly referred to as a 23B+D connection. ISDN-PRI provides a total bandwidth of 1.544 megabits per second and is designed for transmission over a North American-standard T1 line connection. The European standard for ISDN-PRI provides a total of 31 or 32 digital channels. Each of these channels is a 64–kilobit per second B channel, except one that is the D channel for the entire group. In Europe, ISDN-PRI is designed for transmission over a European-standard E1 line connection. A PRI D channel can be used to control one or multiple T1 or E1 lines.

The following figure illustrates the main difference between BRI and PRI, which is the greater number of channels that allows PRI to provide higher bandwidth than the BRI service.

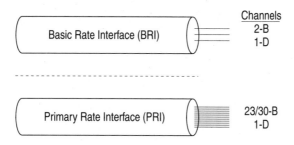

Figure 4.1   **Comparison of ISDN-BRI to ISDN-PRI**

ISDN Hardware

The ISDN user-to-network interface standard defines the hardware components needed for ISDN communication and these components' interfaces to other hardware components. ISDN provides standards for the following components and interfaces:

- Terminal Equipment 1 (TE1). This equipment is workstation equipment, such as the ISDN telephone or ISDN-enabled computer.

- Network Termination 1 (NT1). A device that connects the U interface (the telephone wall jack) to the interior phone circuit on the user premises. The NT1 device converts the two-wire circuit of the U interface to four-wire circuits that allow multiple terminal devices to access ISDN B channels. Typically, the NT1 device provides the Subscriber/Termination interface for ISDN-BRI service.

- Network Termination 2 (NT2). An intelligent device such as a ISDN router that exists between the NT1 and TE1 devices. The NT2 device provides services that map to the Data Link and Network layers of the OSI mode.

- Subscriber/Termination (S/T) Interface. The ISDN standard for the S/T Interface defines the conversion of two-pair to four-pair circuits and also defines distance limitations. The maximum allowable distance between the NT1 device on the user premises and a user computer is approximately 3,500 cable feet.

- U Interface. The telephone wall jack on the user premises. The ISDN standard for the U interface defines the maximum allowable distance between the telephone company's central office equipment and the U interface, which is approximately 18,000 cable feet.

These hardware and interface components are described in the following sections.

Workstation Hardware

There are two types of ISDN hardware devices that you can use to connect your computer to an ISDN line. *Internal ISDN devices* are adapter cards that you put inside your computer. *External ISDN devices* are adapters that you connect to an external port on the back of your computer.

Internal vs. External ISDN Adapters

Internal ISDN cards can take the fullest advantage of your ISDN line. However, internal adapters require you to open your computer to install the card. In addition, in order to install an internal adapter, you need a slot free in your computer that supports the same type of bus (for example, ISA, EISA, or PCI) as the card you want to install.

External ISDN adapters are easy to install and do not require any special software, but they do not provide the same level of performance that internal adapters do. External ISDN adapters are similar to a modem, and the computer communications program attempts to control the external ISDN adapter just as it controls an analog modem, typically with AT commands.

An external ISDN adapter plugs into a computer's serial or parallel port. These ports impose certain limitations. Most computer serial ports do not transmit information faster than 115 kilobits per second, which is less than ISDN's maximum data speed of 128 kilobits per second. These serial ports also impose overhead on the transfer of information between the computer and the external adapter, further slowing data speeds.

An external adapter can also adversely affect the performance of your computer, because an external adapter places heavy requirements on the CPU. To use an external ISDN adapter, it is recommended you use a computer with a 486/33 or faster processor.

Also, interoperability issues can potentially arise with external adapters, because higher-level protocols such as Point-to-Point Protocol (PPP) or authentication are implemented in the modem itself. These protocols are evolving quickly and can be difficult to update in an external adapter.

Adapters and the U and S/T Interfaces

The *U Interface* carries ISDN signals over a single pair of wires between your computer and the telephone central office. This interface is designed to carry ISDN signals over long distances. The *S/T Interface* uses two pairs of wires to deliver the signal from the wall jack to the ISDN adapter in a computer or other ISDN equipment.

If your ISDN adapter supports the S/T Interface, you need to get a device known as a Network Termination 1 (NT1) that converts traffic between the U Interface and the S/T Interface. The NT1 supplies a jack for the U Interface coming from the wall and one or more jacks for the S/T Interface connection to the computer and other ISDN or analog devices, in addition to a connection to an external power supply.

Some ISDN adapters sold in North America connect directly to a U Interface. If a single computer is the only equipment to be connected to an ISDN line, this type of adapter is the easiest to install. Manufacturers may describe such an adapter as having built-in NT1 or simply as a U Interface ISDN adapter.

Wiring

ISDN uses unshielded twisted-pair cable instead of more costly coaxial cable. ISDN lines can be run on existing category 3 wiring to a computer as long as distance limitations are not exceeded. Repeaters can be used when distance limitations are exceeded.

ISDN service from the phone company officially ends at what is called the demarcation point, generally referred to as the demarc. The demarc is usually inside the wall of the customer's office or home. You, the customer, are responsible for the inside wiring from the demarc to your ISDN equipment, including the wall jacks. The telephone company or an electrical contractor can install and maintain the inside wiring for an additional charge.

If you are connecting just one computer to an ISDN line, the wiring requirements can be very simple. Most offices are wired with extra sets of telephone wires, and one of those sets can be used for your ISDN line. However, a number of possible wiring pitfalls exist:

- Your "extra" wires might already be in use for an analog line or lines.
- Your extra wires might be used to power lighted phone buttons.
- Your extra wires might not be connected directly to the demarc.
- The wiring between the ISDN wall jack and the demarc might be "daisy-chain" rather than direct wiring.

Direct wiring between the ISDN wall jack and the demarc, also known as a home run, is recommended. For more information on wiring issues, consult your telephone company or an electrical contractor.

Phone Jacks

The following two types of phone jacks can be used with ISDN telephone lines:

- RJ11, the standard analog phone jack. The RJ11 has four wires. The wire from the wall to the NT1 usually has RJ11 jacks.
- RJ45, a jack slightly wider than the RJ11 that has six wires. The wire from the NT1 to the ISDN adapter usually has RJ45 jacks.

The following figure puts together ISDN hardware and interfaces to illustrate the relationships described in this "ISDN Hardware" section.

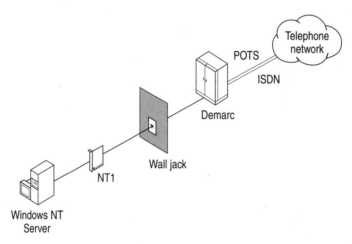

Figure 4.2   ISDN hardware and interfaces

Connecting Multiple Devices to an ISDN Line

Instead of connecting the ISDN line to a single computer, you can also connect an ISDN line to a LAN so all the computers on the LAN share the ISDN line. Doing so requires an ISDN network bridge or router.

You can connect up to eight devices to a single ISDN line. These devices can include network routers and bridges, Group 4 ISDN fax machines, computers, and ISDN telephones, in addition to traditional analog telephone devices.

For example, you might want to have an ISDN adapter in your computer, an ISDN telephone to make voice calls, and a Group 4 ISDN fax machine all connected to the same ISDN line. In such a scenario, incoming data calls go to the computer, voice calls to the telephone, and fax calls to the fax machine.

To support this configuration, you need an NT1 that supports multiple S/T Interface connections. Each device on the ISDN line is connected to the NT1. Each device needs its own Service Profile Identifier (SPID) to ensure the telephone company can route calls to the appropriate device. An example configuration is illustrated in the following figure.

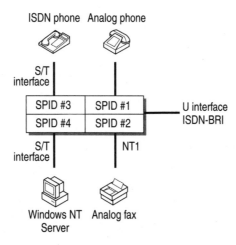

Figure 4.3   Using multiple ISDN devices

Ordering ISDN Service

ISDN is a powerful but complex service and is not yet available throughout the United States. For this reason, getting ISDN can sometimes be confusing or frustrating. Microsoft provides an online service that can guide you through the ordering process. This service and useful information is available for computers running Windows-based operating systems. This service can simplify and streamline the process of getting ISDN for your Windows-based computer, by helping you:

- Identify which telephone companies offer ISDN. Most but not all telephone companies offer this service.
- Check whether the necessary ISDN equipment is installed in your area.
- Learn about the ISDN service options and pricing in your area.
- Send an electronic order for ISDN to your telephone company.
- Automatically tell the phone company how to configure your ISDN line.

To use this online service, connect to the Microsoft World Wide Web site at:
http://www.microsoft.com/windows/getisdn.

Note Even if the right equipment is installed in your area, ISDN may not be available. To determine whether your particular wiring supports ISDN, your telephone company must perform what is known as a line qualification.

Windows NT Architecture Supporting ISDN

Support for ISDN is a built-in feature of Windows NT Server. ISDN requires Transmission Control Protocol/Internet Protocol (TCP/IP) and Point-to-Point Protocol (PPP), which Windows NT Server fully supports. PPP is an industry standard that enables Windows NT–based computers to support remote access networking in multivendor networks.

In addition to providing support for TCP/IP and the TCP/IP-based PPP protocols, Windows NT server architecture supports ISDN by using the services and application programming interfaces (APIs) illustrated in the following figure.

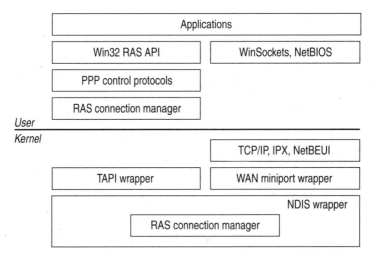

Figure 4.4   ISDN support in the Windows NT server remote access architecture

In the preceding figure, Win32 RAS API stands for the Win32® application programming interface (API) implementation of Remote Access Service. WinSockets stands for the Windows Sockets API; TAPI stands for telephony API; and IPX stands for Internetwork Packet Exchange, a transport protocol.

This architecture is important because, as previously described, internal and external ISDN adapters are differently configured and used by the Windows NT Server operating system. Internal ISDN device drivers provide network driver interface specification (NDIS) and WAN miniport device drivers. These drivers are installed when you configure the ISDN adapter by using the **Adapter** tab in the Network program in Control Panel.

However, external ISDN adapters are attached to the computer by using the serial (COM) port. Because of this, Windows NT Server processes an external ISDN device as a modem and as a result integrates an external ISDN device differently than an internal ISDN device.

Note Vendors of ISDN hardware devices can obtain information about developing NDIS and WAN miniport drivers for their ISDN hardware device drivers by connecting to:
http://www.microsoft.com/hwdev/devdes/isdnwin.html

Point-to-Point Protocol

The Point-to-Point Protocol (PPP) provides a standard method for transporting multiprotocol datagrams over point-to-point links. PPP does so by establishing and configuring different link and network-layer protocols to carry traffic from point to point. Control and data flow modules make up the PPP control protocols as illustrated in the following figure.

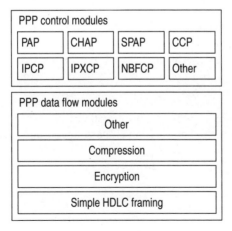

Figure 4.5   Microsoft PPP control modules

The preceding art shows Password Authentication Protocol (PAP), Challenge Handshake Authentication (CHAP), and Shiva Password Authentication Protocol (SPAP), which perform password authentication of RAS clients. Compression Control Protocol (CCP) is used to negotiate encryption with RAS clients. IPCP, IPXCP, NBFCP, and Other are the Internet Protocol (IP), NetWare IPX, NetBIOS Extended User Interface (NetBEUI), and Other protocol modules, which control RAS client sessions. HDLC stands for the High-level Data Link Control protocol.

PPP running under Windows NT Server supports external and internal ISDN adapters. The key difference for PPP between an external ISDN adapter and an internal ISDN adapter is that the external device sends byte-level PPP (also known as asynchronous PPP). The internal ISDN device, which uses an NDIS and WAN miniport driver, sends bit-level PPP (also known as synchronous PPP).

For compatibility with Windows NT Server, Microsoft recommends that external ISDN devices provide an asynchronous-to-synchronous PPP conversion feature. For information about external ISDN devices that can be used on a computer running Windows NT Server, see the *Windows NT Hardware Compatibility List.*

Using Remote Access Service with ISDN

A computer running Windows NT Server with RAS can be used to connect an intranet and remote users to the Internet. The connection to the RAS server computer over the telephone line provides a virtual WAN. Using this connection, local and remote users can access network resources, such as a computer running Internet Information Server.

Because Windows NT Server supports ISDN, you can configure RAS with ISDN connections to the Internet and to remote users. You can optimize the ISDN configuration to allow the RAS server to support the maximum number of remote client connections (256) or to provide the best possible bandwidth for a smaller number of connections.

By using multiple B channels for each Internet or remote client connection, you can maximize the available bandwidth for the connections. However, maximizing the bandwidth by this method reduces the total number of connections that can be supported. You can maximize bandwidth by using PPP Multilink, described in the following section.

Using PPP Multilink with ISDN

The PPP Multilink implementation under Windows NT Server is compliant with the Internet Engineering Task Force (IETF) PPP Multilink standard defined by Request for Comment (RFC) 1717. PPP Multilink protocol provides an inexpensive method that you can use to increase the bandwidth on your existing ISDN and analog telephone lines.

Multilink protocol enables you to combine the bandwidth capabilities of a communication device and telephone line into a single logical pipe. You can use Multilink protocol with analog modems, ISDN, PPTP, or X.25 communication links.

Windows NT Server 4.0 includes RFC-compliant support for the Multilink protocol as part of the Windows NT Server RAS service. Any remote clients that connect to the RAS server must also support a PPP Multilink implementation compliant with RFC 1717.

You can use the Multilink protocol feature only when your computer is configured with multiple WAN adapter devices that can be combined to form the logical PPP pipe over the communication link. The most common use for Multilink is to combine ISDN channels; however, you can also use it to bundle two or more analog modems, or an analog modem and an ISDN line.

For example, you can provide up to 128–kilobit per second wire speeds on a single ISDN-BRI line by combining the two B channels. Each B channel provides a 64–kilobit per second link, and the two combined achieve speeds of up to 128 kilobits per second. You can also combine an analog line with an ISDN line to increase bandwidth.

Note When you combine both B channels under ISDN, you cannot use your second channel for other applications, such as fax or voice calls.

If you use PPP Multilink with ISDN, you must configure your network so that Windows NT–based remote clients connecting to the intranet or the Internet do so by connecting to a server that also supports PPP Multilink, such as a server running Windows NT Server with RAS server.

When using a pool of servers to support remote clients using PPP Multilink, you must also ensure the remote clients connect to the same server for each Multilink session. In other words, if the remote client connects to different servers during an attempted Multilink session, the separate B channel lines cannot be combined across servers. To combine B channels for increased bandwidth, a client's session must occur on one server.

Configuring Windows NT Server for ISDN

Windows NT Server 4.0 and 3.5x provide built-in support for ISDN. To connect to the Internet by using ISDN, you need to install and configure the Dial-Up Networking feature in Windows NT Server.

Before configuring ISDN on a computer running Windows NT Server, you need the following:

- Installed internal or external ISDN adapter

- ISDN telephone line service at the location where you will use dial-up networking to connect to the Internet

- ISDN telephone line service at the remote location to which you want to connect, usually either your Internet service provider (ISP) or a RAS server

In general, it is recommended that you also use PPP with ISDN for connections to the Internet. This protocol is the one typically used to access the Internet over dial-up connections. To use PPP, you must have a PPP account with your ISP. If you currently have a Serial Line Internet Protocol (SLIP) account, you should request your ISP to change the account to PPP.

After you have installed your ISDN adapter and received notice from your telephone company your ISDN service is installed, you can configure Windows NT Server for your ISDN service.

▶ **To configure your ISDN device for ISDN-BRI Service**

1. Click the **Start** button, point to **Settings**, and then click **Control Panel**.

2. Double-click the Network icon.

3. Click the **Adapters** tab.

4. In the **Network Adapters** list, click your ISDN device, and then click **Properties**.

5. Verify that the values selected in the **I/O Port Base Address** and **Interrupt Number** boxes are the values supplied by your ISDN device vendor. If not, click the correct values.

6. In the **Page** list, click **SPID Settings**.

7. In the **Number of Terminals** box, click the terminal number provided by your telephone company. For ISDN-BRI service, this number will be either 1 or 2. For more information, click the **Help** button.

8. In the **SPID 1** box, type the value provided by your telephone company, and click **OK**.

    –Or–

    In the **SPID 2** box, type the value provided by your telephone company, and click **OK**. If the value selected in the **Number of Terminals** box does not equal 2, the **SPID 2** box is unavailable.

9. Click **OK,** and close the Control Panel.

After you have configured ISDN on your computer, you can enable PPP Multilink protocol by using the following procedure.

▶   **To enable Multilink on a RAS server**

1. In Control Panel, double-click the Network icon.

2. Click the **Services** tab.

3. In the **Network Services** list, click **Remote Access Service,** and then click **Properties**.

4. In the **Remote Access Setup** dialog box, click **Network**.

5. In the **Network Configuration** dialog box, select the **Enable Multilink** check box, and then click **OK**.

Alternatives to ISDN

Large companies that connect to the Internet to provide services to a large number of remote users might consider alternative transmission technologies, such as Asynchronous Transfer Mode (ATM), dedicated Frame Relay, or T3 Internet connections. In the near future, new technologies will provide additional options for connecting to the Internet. These technologies include ones such as Asymmetric Digital Subscriber Line (ADSL), which can operate over existing telephone wires, and cable modems that operate over coaxial cable television wiring.

The following table illustrates when ISDN technology can provide adequate bandwidth, based on minimum bandwidth requirements of different application types, and when alternatives to ISDN should be considered.

Table 4.1   Alternatives to ISDN

Application type	Minimum bandwidth required	Acceptable transmission technology
Audio (FM mono quality)	28.8 kilobits per second (Kbps)	Analog
Audio (FM stereo quality)	144 Kbps	ISDN-BRI
Audio (CD quality)	1.544–2.048 megabits per second (Mbps) for ISDN-PRI, T1 or E1;622 Mbps for ATM	ISDN-PRI, T1 or E1; ATM
Data communications	9.6 Kbps–28.8 Kbps for analog; 144 Kbps for ISDN-BRI	Analog; ISDN-BRI
Video (low end)	144 Kbps	ISDN-BRI
Video conferencing	1.544–2.048 Mbps for ISDN-PRI, T1 or E1; 622 Mbps for ATM	ISDN-PRI, T1 or E1; ATM
Video (broadcast quality)	6 Mbps for ISDN-PRI; 622 Mbps for ATM	Dedicated leased lines; ATM
Virtual reality programs	6 Mbps for ISDN-PRI; 622 Mbps for ATM	Dedicated leased lines; ATM

For more information about alternatives to ISDN, see Chapter 3, "Adding Bandwidth for Internet Connectivity."

PART II

Optimizing IIS Server Performance

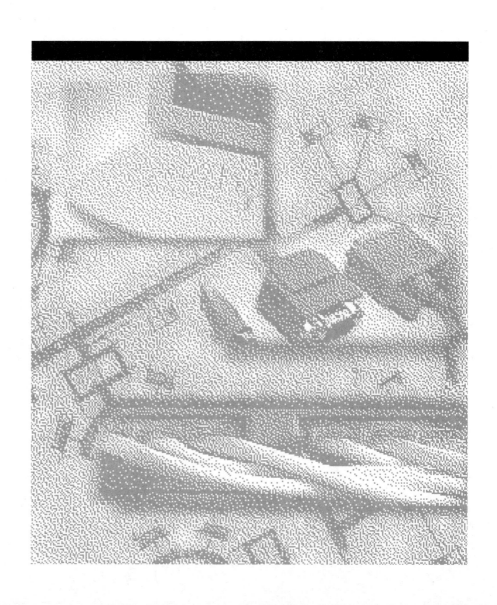

C H A P T E R   5

Monitoring Virtual Memory

The Internet Information Server (IIS) runs as a Windows NT service and takes advantage of the full capability of the Windows NT virtual memory system. Virtual memory uses space on disk to extend the server's physical memory.

This chapter discusses how virtual memory is used on a Windows NT 4.0 server running Internet Information Server 2.0 (IIS). This chapter presents several approaches you can use to monitor and improve memory use. The material is intended as a technical guide for network administrators, but should also be useful for anyone running Internet Information Server—from a single source World Wide Web page publisher to the administrator of a large corporate network for an Internet service provider.

This chapter suggests some tools and techniques for monitoring virtual memory on servers running Internet Information Server. It covers the following topics:

- "Virtual Memory on an IIS Server"
- "Monitoring Server Memory"
- "Monitoring the Working Set of the IIS process"
- "Monitoring the IIS Object Cache"
- "Monitoring the File System Cache"
- "Suggestions for Optimizing Memory on an IIS Server"

Warning To add or modify a Registry value entry, use administrative tools such as Control Panel or System Policy Editor whenever possible. Using a Registry editor (Regedit or Regedt32) to change a value can have unforeseen effects, including changes that can prevent you from starting your system.

Virtual Memory on an IIS Server

The Windows NT virtual memory system extends the server's physical memory by using space on disk. The virtual memory system reserves physical memory for items that are used frequently or are costly to retrieve, and moves unreferenced items to disk. If a process or service needs code or data on disk, the system retrieves the requested pages and delivers them to the process' working set in physical memory — all without intervention from the process. The system will also retrieve contiguous pages, if there is enough physical memory to hold them.

The challenge of a virtual memory system is to minimize disk I/O, which is slow, mechanical, and laborious compared to the speed at which items are written to and retrieved from physical memory. Minimizing disk I/O requires that the system keep as many items as possible in physical memory.

Physical Memory on an IIS Server

A server running Internet Information Server should have sufficient physical memory to keep the following items in physical memory:

- Program code for IIS services. This code occupies only 400K even with HTTP, FTP, and Gopher running simultaneously. This code is part of the *working set* of the Internet Information Server process, Inetinfo.exe, and can be paged to disk.

- Frequently accessed Web page files. The number and size of these files varies widely with the installation. These files are stored in the *file system cache*, an area of physical memory reserved for frequently and repeatedly used pages. The remaining files are stored on disk until needed.

- Frequently used objects. These are objects that are costly to retrieve and are frequently reused by the service, such as file handles, file directory listings, and parsed Internet Database Connector queries and their results. These objects are stored in the *IIS Object Cache*, a cache maintained by the IIS service. The IIS Object Cache is also part of the working set of the Internet Information Server process, Inetinfo.exe, and can be paged to disk.

- IIS Log buffers. When IIS Logging is enabled, Internet Information Server maintains two buffers in which it accumulates log data in ANSI characters before it writes the data to disk. By default, each buffer is 64K. These buffers are part of the working set of the Internet Information Server process. Logged data also appears in the file system cache because data is cached when the buffer contents are written to disk.

- TCB Table. TCP maintains a hash table of transmission control blocks (TCBs) to store data for each TCP connection. A control block is attached to the table for each active connection. The control block is deleted shortly after the connection is closed. The TCB table is part of the operating system's *nonpaged memory pool*. As such, the TCB table must remain in physical memory; it cannot be paged to disk.

- HTTP Connection data structures. HTTP maintains pageable data structures to track its active connections. When these data structures are in physical memory, they are counted as part of the working set of the Internet Information Server process.

- Pool threads. The threads that execute the code for the services are stored in the *nonpaged pool* in physical memory, along with other objects used by the operating system to support Internet Information Server and for other uses. Threads must remain in physical memory; they cannot be paged to disk.

You can measure your server's physical memory and measure the proportion of physical memory used directly or indirectly by Internet Information Server. You can also log the data over time to identify patterns of memory use.

Monitoring Server Memory

Monitoring the physical memory of a server running Internet Information Server involves measuring the size of the areas in physical memory used by IIS and assuring that enough space is available to contain the elements Internet Information Server needs to store. The space should be sufficient for normal operation and for sporadic peaks in demand.

The Windows NT virtual memory system is designed to be self-tuning. The Virtual Memory Manager and Cache Manager adjust the size of the file system cache, the working sets of processes, the paged and nonpaged memory pools, and the paging files on disk to produce the most efficient use of available physical memory. Similarly, the IIS service regulates the size of the IIS Object Cache. Therefore, the primary purpose of monitoring memory in a Windows NT server running Internet Information Server is to make sure that the server has enough physical memory, not to adjust the size of each memory component as might be the case with other operating systems.

How to Monitor Overall Server Memory

Internet Information Server and its component services, HTTP Service (WWW), the File Transfer Protocol (FTP) Service, and Gopher Service, run jointly in a user-mode process called Inetinfo.exe. Like most well-designed user-mode processes, the IIS services derive much of their benefits from the Windows NT operating system architecture, including the Windows NT Security model, RPC communication, messaging, the file systems, and other operating system services. Thus, monitoring memory for Internet Information Server begins with monitoring overall server memory, even on a multipurpose server.

Methods of Monitoring Server Memory

This section is a brief review of the most important memory monitoring techniques. *Windows NT Workstation Resource Guide* includes a detailed discussion of some basic techniques for monitoring memory in Chapter 12, "Detecting Memory Bottlenecks," and Chapter 15, "Detecting Cache Bottlenecks." For more information on the tools discussed in this section, see Chapter 10, "About Performance Monitor," and Chapter 11, "Performance Monitoring Tools" in the *Windows NT Workstation Resource Guide*. Programmers can find additional memory optimizing techniques in the *Win32 Software Development Kit*.

Many performance monitoring tools measure system-wide and per-process memory use. These tools include Task Manager, Process Monitor (Pmon.exe), Process Viewer (Pviewer.exe), Process Explode (Pview.exe), PerfLog (Pdlcnfig.exe and Pdlsvc.exe), and Performance Monitor. PerfLog and Performance Monitor can measure memory use over time.

Here are a few guidelines for using Performance Monitor and PerfLog to monitor overall server memory use:

- *Monitor available memory*. The server must maintain enough available memory to support the operating system and all applications and services it runs. Compare the total physical memory available to Windows NT to the available memory remaining when you are running all server services. To gather more reliable data, log this value over time, making certain to include periods of peak activity. The system attempts to keep available bytes at 4MB or more, but it is prudent to keep at least 5 percent of memory available for peak use.

  To determine the physical memory available to Windows NT, double-click My Computer, and then click **About Windows NT** from the **Help** menu. **Memory Available to Windows NT** is displayed above the **OK** button. Total physical memory is also listed on the **Performance** tab in Task Manager. To start Task Manager, press CTRL+SHIFT+ESC.

  To track available memory, use Performance Monitor or PerfLog to log the Memory: Available Bytes counter.

- *Monitor paging.* Continuous high rates of paging indicate a memory shortage. *Paging* occurs when code or data requested by an application or service is not found in physical memory and must be retrieved from disk. The more memory the server has, the more data the system can store in memory and the more likely it is that the code or data requested is stored in memory. If required data is stored in memory, it does not need to be paged in from disk.

  Paging is measured in several ways:

  - *Numbers of page faults.* Page faults occur when the system cannot find a requested page in the working set of the process that requested the page. The system also counts a page fault on file accesses if the requested page is not found in the file system cache.

    To measure page faults on working sets and on the file system cache, use Performance Monitor or PerfLog to log the Memory: Page Faults/sec and Memory: Cache Faults/sec counters.

  - *Disk reads due to page faults.* All page faults interrupt the processor. Only *hard faults*, those that require reading from disk, delay system response. Monitor hard faults and compare the rate of hard faults to all page faults. In general, a sustained rate of more than five hard faults per second indicates a memory shortage.

    To measure hard faults, use Performance Monitor or PerfLog to log the Memory: Page Reads/sec counter. Use the Memory: Page Faults/sec counter as an indicator of all page faults.

- *Monitor the file system cache.* The file system cache is the working set of the file system. This cache is a reserved area in physical memory where the file system stores its recently used and frequently used data. By default, the system reserves about 50 percent of physical memory for the file system cache, but the system trims the cache if it is running out of memory. A large and effective file system cache is vital to IIS servers, which function like specialized file servers. This topic is discussed in more detail in "Monitoring the File System Cache" later in this chapter.

- *Monitor the size of the paging files.* The paging files on disk back up committed physical memory. The larger the paging file, the more memory the system can commit. Windows NT creates a paging file on the system disk. You can create a paging file on each logical disk, and enlarge existing files.

  To monitor the paging files, use Performance Monitor or PerfLog to log Process: Page File Bytes: Total.

- *Monitor the size of the paged and nonpaged memory pools.* The system's memory pools hold objects created and used by applications and the operating system. The paged pool holds items that can be paged to disk. Items in the non-paged pool must remain in physical memory. The contents of the memory pools are accessible only in privileged mode. On servers running Internet Information Server, the IIS threads that service connections are stored in the nonpaged pool, along with other objects used by the service, such as file handles.

  To monitor the pool space for all processes on the server, use Performance Monitor or PerfLog to log the Memory: Pool Paged Bytes and Memory: Pool Nonpaged Bytes counters. To monitor the pool space used directly by Internet Information Server, log the Process: Pool Paged Bytes: Inetinfo and Process: Pool Nonpaged Bytes: Inetinfo counters for the Inetinfo process.

These general monitoring techniques are useful for any Windows NT Workstation or Server. The following sections discuss techniques for monitoring components specific to the IIS service.

Monitoring the Working Set of the IIS Process

A server running Internet Information Server must have enough physical memory to support the Internet Information Server process. The physical memory visible to a process is called its *working set*. If the working set of the Internet Information Server process is not large enough, IIS is not able to store its code and frequently used data in physical memory. Therefore, the IIS services are delayed by having to retrieve code and data from disk.

The system continually adjusts the size of the working set of a process as the process runs. The amount of space the system provides to the working set depends on the amount of memory available to the system and the needs of the process.

This section describes the working set of the process in which Internet Information Server runs. The section suggests methods for monitoring the size of the Internet Information Server working set over time and explains how to determine whether the working set of the Internet Information Server process is large enough to enable IIS to run efficiently.

About the Inetinfo Working Set

Internet Information Server runs in a pageable user-mode process called Inetinfo.exe. The HTTP, FTP, and Gopher services run in the Inetinfo process and share the threads of the process. The working set of the Inetinfo process is the space in physical memory visible to the Inetinfo process.

Internet Information Server stores its code and frequently used data in the Inetinfo working set. For Internet Information Server to run efficiently, it must be able to maintain all of its code and the most frequently used files in its working set. In addition, the working set of the Inetinfo process should be large enough to contain the IIS Object Cache, data buffers for IIS Logging, and the data structures HTTP uses to track its active connections.

There is no fixed optimal size for the Inetinfo working set. The requirements of the working set vary depending upon the number of connections maintained, the number and size of files, and the use of other supporting services, such as security features and logging.

You can monitor the Internet Information Server process as it runs on your server to determine whether its working set is large enough to support the IIS services.

Monitoring the Inetinfo Working Set

You can monitor the size and effectiveness of a working set of the Inetinfo process by using several tools that monitor processes, such as:

- Process Viewer (Pviewer.exe)
- Process Explode (Pview.exe)
- Process Monitor (Pmon.exe)
- Performance Data Log Service (PerfLog) (Pdlcnfig.exe and Pdlsvc.exe)
- Performance Monitor (Perfmon.exe)

These tools are described in detail in the *Windows NT Workstation Resource Guide,* Chapter 10, "About Performance Monitor," and Chapter 11, "Performance Monitoring Tools."

Using Performance Monitor to Monitor the IIS Working Set

You can use the following Performance Monitor counters to monitor the working set of Inetinfo.exe. Internet Information Server and its component services run in the context of the Inetinfo process. (You can monitor the IIS Object Cache separately. For more information, see "Monitoring the IIS Object Cache" later in this chapter.)

Table 5.1   Performance Monitor Counters for the IIS Working Set

Counter	Indicates
Memory: Available Bytes	The amount of physical memory remaining and available for use, in bytes. This counter displays the amount of memory not currently used by the system or by running processes. This counter displays the last observed value, not an average.
	The operating system attempts to prevent this value from falling below 4MB. The system often trims the working sets of processes to maintain the 4MB minimum available memory.
Process: Working Set: Inetinfo	Size of the working set of the process, in bytes. This counter displays the last observed value, not an average over time.
	The working set is the space in physical memory available to the process. The working set contains recently used code and data. The working set of Inetinfo also contains the IIS Object Cache, buffers for IIS Log data, and the data structures HTTP uses to track connections.
Process: Page Faults/sec: Inetinfo	Hard and soft faults in the working set of the process.
Memory: Page Faults/sec	Hard and soft faults for all working sets running on the system.
Memory: Page Reads/sec	Hard page faults. This counter displays the number of times the disk is read to satisfy page faults. This counter displays the number of read operations, regardless of the number of pages read in each operation.
	A sustained rate of 5 reads/sec or more might indicate a memory shortage.
Memory: Pages Input/sec	One measure of the cost of page faults. This counter displays the number of pages read to satisfy page faults. One page is faulted at a time, but the system can read multiple pages to prevent further faults.

The counters in the preceding table are included in IISMem.pmw, a Performance Monitor workspace settings file on the *Supplement 1* CD.

You should log this data for several days. You can use **Bookmark** in the Performance Monitor log to identify times of unusually high and low server activity.

Analyzing the Working Set Data

The working set of Inetinfo should be large enough to contain the Internet Information Server code and the data IIS references. The Inetinfo working set includes its code, objects in the IIS Object Cache, data structures for tracking connections, buffers for holding IIS Log data, and other data it uses. If the Inetinfo working set is not large enough to contain its code and data, the system must read and write the code and data from disk. Increased disk activity can seriously degrade server performance, particularly if code must be read from disk.

The following sections describe how to use data about the Inetinfo working set to determine if the server has enough memory to support Internet Information Server efficiently.

Available Bytes and the Inetinfo Working Set

If the system has sufficient memory, it can maintain enough space in the Inetinfo working set so that Internet Information Server rarely needs to perform disk operations. One indicator of memory sufficiency is how much the size of the Inetinfo process working set varies in response to general memory availability on the server.

You can use the Memory: Available Bytes counter as an indicator of memory availability and the Process: Working Set: Inetinfo counter as an indicator of the size of the working set of the Internet Information Server process. Be sure to examine data collected over time because these counters display the last value observed, not an average.

Tip   To determine whether a counter reports instantaneous or averaged data, look at its *counter type*. The *counter type* determines how the data Performance Monitor collects from internal counters is calculated and averaged.

For example, the counter type of Memory: Available Bytes, is Perf_Counter_Rawcount. Counters of this type report only the last value observed in each sample interval.

Counters.hlp, a help file for the Performance Monitor counters, lists the counter type of each counter. Counters.hlp also includes a detailed description of each counter type. You can find the most current version of Counters.hlp on the *Supplement 1* CD.

Note how the size of the Inetinfo working set changes in response to changes in available bytes. In general, when available bytes fall, the system attempts to provide more available bytes. To do so, the system recovers bytes by taking bytes from the working sets of processes. This strategy provides more available bytes to the system, but it is likely to increase the rate of page faults for the process because the process must now retrieve data from disk that was once in its working set. When the rate of page faults rises, the system attempts to expand the working set to lower the page fault rate and the size of the working sets fluctuate accordingly.

After you have reviewed data on the varying size of the Inetinfo working set, you can use its page fault rate to determine how large the working set should be to operate efficiently.

Page Faults and the Inetinfo Working Set

There is no recommended value for the number of available bytes or for the size of the Inetinfo working set. The requirements vary widely with each system configuration and the services each system runs. You can determine whether your system has enough available bytes and a large enough Inetinfo working set by monitoring page faults.

The page fault counters for a process are incremented when the process requests code or data that is not found in its working set. The data might be found elsewhere in memory, such as in the file system cache, in the working set of another process, or in transition to disk. The system might also have to read the data from disk.

A sustained high rate of page faults for a process usually indicates that its working set is not large enough to support the process efficiently. If the system doesn't have enough available memory to enlarge the working set, it cannot lower the page fault rate.

Compare your data on the size of the Inetinfo working set to the rate of page faults attributed to the working set. Use the Process: Working Set: Inetinfo counter as an indicator of the size of the working set. Use the Process: Page Faults/sec: Inetinfo counter to indicate the rate of page faults for the Internet Information Server process.

There are two kinds of page faults. The page faults that affect performance significantly are *hard faults*, page faults that require reading from disk to retrieve a referenced page. *Soft faults*, page faults resolved when the page is found elsewhere in physical memory, interrupt the processor but do not affect performance significantly.

A sustained high fault rate of hard faults generally indicates a memory shortage. When the server does not have enough memory to support a sufficiently large working set for the process, the server is not able to lower the page fault rate to an acceptable level and performance is degraded.

Unfortunately, the Process: Page Faults/sec counter includes both hard and soft faults. There are no counters for measuring the hard faults attributable to each process separately. However, Memory: Page Reads/sec and Memory: Pages Input/sec are good indicators of hard faults for the whole system. If the system is incurring large numbers of hard page faults, it is likely that you have a memory bottleneck. Adding memory is likely to improve performance. For more information on memory bottlenecks, see Chapter 6, "Preventing Processor Bottlenecks."

Monitoring the IIS Object Cache

The IIS service maintains the IIS Object Cache, a cache of objects that the HTTP, FTP, and Gopher services use frequently. The Object Cache is also used for objects that are hard to retrieve. The IIS Object Cache is designed to improve the performance of Internet Information Server by keeping these objects readily available to the process. The primary components of the IIS Object Cache are open file object handles and directory listings, but the cache also stores parsed Internet Database Connector queries and their responses, as well as other service-specific objects.

This section describes the IIS Object Cache and suggest methods of monitoring its size and efficiency.

About the IIS Object Cache

The IIS Object Cache is part of the working set of the Internet Information Server process in physical memory. The objects stored in the Object Cache are related to objects in the operating system's nonpaged memory pool. The Object Cache can be paged to disk if memory is not sufficient to support a large enough working set for the Internet Information Server process. It is important to provide enough physical memory to maintain the Object Cache in the working set.

As you might expect, the size of the IIS Object Cache affects its performance. If the cache is not large enough, the system will have to retrieve the objects from disk. If the cache is too large, it will waste space in memory. By default, Internet Information Server allocates 10 percent of physical memory to the IIS Object Cache. This is an optimal size for most configurations. You can change the amount of physical memory allocated to the IIS Object Cache by entering a new value in the **MemoryCacheSize** value entry in the Registry.

For more information on changing the **MemoryCacheSize** value entry, see Regentry.hlp, a Registry help file on the *Supplement 1* CD. **MemoryCacheSize** is also described in the online *Windows NT Server Microsoft Internet Information Server Installation and Administration Guide.*

You can measure the size and effectiveness of the IIS Object Cache by using Performance Monitor.

Using Performance Monitor to Monitor the IIS Object Cache

Performance Monitor includes a set of extensible counters you can use to monitor the IIS services. These counters are installed in Performance Monitor when you run Internet Information Server Setup.

For descriptions of the Internet Information Server counters, in the Performance Monitor **Add to Chart** dialog box, select the counter name, then click the **Explain** button. You can also use Counters.hlp, a help file for the Performance Monitor counters. The most recent version of Counters.hlp is included on the *Supplement 1* CD. Previous versions of Counters.hlp did not include descriptions of the Internet Information Server counters.

Many of the Internet Information Server counters display the last observed value or a cumulative count, not an average value or rate. To determine what a Performance Monitor counter displays, view its counter type in Counters.hlp. The *counter type* determines how the data Performance Monitor collects from internal counters is calculated and averaged. Counters.hlp lists the counter type of each counter and a description of the Performance Monitor counter types.

Performance Monitor includes four performance objects for measuring Internet Information Server performance:

- HTTP Service
- FTP Server
- Gopher Service
- Internet Information Services Global

The Internet Information Services Global performance object contains counters used by all three services. The counters that monitor the IIS Object Cache, which is shared by the services, are part of this performance object.

The following table lists the counters recommended for monitoring the IIS Object Cache. You should log the counters over time to record trends in the size, content, and effectiveness of the IIS Object Cache.

Table 5.2   Performance Monitor Counters for the IIS Object Cache

Counter	Indicates
Internet Information Services Global: Cache Size	Maximum amount of space allocated for the IIS Object Cache, in bytes. This counter does not indicate how much of the space is occupied.
	The default is 10% of physical memory.

	(To change the size of the cache, edit the HKEY_LOCAL_MACHINE\System\
	   CurrentControlSet
	     \Services
	       \Inetinfo
	         \Parameters
	           \MemoryCacheSize

	value entry in the Registry).
Internet Information Services Global: Cache Used	Space in the IIS Object Cache that is currently being used to store objects, in bytes.
	Compare Internet Information Services Global: Cache Used to Internet Information Server: Cache Size.
Internet Information Services Global: Cache Hits Internet Information Services Global: Cache Misses Internet Information Services Global: Cache Hits %	A measure of the efficiency of the IIS Object Cache. Internet Information Services Global: Cache Hits and Internet Information Services Global: Cache Hits % (Internet Information Services Global: Cache Hits/ (Internet Information Services Global: Cache Hits + Internet Information Services Global: Cache Misses)) demonstrate how often data sought in the IIS Object Cache is found. Internet Information Services Global: Cache Misses indicates how often the system must search elsewhere in memory or on disk to satisfy a request.
	Internet Information Services Global: Cache Hits and Internet Information Services Global: Cache Misses display the total number of hits and misses since the service started. These values always remain the same or increase over time.
	Internet Information Services Global: Cache Hits % displays an instantaneous value, not an average over time.

Table 5.2   Performance Monitor Counters for the IIS Object Cache *(Continued)*

Counter	Indicates
Internet Information Services Global: Cache Flushes	How many times an object was deleted from the IIS Object Cache, either because it timed out, or because the object changed.
Internet Information Services Global: Objects	The number of objects currently stored in the IIS Object Cache.
Internet Information Services Global: Cached File Handles Internet Information Services Global: Directory Listings	Internet Information Services Global: Objects = Internet Information Services Global: Cached File Handles + Internet Information Services Global: Directory Listings + other objects, such as IDC queries and responses.

These counters are included in IISCache.pmw, a Performance Monitor workspace settings file on the *Supplement 1* CD. The workspace sets up a chart and a report of the counters.

Troubleshooting the Internet Information Services Counters

When you are monitoring a server remotely, the Internet Information Services Global, HTTP Service, FTP Server, and Gopher Service performance objects and counters appear in Performance Monitor only when the related IIS service is running on the computer being monitored. If you do not see these objects in the **Add to Chart** dialog box, close Performance Monitor on your computer, start the IIS service on the computer being monitored, and then start Performance Monitor again.

If the objects and counters still do not appear in the **Add to Chart** dialog box, or if they appear intermittently, make certain that no one else is using Performance Monitor to monitor the remote computer. All remote users must restart Performance Monitor after the IIS service is started for any of them to see the Internet Information Server counters. Also, check the Event Viewer application event log for errors. Errors in the service or in loading the counters can also prevent Performance Monitor from displaying the counters.

For more information on troubleshooting extensible Performance Monitor counters, see "Troubleshooting Features" in *Windows NT Workstation Resource Guide*, Chapter 10, "About Performance Monitor."

Analyzing the IIS Object Cache Data

The Performance Monitor counters for Internet Information Server monitor three different aspects of the IIS Object Cache: its contents, its size, and its performance. This section explains how to interpret the data you collect by using the Performance Monitor Internet Information Server counters.

Analyzing IIS Object Cache Contents

You can use the Performance Monitor counters to reveal the contents of the IIS Object Cache. The Internet Information Services Global: Objects counter counts all objects. The Internet Information Services Global: Cached File Handles and Internet Information Services Global: Directory Listings counters are subsets of the Internet Information Services Global: Objects counter. At any given time, the difference between the total number of objects and the sum of Internet Information Services Global: Cached File Handles and Internet Information Services Global: Directory Listings is equal to the number of other objects stored in the cache. Internet Information Services Global: Directory Listings are most important to servers running FTP service.

When interpreting the counters, remember that they show the most recently observed value, not an average.

The primary reason to count cache contents is to relate the contents to the size of the cache.

Analyzing the Size of the IIS Object Cache

The size of the IIS Object Cache is not a common problem, but it is worth monitoring because the cache is not efficient if it is too small.

Compare Internet Information Services Global: Cache Used to Internet Information Services Global: Cache Size over time. These are instantaneous values, not averages, so it is important to use a large data sample. If the Internet Information Services Global: Cache Used to Internet Information Services Global: Cache Size ratio is more than .9, and you have sufficient available memory (which you can determine by using Memory: Available Bytes), you might consider increasing the maximum size of the cache to 5MB. Alternatively, if the ratio of Internet Information Services Global: Cache Used to Internet Information Services Global: Cache Size remains less than .2 over time, consider reducing the cache size.

To change the size of the cache, use the **MemoryCacheSize** value entry in the Registry. It is located in:

HKEY_LOCAL_MACHINE\System
  \CurrentControlSet
    \Services
      \Inetinfo
        \Parameters.

After changing the value, restart the service, log the IIS Object Cache counters again, and watch for changes in performance.

Analyzing the Performance of the IIS Object Cache

Cache performance is judged by how often objects sought in the cache are found there. Frequent cache misses harm performance if they result in disk I/O. There are no fixed standards for cache performance, although a value of 80 to 90 percent for Internet Information Services Global: Cache Hits % is considered to be excellent for sites with many static files. If Internet Information Services Global: Cache Hits and Internet Information Services Global: Cache Hits % are very low or Internet Information Services Global: Cache Misses is quite high, the cache might be too small to function effectively. Adding memory increases the cache size and should improve its performance.

Cache flushes can also affect the performance of the IIS Object Cache. Cache flushes are regulated, in part, by an internal timer. The timer activates the *object-cache scavenger* which deletes expired objects. Objects are flushed from the cache if they change or if they time out before they are reused. If the timer is too quick, objects can be flushed from the cache too frequently. If the timer is too slow, objects can be wasting precious physical memory space.

To measure cache flushes, compare the number of cache flushes over time to the number of cache misses and to the rate of page faults of the IIS process (as indicated by the Process: Page Faults/sec: Inetinfo counter. It is important to observe these values over time. Like the other Internet Information Server counters, Internet Information Services Global: Cache Flushes displays an instantaneous value, not an average. If a high rate of cache flushes is associated with elevated cache misses and page faults, the cache might be flushed too frequently.

If you suspect that cache flushes are occurring too rapidly or too infrequently, you might want to change the rate at which unreferenced objects are flushed from the Internet Information Server cache. Make sure you have ample memory before increasing the time between flushes. To change the flush rate, use the **ObjectCacheTTL** value entry in the Registry. It is located in:

HKEY_LOCAL_MACHINE\System
   \CurrentControlSet
    \Services
     \Inetinfo
      \Parameters.

For more information about **ObjectCacheTTL**, see Regentry.hlp, the Registry help file, on the *Supplement 1* CD.

Monitoring the File System Cache

The *file system cache* is an area of physical memory reserved for frequently and repeatedly used file system data (it does not store code pages). This cache is maintained by the Windows NT Cache Manager for use by all processes. Processes map or copy files into the cache, depending on how they will use the files. If a process finds a page it needs in the cache, it can avoid costly disk I/O.

Servers running Internet Information Server are well suited to take advantage of the performance gains provided by the cache. Therefore, it is important that you provide enough physical memory to the server to allow the operating system to maintain the cache at an optimal size.

This section explains how Internet Information Server uses the file system cache, how to monitor the size and efficiency of the cache, and how to interpret the data you collect.

How IIS Uses the File System Cache

The IIS services rely on the operating system to store and retrieve frequently used Web pages and other files from the file system cache. The file system cache is particularly useful for servers of static Web pages. Web pages tend to be used in repeated, predictable patterns. Files read repeatedly are more likely to be found in the cache.

Also, Internet Information Server always reads sequentially. Sequential reading takes advantage of a Windows NT Cache Manager feature called a read ahead. A *read ahead* occurs when the Cache Manager's predictive algorithms detect sequential reading and begin to read larger blocks of data in each read operation. Read aheads can provide a significant performance boost to the process.

The IIS services use the file system cache and the IIS Object Cache. Sometimes, the caches are used together. When a thread of an IIS service needs to open a file, the thread requests a file handle from the operating system. When the thread receives the handle, the thread uses the handle to open the file. Then, if space permits, the thread stores the handle in the IIS Object Cache and the system stores the file data in the file system cache. Later, if that thread, or any other thread, needs the file, the file handle can be retrieved from the IIS Object Cache and the file contents can be retrieved from the file system cache.

The performance of IIS servers can benefit substantially from the file system cache, but only when the cache is large enough to hold all of the files the server needs. You can measure the size and effectiveness of the file system cache by using Performance Monitor.

Using Performance Monitor to Monitor the File System Cache

Performance Monitor includes several counters in the Memory and Cache performance objects that monitor the size and effectiveness of the file system cache. The following table lists these counters.

Table 5.3   Performance Monitor Counters for the File System Cache

Counter	Indicates
Memory: Cache bytes	The size of the cache, in bytes. This counter displays the last observed value; it is not an average.
Memory: Cache faults/sec	How often data sought in the file system cache is not found there. The count includes faults for data found elsewhere in memory, as well as faults that require disk operations to retrieve the requested data.
	This counter displays the number of faults, without regard for the number of pages retrieved in response to the fault.
Cache: MDL Reads/sec	How often the system attempts to read large blocks of data from the cache.
	Memory Descriptor List (MDL) Reads are read operations in which the system uses a list of the physical address of each page to help it find the page.
	MDL reads are often used to retrieve cached Web pages and FTP files.

Table 5.3   Performance Monitor Counters for the File System Cache *(Continued)*

Counter	Indicates
Cache: MDL Read Hits %	How often attempts to find large sections of data in the cache are successful. You can use the Cache: MDL Read Hits % counter to calculate the percentage of MDL misses. Misses are likely to result in disk I/O.
Cache: Data Maps/sec	How often pages are mapped into the cache from elsewhere in physical memory or from disk. To measure the percentage of data maps from elsewhere in physical memory, use Cache: Data Map Hits %. The inverse of Cache: Data Map Hits % indicates data maps from disk.
Cache: Read Aheads/sec	A measure of sequential reading from the cache. When the system detects sequential reading, it anticipates future reads and reads in larger blocks of data. The read ahead counters are a useful measure of how effectively an application uses the cache.
Memory: Page Faults/sec	Hard and soft faults in the working set of the process. This counter displays the number of faults, without regard for the number of pages retrieved in response to the fault.
Memory: Page Reads/sec	Hard faults in the working sets of processes and in the file system cache.

These counters are included in IISMem.pmw, a Performance Monitor workspace settings file on the *Supplement 1* CD. You should log this data for several days. You can use bookmarks in Performance Monitor to note times of unusually high and low server activity.

Analyzing the File System Cache Data

You can use the data you collect in Performance Monitor to evaluate whether your server has enough memory to support an effective file system cache. This evaluation consists of the following three steps:

- Determine how the size of your server's file system cache varies over time.
- Determine the extent to which the performance of your server's cache varies with the size of the cache.
- Verify that the server has enough memory to support an effective cache even when the server is most active.

The following sections provide information to help you with this evaluation.

Analyzing Cache Size Data

The Windows NT Cache Manager adjusts the size of the file system cache based on whether a computer is a workstation or a server, the amount of physical memory in the computer, and the applications and services the computer is supporting. In general, it is counterproductive to override the Cache Manager and manipulate the cache size directly. If the cache is too small to be effective, it is best to increase the amount of physical memory on the computer, or to redistribute memory-intensive applications to other servers.

The Performance Monitor Memory: Cache Size counter is a useful indicator of the size of the file system cache. Task Manager also displays the size of the file system cache in the **File Cache** field of its **Performance** tab.

You can use also use Performance Monitor or PerfLog to log the Memory: Cache Size counter. A log of cache size reveals how the size of the file system cache changes over time. Compare this data to a measure of general memory availability, such as data from the Memory: Available Bytes counter. In general, when memory is scarce, the system trims the cache and when memory is ample, the system enlarges the cache.

Note the points in the log when the cache is smallest. Keep track of how small the cache gets and how often the cache is small. Also, note how much system memory is available when the cache size is reduced. This data is useful when associating the size of the cache to its performance.

Analyzing Cache Performance Data

You can use the Performance Monitor data to evaluate the performance of the file system cache on your server. The file system cache is judged based on how often files sought in the cache are found there. A *hit* is recorded when requested files are found in the cache. A *miss* or *fault* is recorded when requested files are not found. Misses and faults indicate how often the system needs to do extra work to retrieve files from somewhere other than the cache.

To evaluate the performance of your server's file system cache, chart a Performance Monitor log of Cache: MDL Read Hits %. The file system cache is performing well when this value is highest. Values near 100 percent are not uncommon on IIS servers with ample memory. Subtract the percentage of hits from 100 percent to determine the number of misses. Misses on MDL reads usually require disk operations to find the requested data.

MDL Reads are the most common type of read used for retrieving many contiguous pages. Typically, MDL Reads are the most common read operation on servers running Internet Information Server. To determine which type of cache read is most common on your server, create a Performance Monitor report of the rates of different types of cache reads. Include the Cache: Copy Reads/sec, Cache: Data Maps/sec, Cache: Fast Reads/sec, Cache: MDL Reads/sec, and Cache: Pin Reads/sec.

You can also use the Memory: Cache Faults/sec counter to indicate how often data sought in the file system cache is not found there. This value should be as small as possible. The Memory: Page Faults/sec and Memory: Page Reads/sec counters are included to help you relate the fault rate of the cache to the fault rate in the system as a whole. Memory: Cache Faults/sec is a component of Memory: Page Faults/sec. The ratio of Memory: Cache Faults/sec to Memory: Page Faults/sec indicates the proportion of faults occurring in the cache as opposed to the working sets of processes.

A high rate of cache faults can indicate a memory shortage. But it can also indicate a less than optimal organization of data on disk. If the files used in sequence are stored on the same logical partitions of the same disk, they are more likely to benefit from the Windows NT Cache Manager's optimizing strategies, such as read aheads. The Memory: Read Aheads/sec counter displays the rate of sequential reading from the cache.

Comparing Cache Size and Performance Data

You can determine the extent to which the performance of the file system cache varies with the size of the cache. Compare the size of the cache over time to the rate at which data sought in the cache is found there.

Use the Memory: Cache Bytes counter as an indicator of the size of the cache. Use Memory: Cache Faults/sec as an indicator of the rate of cache misses, and Cache: MDL Read Hits % as an indicator of the rate of cache hits.

If Memory: Cache Faults/sec rises and Cache: MDL Read Hits % falls when the file system cache is smaller, the cache might be too small to be of much benefit to the server. A less effective file system cache is likely to degrade the performance of an IIS server significantly, especially if the size of the cache is often reduced due to a general memory shortage.

If cache performance is poor when the cache is small, use the data you have collected to infer why the cache size is reduced. Choose a period when the cache is small and note the available memory on the server and the processes and services running on the server, including the number of simultaneous connections supported.

When you add physical memory to your server, the system allocates more space to the file system cache. A larger cache is almost always more efficient. In addition, defragmenting your disks makes it more likely that related pages are copied into the cache together and this improves the hit rate of the cache. Finally, consider reducing the workload on the server by moving some of the load to another server.

Suggestions for Optimizing Memory on an IIS Server

Servers running Internet Information Server, like all high-performance file servers, benefit from ample physical memory. Generally, the more memory you add, the more the servers use and the better they perform. Most IIS servers perform acceptably with 32MB of memory. However, if you are running memory-intensive applications, like Common Gateway Interface (CGI) applications, you might need up to five times more memory to prevent a memory bottleneck.

Here are a few suggestions for optimizing memory performance without adding memory:

- Improve data organization. Keep related Web files on the same logical partitions of a disk. Keeping files together improves the performance of the file system cache and reduces the size of the process's working set. Also, defragment your disks. Even well organized files can take more time to retrieve if they are fragmented.

- Try disk mirroring or striping. The optimum configuration is to have enough physical memory to hold all static Web pages. However, if pages must be retrieved from disk, use mirroring or striping to make reading from disk sets faster.

- Replace or convert CGI applications. CGI applications use three to five times more processor time and memory space than equivalent ISAPI extensions. If you cannot or choose not to replace your CGI applications or to convert them to ISAPI extensions, you might need to add additional processors and memory. For more information on CGI and ISAPI applications, see Chapter 9, "Monitoring Dynamic Page Generation."

- Enlarge paging files. Add paging files and/or increase the size of your paging files. Windows NT creates one paging file on the system disk, but you can create a paging file on each logical partition of each disk.

- Resize the IIS Object Cache. If the system has enough memory, and most of the IIS Object Cache is used, consider increasing the size of the IIS Object Cache (**MemoryCacheSize**) or lengthening the period that an unused object can remain in the cache (**ObjectCacheTTL**). Alternatively, if memory is scarce and the contents of the object cache are volatile, consider reducing the size of the object cache or increasing the rate at which the cache is flushed.

- Change the balance of the cache to working set. By default, Windows NT servers are configured to give preference to the file system cache over the working sets of processes when allocating memory space. Although IIS servers benefit from a large file system cache, the **Maximize Throughput for File Sharing** option often causes the Internet Information Server pageable code to be written to disk, which results in lengthy processing delays. To avoid these processing delays, set Server properties to the **Maximize Throughput for Network Applications** option.

▶   **To change Server properties:**

1. Double-click the Network icon in Control Panel.

2. Click the **Services** tab.

3. Click **Server** to select it, and then click the **Properties** button.

4. Click **Maximize Throughput for Network Applications**, and then click **OK**.

5. Restart the computer.

- Limit connections. If your server is running out of memory, limiting the number of connections on the server might help because some physical memory is consumed by the data structures the system uses to keep track of connections.

    Administrators can use the Internet Service Manager to limit the number of connections. On the property page for each service, click the **Service** tab, then change the value in the **Maximum Connections** field. The following table shows the default values for maximum connections by service.

Table 5.4   Default Values for Maximum Connections

Service	Default Maximum Connections
FTP	1,000
Gopher	1,000
WWW (HTTP)	100,000

C H A P T E R   6

Preventing Processor Bottlenecks

Servers running Internet Information Server (IIS) rely on the speed and efficiency of their processors. The Internet Information Server code is multithreaded for efficient scaling on single-processor and multiprocessor computers and is largely self-tuning. Nonetheless, processor bottlenecks are a potential problem on very active servers running Internet Information Server, even on servers with multiple processors.

A *processor bottleneck* occurs when one or more processes occupy nearly all of the processor time of all processors on the computer. In a bottleneck, the ready threads of processes must wait in a queue for processor time. All other activity comes to a halt until the queue is cleared. Processor bottlenecks can occur on multiprocessor computers when only a single processor is exhausted, if the work in the queue cannot be or is not distributed to the other processors. By definition, adding or improving other components of the computer, such as memory, disks, or network connections, does not overcome the performance problem.

This chapter discusses strategies for long-term monitoring of processor activity and processor queues. The chapter describes how Internet Information Server uses server processors, and how you can monitor and measure processor activity. The chapter concludes with suggestions for preventing processor bottlenecks.

The sections in this chapter are as follows:

- "Monitoring Server Processors"
- "Monitoring Connections"
- "Monitoring Threads"
- "Monitoring Interrupts and DPCs"
- "Suggestions for Improving Processor Performance on an IIS Server"

This chapter focuses on issues specific to Windows NT 4.0 Servers running IIS services. For more general information on monitoring and tuning processors, see *Microsoft Windows NT Workstation Resource Kit*, Chapter 13, "Detecting Processor Bottlenecks" and Chapter 16, "Monitoring Multiple Processor Computers." For a detailed discussion of the challenges involved in monitoring volatile processes and threads, see the section "Monitoring Processes and Threads," in Chapter 10, "About Performance Monitor," in the *Windows NT Workstation Resource Kit*.

Warning To add or modify a Registry value entry, use administrative tools such as Control Panel or System Policy Editor whenever possible. Using a Registry editor (Regedit or Regedt32) to change a value can have unforeseen effects, including changes that can prevent you from starting your system.

Monitoring Server Processors

The processors in a server running Internet Information Server must support the operating system and processes unrelated to Internet services, as well as IIS processes. The processors must also support applications related to Internet services, such as those that assemble data from SQL Server databases or generate dynamic Web pages.

You have a choice of several tools you can use to monitor processor performance. Task Manager, Microsoft Web Capacity Analysis Tool (WCAT), PerfLog, and Performance Monitor are commonly used to monitor processors on Windows NT servers. Also, Pentium counters, extensible counters that monitor the inner workings of Intel Pentium (P5) and Pentium Pro (P6) processors, are available on the *Windows NT Workstation Resource Kit* and *Windows NT Server Resource Kit* CDs. Remember that all tools use system resources. Monitor the processor use of the process in which the tool runs. Then, before you analyze your data, subtract the processor time of the tool process from the data.

Using Performance Monitor to Monitor Processor Activity

You can use PerfLog to log data from the following counters automatically on a regular or periodic basis, or use Performance Monitor to log the System and Processor objects.

Table 6.1   Performance Monitor Counters for Processor Activity

Counter	Indicates
System: Processor Queue Length	Threads waiting for processor time. If this value exceeds 2 for a sustained period of time, the processor may be a bottleneck.
System: % Total Processor Time	The sum of processor use on each processor divided by the number of processors.
Processor: % Processor Time	Processor use on each processor. This counter reveals unequal distribution of processor load.
Processor: % Privileged Time	Proportion of the processor's time spent in privileged mode. In Windows NT, only privileged mode code has direct access to hardware and to all memory in the system. The Windows NT Executive runs in privileged mode. Application threads can be switched to privileged mode to run operating system services.
Processor: % User Time	Proportion of the processor's time spent in user mode. User mode is the processor mode in which applications, like the IIS services, run.
Process: % Processor Time	The processor use attributable to each processor.

You can use the preceding Performance Monitor counters to monitor general processor performance. These counters are included in IISProc.pmw, a Performance Monitor workspace settings file on the *Windows NT Server Resource Kit Supplement 1* CD.

Paging and Processor Bottlenecks

The most common cause of an apparent processor bottleneck is a memory bottleneck. If the system does not have enough physical memory to store the code and data programs need, the processor spends substantial time *paging*. Before adding or upgrading processors or disks, you should monitor the memory in your server. For more information about monitoring memory, see Chapter 5, "Monitoring Virtual Memory."

Analyzing Processor Activity Data

Of the counters listed, the System: Processor Queue Length counter is the most important counter for analyzing processor activity data. The System: Processor Queue Length counter displays the number of ready threads in the single queue shared by all processors. Sustained high rates of processor activity, which leave little excess capacity to handle peak loads, are often associated with processor bottlenecks. Processor activity, by itself, indicates only that the resource is used, not that maximum use of the resource is a problem. However, a long, sustained queue indicates that ready threads are being kept waiting because a processor cannot handle the load.

A sustained processor queue length of 2 or more threads (as indicated by the System: Processor Queue Length Counter) typically indicates a processor bottleneck. You might consider setting a Performance Monitor alert to notify the Administrators when the processor queue length reaches an unacceptable value.

The Processor: % Processor Time counter is most often used as a general measure of processor activity on both single-processor and multiprocessor computers. System: % Total Processor Time is included for monitoring system-wide processor use on multiprocessor computers. On single-processor computers, System: % Total Processor Time always equals Processor: % Processor Time. On multiprocessor computers, System: % Total Processor Time represents the active time of all processors divided by the number of processors.

If the server workload is shared equally among all processors, System: % Total Processor time is an excellent measure of processor activity. However, this counter hides bottlenecks resulting from unequal processor loads. (If one processor is 100% busy and three other processors are idle, the % Total Processor Time is 25%.)

Windows NT is designed for efficient scaling and includes several strategies for balancing processor load. Applications can create an imbalance by setting a processor affinity, which binds a process to a single processor. For detailed processor monitoring, you need to chart Processor: % Processor Time for each processor on the computer.

You might encounter the following challenges in analyzing your processor data:

- A large processor queue when all processors are busy. Create a histogram of Process: % Processor Time for each process. The histogram shows the processor time consumed by each process.

- A single bar rises above all of the others. The process represented by the bar might be consuming a disproportionate share of processor time and causing a bottleneck. Consider replacing the application running in the process, or moving the process to another server.

- The processors are being shared equally by several processes. Consider upgrading or adding processors. Multithreaded processes benefit most from additional processors.

For more information on processor use by applications related to Internet Information Server, see Chapter 9, "Monitoring Dynamic Page Generation."

Monitoring Connections

Internet Information Server is designed to support millions of connections. In fact, the internal default for the maximum number of simultaneous connections is 2 million connections. (This default is overriden by the Internet Service Manager, but administrators can change it.) Nonetheless, large numbers of simultaneous connections can overload the processors.

It is important to monitor connections on your Internet Information Server. In particular, it is important to determine how your server responds when it is managing different numbers of connections. When you have collected data on connection trends, you can associate data about general server performance with the number of connections being served.

This section discusses why connections have performance overhead, how you can use Performance Monitor and other tools to measure the overhead, and how to interpret the data you gather.

The Performance Overhead of Connections

Each connection that an IIS service establishes consumes some processor time. The network adapter card interrupts the processor to signal that a client has requested a connection. Further processing is required to establish and maintain the connection, to fulfill client requests sent on the connection and, when the connection is closed, processing is required to delete the structures that serviced the connection. Each time a connection is established, the load on the server increases.

One aspect of connection overhead is the time it takes to search the Transmission Control Block (TCB) table. TCP creates and maintains transmission control blocks (TCBs) to store data about connections. This might include data about the precedence of the connection and its local and remote socket numbers. The TCBs are stored in a hash table for efficient control. The hash table is stored in the operating system's nonpaged memory pool.

Internet Information Server 2.0 includes several features to optimize its handling of connections. Among these features are HTTP keep-alives.

HTTP keep-alives maintain a connection even after the connection's initial request is complete. This feature keeps the connection active and available for subsequent requests. Keep-alives are implemented to avoid the substantial cost of establishing and terminating connections. Both the client and the server must support keep-alives. Keep-alives are supported by Internet Information Server version 1.0 and later and Internet Explorer version 2.0 and later.

HTTP keep-alives are different from and independent of Transmission Control Protocol/Internet Protocol (TCP/IP) keep-alives. TCP/IP keep-alives are messages sent to determine whether an idle connection is still active.

HTTP keep-alives are enabled in Internet Information Server by default. Although keep-alives significantly improve bandwidth performance on most servers, you can modify or eliminate them if they are not needed. You can also measure their effect on the performance of your system. To test their effect on the server, you can disable them, but it is recommended that you reenable them when the test is concluded to maintain the performance of the server.

You can disable keep-alives by adding the **AllowKeepAlives** value entry to the Registry and setting its value to 0. To reenable keep-alives, delete the **AllowKeepAlives** value entry, or set it to 1. You must place **AllowKeepAlives** in:

HKEY_LOCAL_MACHINE\System
  \CurrentControlSet
   \Services
    \W3SVC
     \Parameters

Using IIS Logging to Monitor Connections

You can use the Internet Information Server Logging to monitor the number of connections your server handles and to track patterns of client demand for your server. For more information about configuring and interpreting Internet Information Server logs, see the online *Windows NT Server Microsoft Internet Information Server Installation and Administration Guide.*

Using Performance Monitor to Monitor Connections

Performance Monitor can monitor the number of simultaneous connections to the IIS services and the processor use of the process in which the IIS services run. The following table lists the Performance Monitor counters that monitor connections to Internet Information Server.

Table 6.2   Performance Monitor Counters for IIS Service Connections

Counter	Indicates
HTTP Service: Current Connections FTP Server: Current Connections Gopher Service: Current Connections	The number of connections maintained by the service during the most recent sample interval.
HTTP Service: Maximum Connections FTP Server: Maximum Connections Gopher Service: Maximum Connections	The largest number of connections maintained simultaneously since the server was started.

These Performance Monitor counters are included in IISProc.pmw. Because these counters display the last value they observe, and not an average, you must log these values over time to collect reliable data.

Also, these counters are likely to exaggerate the number of simultaneous connections because some some entries might not yet be deleted even though the connection is closed.

Note   The HTTP Service, FTP Server, and Gopher Service counters collect data at the OSI Application Layer. Counts of TCP/IP connections might not equal HTTP, FTP, and Gopher connections if the connection was blocked, rejected, or reset between the Transport and Application Layers. For details on monitoring connections at lower layers, see Chapter 7, "Monitoring Bandwidth and Network Capacity."

Analyzing Connection Data

By monitoring numbers of connections you can identify patterns of client demand for your server. Classify the data in your Performance Monitor logs into intervals by the numbers of connections served during the interval. Observe the length of the processor queue and the processor use on each processor during periods of small, moderate, and large numbers of connections. This data shows how your configuration responds to each load level.

You can identify a processor bottleneck at each interval by:

- A long, sustained processor queue (more than two threads).
- High use rates on one or more processors.
- A curve in the graph of the Current Connections counter on any IIS service performance object that reaches a high value and then forms a plateau. This pattern often indicates that additional connections are being blocked or rejected.

To prevent processor bottlenecks, make certain that a lengthy processor queue isn't forming when you serve large numbers of connections. Typically, you can avoid a bottleneck during peak time by setting the connection limit to twice the average value of Current Connections. If the processor regularly becomes a bottleneck when servicing large numbers of connections, you might consider upgrading or adding processors, or limiting the maximum number of connections on the server. Limiting connections might cause the server to block or reject connections, but it helps to ensure that accepted connections are processed promptly.

The maximum number of connections is set separately for each service. Adminstrators can use the Internet Service Manager to limit the number of connections. On the property page for each service, click the **Service** tab, then change the value in the **Maximum Connections** field. The following table shows the default values for maximum connections by service.

Table 6.3   Default Values for Maximum Connections

Service	Default Maximum Connections
FTP	1,000
Gopher	1,000
WWW (HTTP)	100,000

Monitoring Threads

Internet Information Server runs in a multithreaded process designed for efficient scaling on single-processor and multiprocessor systems. *Threads* are the objects in each process that run the process code on the processor. On single processor systems, the threads of the Internet Information Server process are switched on and off of the processor in order of priority. On multiprocessor systems, Internet Information Server can run more than one thread simultaneously.

In the Internet Information Server process, there is no simple association between threads and connections or threads and requests. Nor is there an easily quantified relationship between the optimum number of threads in the process and the number of files served, the number of requests filled, or the number of connections maintained.

The relationship between threads, connections, and requests is more complex with Internet Information Server because IIS uses the *worker thread* model, rather than the simpler, but less efficient, *thread per client* model. Instead of dedicating a thread to each connection or request, Internet Information Server dedicates one thread, the *worker thread*, to the task of accepting and monitoring all connections. This frees other threads to do the remaining work of the application, such as authenticating users; parsing client requests; locating, opening, and transmitting files; and managing internal data structures. As a result, several threads can service a single connection and each request from a connection might be serviced by different threads.

Even though you cannot associate individual threads and connections or requests, you can:

- Count the number of threads in the Internet Information Server process.
- Measure the amount of processor time each thread gets.
- Associate the number of threads (and processor activity) with the number of current connections, number of files served, and other measures of server activity and performance.

Several tools monitor the threads in a process, including Process Viewer, Process Explode, PerfLog, and Performance Monitor. Individual threads are difficult to monitor, especially if they frequently start and stop. Threads are also costly to measure. Be sure to monitor the overhead (by using Process: % Processor Time) of the process in which your tool runs and subtract it from the data you collect. For a detailed discussion of this issue, see the *Windows NT Workstation Resource Guide*, Chapter 10, "About Performance Monitor," "Monitoring Processes and Threads."

Using Performance Monitor to Monitor IIS Threads

You can use Performance Monitor to monitor the threads in the Internet Information Server process. The following table lists the Performance Monitor counters that monitor threads. These counters are included in IISProc.pmw. You can add to this list any counters you will use to associate numbers of threads with performance, such as HTTP Service: Current Connections, HTTP Service: Bytes/sec, or Server: Logon/sec.

Table 6.4   Performance Monitor Counters for Monitoring IIS Threads

Counter	Indicates
Process: Thread Count: Inetinfo	The number of threads created by the process. This counter does not indicate which threads are busy and which are idle.
	This counter displays the last observed value, not an average.
Thread: % Processor Time: Inetinfo => *Thread #*	How much processor time each thread of the Inetinfo process is using. If a log of this counter over time shows that threads are consistently idle, it may be prudent to reduce the number of threads per processor.
Thread: Context Switches/sec: Inetinfo => *Thread #*	How many times the threads of the IIS service are switched on to and off of a processor. This counter is an indicator of the activity of the threads of the IIS service process.

Analyzing the IIS Thread Data

You can chart the Process: Thread Count: Inetinfo value over time to see how many threads the Inetinfo process creates and how the numbers of threads vary. Then, observe the processor time for each thread in the process (Thread: % Processor Time: Inetinfo => *Thread #*) during periods of high, medium, and low server activity (as indicated by the other performance measures).

You should also observe the patterns of context switches over time. Context switches indicate that the microkernel has switched the processor from one thread to another. A context switch occurs each time a new thread runs, and each time one thread takes over from another. A large number of threads is likely to increase the number of context switches. Context switches allow multiple threads to share the processor, but they also interrupt the processor and might interfere with processor performance, especially on multiprocessor computers.

Optimizing Thread Values

By default, the Internet Information Server process creates up to 10 threads per processor. Internet Information Server continually adjusts the number of threads in its process in response to server activity. For most systems, this tuning is sufficient to maintain the optimum number of threads, but you can change the maximum number of threads per processor, if your system requires it.

If the threads in the Internet Information Server process appear to be overworked or underutilized, consider these tuning strategies:

- If nearly all of the threads of the Internet Information Server process are busy nearly all of the time, and the processors are at or near their maximum capacity, consider distributing the workload among more servers.

  You can also add processors, but do so cautiously. Unnecessary or underused processors will degrade performance, not improve it.

- If nearly all threads appear busy, but the processors are not always active, consider increasing the maximum number of threads per processor. Increasing the number of threads is typically an interim solution used while a bottleneck in another subsystem is being resolved.

  Do not increase the maximum number of threads unless you have processors with excess capacity. More threads on the same number of processors cause more interrupts and context switches, and result in less processor time per thread.

- If many threads are continuously idle, you might save processor time and memory by reducing the number of threads in the process.

To adjust the maximum number of threads in the IIS service process, use a Registry editor to add the **MaxPoolThreads** value entry to the Registry. **MaxPoolThreads** does not appear in the Registry unless it is added. It must be added to the following:

HKEY_LOCAL_MACHINE\System
   \CurrentControlSet
     \Services
       \Inetinfo
         \Parameters

MaxPoolThreads is calculated in units of threads-per-processor. If this value entry does not appear in the Registry, Internet Information Server allocates a maximum of 10 threads per processor. Do not set this value below 5 or above 20. For more information on **MaxPoolThreads**, see Regentry.hlp on the *Windows NT Workstation Resource Guide 4.0* CD.

Continue monitoring the system carefully to make sure that changing the numbers of threads achieves the desired effect.

Monitoring Interrupts and DPCs

One of the processor's tasks is to service interrupts and DPCs from all of the computer's subsystems. On a busy server running Internet Information Server, much of the processor's time can be spent servicing interrupts and DPCs, especially from the disk subsystem and the network adapter cards.

This section describes some methods of measuring how much time your server's processors are spending handling interrupts and DPCs from the network adapter cards. It discusses how network card interrupts and DPCs are distributed among processors in multiprocessor computers, and suggests some methods of tuning DPC distribution to improve processor performance.

Describing Interrupts and DPCs

Interrupts are very high-priority signals that halt the processor's activity and prepare the processor for a new activity, if only very briefly. Interrupts consume processor time and disrupt the processor's work, but they are essential to a preemptive multitasking system.

Client connections involve many interrupts. The network adapter card generates an interrupt when it receives a new packet or completes a transmission. The system collects some very basic information and then adds one or more *deferred procedure calls* (DPCs) to the queue to handle the next steps in the process.

DPCs are similar to interrupts except that they have a lower Interrupt Request Level (IRQL). (IRQL is the priority scale used for objects like interrupts. It is different from the priority scale that the microkernel uses to schedule processes and threads.) Unlike interrupts, DPCs can be delayed, allowing the processor to complete higher priority work. When the DPC gets processor time, the work of establishing the connection can proceed.

Interrupts and Processor Performance

Commonly used server processors, such as Intel 486, Intel Pentium and Pentium Pro, and RISC processors, can handle thousands of interrupts and DPCs without being consumed by the task. However, each interrupt takes time away from the other work of the processor. An active server running Internet Information Server at high bandwidth can interrupt the processor enough to impede performance.

To help improve processor performance, some newer network card drivers provide an advanced feature known as *interrupt moderation*. When the driver detects a high rate of interrupts from the network adapter card, the interrupt moderation code disables interrupts and accumulates the interrupts in a buffer instead of sending them to the processor. When the processor has completed its work, the interrupts are reenabled.

Monitoring interrupts and DPCs is an important part of monitoring processor performance (and network adapter card performance) on a server running Internet Information Server. On a single processor system, a very high level of interrupts might indicate an errant network card or disk adapter, as well as an overworked processor. On a multiprocessor system, data about interrupts and DPCs might also reveal a poor distribution of workload among processors.

Using Performance Monitor to Monitor Interrupts and DPCs

You can use Performance Monitor to monitor the interrupts and DPCs in the Internet Information Server process. The following table lists the Performance Monitor counters that monitor interrupts and DPCs. These counters are included in IISProc.pmw.

When monitoring, chart these counters along with standard measures of processor time, such as System: Processor Queue Length and Process: % Processor Time: Inetinfo. If you are monitoring a multiprocessor computer, be sure to include Processor: % Processor Time. This counter displays the processor use of each processor over time. You might also include Processor: % Privileged Time because interrupts and DPCs are processed in privileged mode.

Table 6.5   Performance Monitor Counters for Interrupt and DPC Monitoring

Counter	Indicates
Processor: % Interrupt Time	How much time the processor is spending processing interrupts. Interrupts are generated when a client requests a connection or sends data.
	If processor time is more than 90% and this value is greater than 15%, the processor is probably overburdened with interrupts.
Processor: Interrupts/sec	The rate at which the processor is handling interrupts.
Processor: % DPC Time	How much time the processor is spending processing deferred procedure calls (DPCs). DPCs originate when the processor performs tasks requiring immediate attention, and then defers the remainder of the task to be handled at lower priority. DPCs represent further processing of client requests.
Processor: DPCs queued/sec	The rate at which DPCs are added to the processor's queue. (This counter does not measure the number of DPCs in the queue.)
Pentium: Interrupts/sec (Pentium, but not Pentium Pro, processors)	Only taken INTR and NMI hardware interrupts.
Pentium: Hardware interrupts received/sec (Pentium Pro processors only)	The rate at which hardware interrupts are detected by the processor's internal counters.

Note The Pentium performance object includes counters that display data on interrupts and DPCs. Pentium counters are extensible Performance Monitor counters designed to monitor Pentium processors. The counters are included on the *Windows NT Workstation Resource Kit* CD in the Performance Tools group. You must install the Pentium counters before you can use them. For detailed instructions, see P5Perf.txt on the *Windows NT Workstation Resource Kit* CD.

Analyzing Data on Interrupts and DPCs

When you have collected data on interrupts and DPCs that is representative of the general activity on your server, you can use the guidelines in this section to help you interpret the data.

Analyzing Interrupt and DPC Rates

You can observe the rates of interrupts and DPCs during periods of high, medium, and low server activity. Note the rate of interrupts and DPCs when processor use is very high, especially when a processor queue is developing.

A very high rate of interrupts can indicate a problem with a component that generates interrupts, such as the disk subsystem or a network adapter card. Test your components and rule out a hardware problem before proceeding.

Analyzing Processor Time

You should observe the proportion of the processor's time that is spent servicing interrupts and DPCs. Compare the values of the Processor: % Interrupt Time and Processor: % DPC Time counters to Processor: % Processor Time.

If a busy processor is spending the majority of its time servicing interrupts and DPCs, the processor probably cannot function effectively and a processor bottleneck is likely to develop. Consider upgrading or adding processors to handle the workload.

Alternatively, if the processor has some excess capacity (if Processor: % Processor Time < 85%), or if it is spending a relatively small amount of its time (if Processor: % Interrupt Time and Processor: % DPC Time < 20%) servicing interrupts and DPCs, you probably do not have a problem with interrupts and DPCs.

Analyzing the Distribution of Interrupts and DPCs on Multiprocessor Computers

The most common interrupt-related problem on multiprocessor computers is not the rate of interrupts and DPCs, but their distribution among processors. To determine whether you have a distribution problem:

- Observe the proportion of time each processor is spending servicing interrupts and DPCs.

- Observe the rate of interrupts and DPCs for each processor.

- Note whether interrupts and DPCs are distributed equally among all processors or whether one or more processors are servicing all of the interrupts or DPCs.

A busy processor that is servicing all of the system's interrupts or DPCs is likely to become a bottleneck. The source of the problem is not the number of interrupts or DPCs but the way that interrupts and DPCs are distributed among the processors.

The following sections describe common strategies for distributing interrupts and DPCs on Windows NT servers.

Interrupt Distribution

Different processor platforms use different methods to distribute interrupts. The distribution of interrupts from network adapter cards is controlled by the Hardware Abstraction Layer (HAL) for each processor platform. The interrupt scheme implemented by the HAL depends on the capability of the processor. Some processors include interrupt control hardware, such as the Advanced Programmable Interrupt Controller (APIC) on newer Pentium and Pentium Pro processors. The APIC allows processors to route interrupts to other processors on the computer.

You cannot control or modify the distribution of network card interrupts on your computer. The information in this section is included to help you interpret the interrupt data you collect and, in particular, to explain one of the reasons why one processor might be busier than the others. Monitoring the processor that services the majority of interrupts can help you anticipate or prevent a bottleneck.

There are many different strategies for distributing interrupts on multiprocessor computers. Common strategies are:

- *No distribution.* The traditional method for managing interrupts is to send all interrupts from all network cards to a single processor, usually the first (lowest-numbered) processor. If your data shows that all interrupts are being serviced by a single processor, your system might use this method.

- *Static distribution.* Some systems distribute network card interrupts among processors statically, that is, the distribution doesn't change. These systems associate each network adapter card with a processor. The interrupts generated by the network card are always sent to the network card's associated processor, regardless of whether the processor is busy or idle.

  Typically, these systems associate the first (lowest-numbered) network card with the first (lowest-numbered) processor and each subsequent network card with each subsequent processor. If there are more network cards than processors, the system begins its assignments again with the first processor.

  If your data shows that interrupts are distributed rather evenly among processors, you might have a system that provides static distribution. However, if one of the network cards is idle or not used, static distribution results in unequal distribution of interrupts.

- *Dynamic distribution.* Some systems distribute interrupts to processors dynamically based on one or more elements of system data, such as processor activity. The interrupts generated by a network card can be sent to any one of the processors.

  If your data shows that interrupts are almost always distributed evenly, you might have a system that provides dynamic distribution.

Distribution of interrupts to all processors, whether statically or dynamically, is commonly known as *symmetric interrupt distribution.* Symmetric interrupt distribution is designed to improve scaling and to prevent a single processor from becoming a bottleneck while other processors have excess capacity. It is available on the Microsoft Windows NT 4.0 HAL for Pentium and Pentium Pro processors. For specific information on the distribution method used for your processor platform, consult your system vendor.

Strategies for producing the most efficient interrupt distribution systems are evolving. You cannot change the interrupt distribution scheme on your computer, but you can coordinate the distribution of DPCs with the distribution of interrupts.

DPC Distribution

The distribution of DPCs generated by network cards is a function of Ndis.sys, the Windows NT implementation of the Network Driver Interface Specification (NDIS). Ndis.sys is a wrapper that shields the details of the network adapter card from the rest of the operating system. Ndis.sys controls DPC distribution on all network cards that use miniport drivers, which is nearly all of them.

Ndis.sys attempts to balance the processor workload generated by interrupts. By default, Ndis.sys associates each network card with a processor and directs all DPCs from a network card to the processor associated with that network card. Ndis.sys attempts to compensate for the burden placed on the lowest-numbered processor by associating the first network card with the highest-numbered processor. Each subsequent network card is associated with the next processor in descending order of processor number.

On many systems, this strategy balances the load. If a server that does not distribute interrupts has two processors and one network card, Processor 0 services the interrupts and Processor 1 services the DPCs.

Unfortunately, this distribution strategy doesn't always work as planned:

- DPCs evolve from interrupts. When a DPC is generated from an interrupt, the DPC must be switched to another processor. The switch requires an interprocessor interrupt from the sending processor to the receiving processor. These very high priority interprocessor interrupts consume additional processor time.

- Information gathered when the interrupt is processed is stored in the processor cache. When the DPC generated from the interrupt is switched to another processor, the data in the cache of the sending processor is flushed and must be collected anew by the receiving processor.

- On many platforms, interrupts are distributed among all processors. Leaving the DPC on the processor that handled the interrupt reduces the number of interprocessor interrupts and allows the DPC to use data stored in the processor cache when the interrupt was serviced.

Fortunately, if DPC distribution is a problem in your system, you can improve system performance by optimizing DPC distribution.

Optimizing DPC Distribution

The solutions to poor DPC distribution differ depending on whether the system distributes interrupts symmetrically:

- *No distribution.* If you are administering a multiprocessor server that does not distribute interrupts symmetrically, monitor the highest-numbered processor carefully. If the processor frequently operates at capacity (if Processor: % Processor Time = 100%) and more than half of its time is spent servicing DPCs (if Processor: % DPC Time > 50%), you can improve the performance of your system by one or more of the following methods:

  - Upgrading to a system that distributes interrupts.

  - Adding network adapter cards so that you have one network adapter card for each processor. Ndis.sys then distributes DPCs to all processors. Generally, you should only add a network adapter card if you also need the bandwidth because each additional network card has some intrinsic overhead.

  - Adjusting the NDIS Processor Affinity Mask to allow or prevent certain processors from servicing DPCs. This is not recommended unless you are very familiar with this process. A less-than-optimal mask can degrade processor performance. You can change the Processor Affinity Mask by editing the **ProcessorAffinityMask** value entry in the Registry.

- *Symmetric distribution.* If you are administering a multiprocessor server that distributes interrupts to all processors, whether statically or dynamically, you can improve performance by setting the value of the **ProcessorAffinityMask** value entry in the Registry to zero. If the value of **ProcessorAffinityMask** is zero, network cards are not associated with processors, and DPCs remain on the processor that handled the interrupt. **ProcessorAffinityMask** is located in:

HKEY_LOCAL_MACHINE\System
   \CurrentControlSet
     \Services
      \NDIS
       \Parameters

ProcessorAffinityMask is described in the Regentry.hlp file on the *Supplement 1* CD. (It is not included in previous versions of Regentry.hlp.)

Suggestions for Improving Processor Performance on an IIS Server

The IIS services run in a multithreaded process designed to operate efficiently on single-processor and multiprocessor computers. An Intel 486, Intel Pentium or Pentium Pro, or RISC processor should be sufficient to handle more than a thousand simultaneous connections. Servers with more activity benefit from multiple processors.

If your data on processor performance indicates that processor queues are developing regularly or while servicing large numbers of connections, monitor the memory of your server. Rule out a memory bottleneck or add more memory before (or in addition to) adding or upgrading processors.

In addition, consider the following suggestions for improving processor performance:

- *Redistribute the workload.* If nearly all of the threads of the Internet Information Server process are busy nearly all of the time, and the processors are at or near their maximum capacity, consider distributing the workload among more servers, or redistributing tasks among servers. You can also add processors, but do so cautiously. Unnecessary or underused processors will degrade performance, not improve it.

- *Add processors.* If the workload is distributed evenly, and all threads in the Internet Information Server process continue to be busy nearly all of the time, or if a processor queue forms when the number of connections rises, add and/or upgrade processors. You can avoid a processor bottleneck during peak use by calculating the processor use on your system when the number of current connections is at its average, and allowing enough processing power to handle twice the average number of connections.

- *Upgrade the L2 cache.* When adding or upgrading processors, choose processors with a large secondary (L2) cache. File server applications, such as Internet Information Server, benefit from a large processor cache because their instruction paths involve many different components. A large processor cache (2MB) is recommended to improve performance on active servers running Internet Information Server.

- *Improve DPC handling.* Platforms that distribute interrupts to all processors do not benefit from the Windows NT default DPC affinity. If you are administering a multiprocessor computer that distributes interrupts symmetrically, such as an Intel Pentium or Pentium Pro (P6) system for Windows NT 4.0, set the value of the **ProcessorAffinityMask** value entry in the Registry to zero. DPCs will be handled by the same processor that handled the interrupt from which the DPC evolved.

- *Add network adapter cards.* If you are administering a multiprocessor system that does *not* distribute interrupts symmetrically, you can improve the distribution of the processor workload by adding network cards so that there is one network card for every processor. Generally, you only add network cards when you need to improve the throughput of your system. Network cards, like any additional hardware, have some intrinsic overhead. However, if one of the processors is nearly always active (if Processor: % Processor Time = 100%) and more than half of its time is spent servicing DPCs (if Processor: % DPC Time > 50%), then adding a network card is likely to improve system performance.

- *Upgrade Network Adapter Cards.* If you are adding or upgrading network adapter cards, choose cards with drivers that support interrupt moderation. Interrupt moderation prevents the processor from being overwhelmed by bursts of interrupts. Consult the driver manufacturer for details.

- *Limit Connections.* If you cannot upgrade or add processors, consider reducing the maximum number of connections that each IIS service accepts. Limiting connections might result in connections being blocked or rejected, but it helps ensure that accepted connections are processed promptly.

  To change the number of connections, use the Internet Service Manager Properties page for each service. Reduce the number in the **Maximum Connections** field until the server can handle twice the average number of connections without developing a long processor queue.

- *Redesign the Web site.* You can improve performance and reduce the processor workload by substituting static web pages for dynamic pages and eliminating large bitmapped images.

- *Adjust the Maximum Number of Threads.* Internet Information Server tunes the number of threads in its process dynamically. The dynamic values are usually optimal. In extreme cases of very active or underused processors, you might want to adjust the maximum number of threads in the Inetinfo process. If you change the maximum number of threads, continue careful testing to make sure that the change has improved performance. The difference is usually quite subtle.

On a large network of Intranet and Internet servers, the processors in each server are vital components. However, they work with memory, disks, and the network as an integrated unit. For more detailed information on monitoring and tuning techniques, see Chapter 7, "Monitoring Bandwidth and Network Capacity."

C H A P T E R   7

Monitoring Bandwidth and Network Capacity

The primary functions of an Internet Information Server are to establish connections for its clients, to receive and interpret requests, and to deliver files—all as quickly as possible. The pace at which these vital functions are performed depends, in large part, on two factors: the effective bandwidth of the link between the server and the network and on the capacity of this link and the server to support network resources.

This chapter examines bandwidth and network capacity on an Internet Information Server and suggests methods you can use to measure and improve transmission rates and connection handling on your server. This chapter is not intended as a comprehensive guide to network monitoring. Instead, it is a limited presentation of the network-related issues that are important on servers running Internet Information Server (IIS).

This chapter includes the following sections:

- "Defining Bandwidth and Network Capacity." This section defines the terms *bandwidth* and *network capacity*.

- "Monitoring Transmission Rates." This section describes the Performance Monitor counters available for measuring transmission rates. Transmission rates are a primary measure of bandwidth on an Internet Information Server.

- "Monitoring File Transfers." This section describes the Performance Monitor counters that display the number of files and directory listings sent and received by each IIS service. These counters can be used to determine the level of a particular service's network activity or the effect of file activity on server components.

- "Monitoring TCP Connections." This section describes the Performance Monitor counters on the TCP object that monitor the rate at which Transmission Control Protocol (TCP) connections are established, failed, and reset. The ability to establish and maintain connections is a primary indicator of the effective network capacity of a server.

- "Using Network Monitor to Monitor Bandwidth." Network Monitor enables you to examine the packets sent and received by the local computer. It is an optional tool included with Windows NT Server. This section suggests some Network Monitor fields to watch when measuring bandwidth.
- "Limiting Bandwidth." On multipurpose servers, you might want to limit the proportion of the server's bandwidth used by IIS services. Doing so prevents Internet Information Server from consuming network capacity required by other services. This section explains how to limit the share of the network used by the Internet Information Server, and how to monitor the results.
- "Suggestions for Maximizing Bandwidth." This section provides some suggestions for improving the performance of your server with its current equipment.

Defining Bandwidth and Network Capacity

Bandwidth and network capacity are measures of the effective performance of the communication links that connect the server computer to the network. Effective performance refers to performance judged by actual, observed values, as opposed to theoretical values that might be achieved in an ideal environment. A server's effective performance is determined by the individual capacity of each network segment and by the ability of the server to respond to requests.

Bandwidth refers to the rate at which data is transmitted and received over a communication link between a computer and the network. Bandwidth is measured in several different ways:

- The rate at which bytes are transferred to and from the server.
- The rate at which data packages are sent by the server. Data packages include frames, packets, segments, and datagrams.
- The rate at which files are sent and received by the server.

Effective bandwidth varies widely depending upon the transmission capacity of the link, the server configuration, and the server workload. The values for a single server also change as it operates, in response to demand and to competition for shared network resources.

Network capacity is a broader term that refers to the ability of the server and the communication link to carry network traffic and support multiple resources. Network capacity is measured, in part, by the number of connections established and maintained by the server.

The following sections describe in more detail the methods you can use to measure bandwidth and network capacity on your server.

Monitoring Transmission Rates

The simplest measure of the effective bandwidth of a server is the rate at which the server sends and receives data. Performance Monitor displays counts of data transmissions that are collected by many components of the server computer. The components that collect data each reside in different Open Systems Interconnectivity (OSI) layers:

- Counters on the HTTP Service, FTP Server, and Gopher Service performance objects measure data transmitted at the OSI Application Layer. (HTTP stands for hypertext transfer protocol; FTP stands for File Transfer Protocol.)
- Counters on the TCP object measure data transmitted at the Transport Layer.
- Counters on the IP object measure data at the Network Layer. (IP stands for Internet Protocol.)
- Counters on the Network Interface object measure data at the Data Link Layer.

As a result of their different positions in the OSI stack, the counters display different data. For example, the counters at the Application Layer count the bytes sent before the data is divided into packets and prefixed with protocol headers and control packets. Counters at the Application Layer measure data in this way because the data is in this form when the application sends it. Counts at the Application Layer also do not include retransmitted data.

In addition, the counters display the data in units native to the component measured. For example, the HTTP Service object displays data in bytes, and the TCP object displays data in segments.

The next section lists and describes the Performance Monitor counters you can use to measure data sent and received by your server. The following section also offers help in interpreting the data you collect.

Using Performance Monitor to Monitor Transmission Rates

The following tables list and describe some of the Performance Monitor counters that can be used for measuring transmission rates. The counters in this table display the transmission rate observed during the last sample interval. They do not display a rolling or cumulative average of the rate. Also, the counters that represent sums of other counters, such as IP: Datagrams/sec, are simple sums of the other counters' values. They are not weighted sums.

For more information about how counter values are calculated, check the counter type of the counter. A counter type determines how Performance Monitor calculates and displays that particular counter. Counters.hlp, a Help file for the Performance Monitor counters, lists and describes the counter type of each counter. Counters.hlp is included on the *Microsoft Windows NT Server Resource Kit Supplement 1* CD.

Note   You must install Simple Network Management Protocol (SNMP) to activate the counters on the TCP, IP, and Network Interface performance objects in Performance Monitor.

The following table lists and describes counters at the Application Layer.

Table 7.1   Performance Monitor Counters for Measuring Transmission Rates at the Application Layer

Counter	Indicates
HTTP Service: Bytes Sent/sec	The rate at which the HTTP server application is sending data, in bytes.
HTTP Service: Bytes Received/sec	The rate at which the HTTP server application is receiving data, in bytes.
HTTP Service: Bytes Total/sec	The rate at which the HTTP server application is sending and receiving data, in bytes.
	HTTP Service: Bytes Total/sec is the sum of HTTP Service: Bytes Sent/sec and HTTP Service: Bytes Received/sec.
FTP Server: Bytes Sent/sec	The rate at which the FTP server application is sending data, in bytes.
FTP Server: Bytes Received/sec	The rate at which the FTP server application is receiving data, in bytes.
FTP Server: Bytes Total/sec	The rate at which the FTP server application is sending and receiving data, in bytes.
	FTP Server: Bytes Total/sec is the sum of FTP Server: Bytes Sent/sec and FTP Server: Bytes Received/sec.
Gopher Service: Bytes Sent/sec	The rate at which the Gopher server application is sending data, in bytes.
Gopher Service: Bytes Received/sec	The rate at which the Gopher server application is receiving data, in bytes.
Gopher Service: Bytes Total/sec	The rate at which the Gopher server application is sending and receiving data, in bytes.
	Gopher Service: Bytes Total/sec is the sum of Gopher Service: Bytes Sent/sec and Gopher Service: Bytes Received/sec.

The following table lists and describes counters on the TCP object.

Table 7.2   Performance Monitor Counters for Measuring Transmission Rates at the Transport Layer

Counter	Indicates
TCP: Segments Sent/sec	The rate at which TCP segments are sent by using the TCP protocol.
TCP: Segments Received/sec	The rate at which TCP segments are received by using the TCP protocol.
TCP: Segments/sec	The sum of Segments Sent/sec and Segments Received/sec.
TCP: Segments Retransmitted/sec	The rate at which segments are transmitted that contain one or more bytes TCP recognizes as having been transmitted before.

Segments Retransmitted/sec is a proper subset of Segments Sent/sec and Segments/sec. To determine the proportion of transmissions caused by failed transmission attempts, divide Segments Retransmitted/sec by Segments Sent/sec.

The following table lists and describes counters on the IP object.

Table 7.3   Performance Monitor Counters for Measuring Transmission Rates at the Network Layer

Counter	Indicates
IP: Datagrams Sent/sec	The rate at which IP datagrams are sent by using the IP protocol. This counter does not include datagrams forwarded to another server.
IP: Datagrams Received/sec	The rate at which IP datagrams are received from IP by using IP protocol. This counter does not include datagrams forwarded to another server.
IP: Datagrams/sec	The sum of IP: Datagrams Sent/sec and IP: Datagrams Received/sec.
IP: Datagrams Forwarded/sec	The rate at which IP datagrams are forwarded to their final destination by the server.

The sum of IP: Datagrams/sec and IP: Datagrams Forwarded/sec represents the rate at which all IP datagrams are handled by the server.

The following table lists and describes counters on the Network Interface performance object.

Table 7.4   Performance Monitor Counters for Measuring Transmission Rates at the Data Link Layer

Counter	Indicates
Network Interface: Bytes Sent/sec: NIC#	The rate at which bytes are sent over each network adapter (that is, over each network interface card, or NIC). The counted bytes include framing characters.
Network Interface: Bytes Received/sec: NIC#	The rate at which bytes are received over each network adapter. The counted bytes include framing characters.
Network Interface: Bytes Total/sec: NIC#	The sum of Network Interface: Bytes Sent/Sec and Network Interface: Bytes Received/sec.

The Network Interface counters display data about the network adapters on the server computer. The first instance of the Network Interface object (Instance 1) that you see in Performance Monitor represents the loopback. The *loopback* is a local path through the protocol driver and the network adapter. All other instances represent installed network adapters.

These counters are included in IISNet.pmw, a Performance Monitor workspace settings file on the *Supplement 1* CD.

Analyzing Transmission Rate Data

The data provided by these counters is collected by different methods, is displayed in different units, and represents the view of different system objects. Some guidelines for interpreting the data follow:

- The IIS service counters display the number of bytes transmitted on behalf of each service that server provides. To calculate the total number of bytes sent or received by all IIS services, sum the values for each service. You can determine the proportion of bytes transmitted by each service by computing the ratio of bytes for one service to the sum of bytes for all services, or for the network.

- Data collected by the IIS service counters underestimates the total number of bytes actually being transmitted to the network by the IIS services. These values are collected at the Application Layer, so they measure data only. They do not measure protocol headers, control packets, or retransmitted bytes.

    In general, the bytes counted by the services represent approximately 60 to 70 percent of the total number of bytes transmitted by the services on the network. If the sum of bytes for all services accounts for two-thirds or more of total network bandwidth, you can assume your network is running at or near the total capacity of its communications link.

- Counters on the TCP and IP performance objects display the rate at which data is sent and received on a Transmission Control Protocol/Internet Protocol (TCP/IP) connection at the Transport and Network layers, but they do not count in bytes. Counters on the IP performance object display data in datagrams, and counters on the TCP performance object display data in segments. It is difficult to convert segments to bytes because the bytes per segment can vary from 8K to 64K; the number of bytes per segment depends upon the size of the TCP/IP receive window and the maximum segment size negotiated when each connection is established.

- Counters on the Network Interface performance object display the rate at which bytes are transmitted over a TCP/IP connection by monitoring the counters on the network adapter at the Data Link Layer. The values of these Network Interface counters include all prepended frame header bytes and bytes retransmitted. These values provide a relatively accurate estimate of the numbers of bytes transmitted over the network, but they do not relate the bytes transmitted to a specific IIS service.

Despite the difficulty of comparing these counters to each other, they can all be related to other performance measures, such as the total number of connections served at a given bandwidth, or processor use at different throughput rates.

Monitoring File Transfers

Each World Wide Web page sent by Internet Information Server results in the transfer of at least one file. Most static Web pages include multiple files, such as a file of text and one or more files of graphics.

Performance Monitor includes counters for each IIS service. These counters display the number of files sent and received by the HTTP service and the FTP server, and the number of files and directory listings sent by the Gopher service. The file counters are listed and described in the following table.

Table 7.5   Performance Monitor Counters for IIS File Transfers

Counter	Indicates
HTTP Service: Files Sent FTP Server: Files Sent Gopher Service: Files Sent	The number of files sent by the service since the service was started.
HTTP Service: Files Received FTP Server: Files Received	The number of files received by the service since the service was started.

Counter	Indicates
HTTP Service: Files Total FTP Server: Files Total	The number of files sent and received by the service since the service was started. Files Total is the unweighted sum of Files Sent and Files Received.
Gopher Service: Directory Listings Sent	The number of directory listings sent by the Gopher service since the service was started.

The file counters for a particular service can be used as indicators of the network activity of that service. They can also be associated with other performance measures to determine the effect of high and low rates of file activity on server components.

Note, however, that the file counters for an IIS service display cumulative totals on all traffic since the service was started, regardless of when Performance Monitor was started. The counters do not display current values or the rate at which files are transmitted.

To calculate file transmission rates, you can use Performance Data Log Service (PerfLog) to log the file counters. PerfLog automatically logs the time at which measurement is taken. After you have generated a PerfLog log, you can use the PerfLog output files as input to a spreadsheet that associates the time of the measurement and the file count to derive the transmission rates. For more information on PerfLog, see Chapter 11, "Performance Monitoring Tools," in *Microsoft Windows NT Workstation Resource Kit: Windows NT Workstation Resource Guide* and the Help file Pdlcnfig.hlp on the *Windows NT Server Resource Kit* CD.

Monitoring TCP Connections

If the bandwidth of your server is insufficient to handle its workload, it is likely that clients will be aware of it before the server is. Client requests to the server will be rejected or will time out, or response will be delayed. On the server side, the indicators are less clear. The server will continue to establish connections, receive requests, and transmit data.

Bandwidth shortages are not uncommon. They have even been observed on dedicated Internet Information Servers with dedicated T1 lines. Traffic generated by an Internet Information Server alone can easily saturate a 1.5–megabytes per second T1 line.

You can detect a bandwidth shortage on your server (perhaps even before clients do) by monitoring the success and failure of connections established and rejected by TCP. When the bandwidth is ample, the server can establish and serve connections before they time out. If bandwidth is not sufficient, the connections fail.

The following section describes the Performance Monitor counters recommended for monitoring the success and failure of connections on your server.

Using Performance Monitor to Monitor TCP Connections

Performance Monitor includes many counters that monitor connections. The counters on the TCP object are the best indicators of the success of connection requests.

The counters on the HTTP Service, FTP Server, and Gopher Service performance objects monitor connections maintained by each IIS service. The counters on these objects display only successful connection requests. They do not display failed attempts to connect to these IIS services. Like all counters at the Application Layer, they do not have information about connections until the connections are established. Performance Monitor counters that display the number of simultaneous connections maintained by Internet Information Server are discussed in Chapter 6, "Preventing Processor Bottlenecks."

The following table lists and describes the Performance Monitor counters that monitor the success and failure of connections to TCP.

Table 7.6   Performance Monitor Counters for Monitoring TCP Connection Successes and Failures

Counter	Indicates
TCP: Connections Established	The number of simultaneous connections supported by TCP (at last observation). This counter displays the number of connections last observed to be in the ESTABLISHED or CLOSE-WAIT state. It displays the last observed value only; its value is not an average.
TCP: Connection Failures	The number of connections that have failed since the service was started (regardless of when Performance Monitor was started). TCP counts a connection as having failed when it goes directly from sending (SYNC-SENT) or receiving (SYNC-RCVD) to CLOSED or from receiving (SYNC-RCVD) to listening (LISTEN).
TCP: Connections Reset	The number of connections reset since the service was started (regardless of when Performance Monitor was started).
	TCP counts a connection as having been reset when it goes directly from ESTABLISHED or CLOSE-WAIT to CLOSED.

These counters are included in IISNet.pmw, a Performance Monitor workspace file on the *Supplement 1* CD.

Analyzing TCP Connection Data

At the TCP level, you should monitor the TCP: Connections Established counter regularly. You might notice a pattern in which the counter value often reaches, but rarely exceeds, a maximum (that is, the graphed line rises and then plateaus at a peak). If so, the peak value is likely to indicate the maximum number of connections that can be established with the current bandwidth and application workload. If you observe such a pattern, the server probably cannot support any greater demand.

Failure to support current or increasing demand also might be evident from the number of connection failures and resets. The counters that monitor failures and resets show cumulative values, but you can set Performance Monitor alerts on the values or use PerfLog to log values over time. You can then use a spreadsheet to calculate the rates at which connections are rejected and reset. An increasing number of failures and resets or a consistently increasing rate of failures and resets might indicate a bandwidth shortage.

Be cautious when interpreting the number of reset connections shown by the TCP: Connections Reset counter. Resets do not always indicate dropped or failed connections. Many browsers try to minimize connection overhead by routinely closing connections by sending a TCP reset (RST) packet, rather than by closing the connection with a normal close operation. The TCP: Connections Reset counter does not distinguish between connections reset because they are dropped and those reset to close connections abruptly.

Using Network Monitor to Monitor Bandwidth

Network Monitor is a tool that lets you monitor the data sent and received by the local computer. It provides many capabilities, including enabling users to:

- Capture or trace data and filter it based on different attributes.
- Monitor throughput based on bytes or frames.
- Monitor bandwidth based on the percentage of the network used.
- Monitor errors, a possible consequence of an overloaded network.

The Windows NT Server CD includes Network Monitor as an optional Windows NT tool.

▶ **To install Network Monitor**

1. Double-click the Network icon in Control Panel.
2. Click the **Services** tab, and then click **Add**.
3. In the **Network Service** box, double-click **Network Monitor Tools and Agent**.

Network Monitor comes with a Help file (Netmon.hlp) and a glossary (Nmgloss.hlp). It is also documented in detail in Chapter 10, "Monitoring Your Network," in *Microsoft Windows NT Server Concepts and Planning*.

For an overall view of bandwidth, use the **Network Monitor Frames Per Second** and **Bytes Per Second** status bars. Use the **% Network Utilization** status bar to view monitor network capacity used. The **# Frames Dropped** field indicates the number of frames that are not processed because the buffers on the network adapters are full. Frame-dropping occurs when the processor cannot handle the traffic generated by the network.

Limiting Bandwidth

If the bandwidth on your server is not sufficient to handle the load imposed by Internet Information Server, you can limit the amount of bandwidth Internet Information Server uses. Limiting bandwidth guarantees that some proportion of the server's bandwidth remains available to other server services. This Internet Information Server feature is intended for servers that handle electronic mail or are domain or file servers, in addition to running Internet Information Server.

The following sections explain how to limit the bandwidth used by IIS services, how to monitor the effect of the limitation, and how to interpret the monitoring data you collect.

Enabling the Bandwidth Throttler

Use the Bandwidth Throttler in Internet Server Manager to limit the bandwidth available to Internet Information Server. You can enable the Bandwidth Throttler from the property page for any of the three IIS services. The limit you set applies to the combined bandwidth used by all three IIS services, regardless of which property page you set it from.

▶ **To enable the Bandwidth Throttler**

1. On the **WWW Service Properties**, **FTP Service Properties**, or **Gopher Service Properties** page, click the **Advanced** tab, then click **Limit Network Use by all Internet Services on this computer**.

2. In the **Maximum Network use** box, type the maximum amount of bandwidth you want the combined IIS services to use, in kilobytes per second.

You do not need to restart the server or the service to activate the Bandwidth Throttler. The Bandwidth Throttler is enabled dynamically. Because you do not need to restart the server, you can enable and disable the Bandwidth Throttler or change the value of **Maximum Network use** as needed. For example, you can restrict use of bandwidth by Internet Information Server during peak morning hours to make more bandwidth available for electronic mail.

Note The value that you enter in the **Maximum Network use** box is stored in the **BandwidthLevel** value entry in the Registry. **BandwidthLevel** does not appear in the Registry until you enable the Bandwidth Throttler. If you later disable the Bandwidth Throttler, the value of **BandwidthLevel** is set to 0xFFFFFFFF.

You can enable the Bandwidth Throttler by adding the **BandwidthLevel** value entry to the Registry and setting **BandwidthLevel** to a value lower than 0xFFFFFFFF. However, if you edit the Registry, you must stop and restart the server to make the change effective.

For more information on **BandwidthLevel**, see Regentry.hlp, the Registry Help file, on the *Supplement 1* CD.

Warning To add or modify a Registry value entry, use administrative tools such as Control Panel or System Policy Editor whenever possible. Using a Registry editor (Regedit or Regedt32) to change a value can have unforeseen effects, including changes that can prevent you from starting your system.

Setting Maximum Network Use

The value you set for **Maximum Network use** depends upon the following factors:

- The total capacity of the communication link between the server and the network. For example, a 10 Base T Ethernet cable has a maximum capacity of 10 megabytes per second.

- The average and maximum transmission rates to and from the server. Use the information in the "Monitoring Transmission Rates" section of this chapter to determine the rates for your server.

- The average and maximum numbers of connections maintained by the server. Use the information in the "Monitoring TCP Connections" section of this chapter to determine the rates for your server.

- The requirements of the applications and services that share the communication link with Internet Information Server. You can use Performance Monitor, PerfLog, Task Manager, and Network Monitor to monitor the transmission rates and connections maintained by other services.

When calculating a value for the **Maximum Network use** box, remember that the Bandwidth Throttler is calibrated in numbers of kilobytes per second. If you wish to limit the bandwidth used by Internet Information Server to a fixed proportion of the link, you must convert the desired value from megabits per second to kilobytes per second.

Also, the Bandwidth Throttler is part of the Internet Information Server. As such, it counts bytes at the OSI Application Layer. It does not have information on the bytes generated at lower levels, such as those for protocol headers, control packets, or retransmissions. When selecting a value for the **Maximum Network use** box, remember that for every byte sent by Internet Information Server, at least 1.5 bytes (8 bits + 4 control bits) are transmitted across the network. If the network frequently retransmits data because of errors, the actual number of bytes transmitted for each byte sent by Internet Information Server is even more than 1.5 bytes. Be sure to factor this difference into your calculation of the desired bandwidth for IIS services.

For example, you might limit the bandwidth Internet Information Server uses to half of the capacity of a 1.544–megabit per second T1 line. First, convert megabits per second to kilobytes per second:

```
(1.544 Megabits per second * 1024) / (8 bits per byte) = 197.6 KB/sec
```

Next, divide by two to determine a value equal to half of the transmission capacity of the line:

```
197.6 KB/sec / 2 = 98.8 KB/sec
```

Then account for the extra bytes generated by protocol headers and control packets:

```
98.8 KB/sec / 1.5 bytes transmitted for every IIS byte sent = 65.9
KB/sec.
```

However, limiting bandwidth can result in connections being blocked or rejected. You can use Performance Monitor to monitor the effect of limiting bandwidth.

Monitoring the Bandwidth Throttler

When you enable the Bandwidth Throttler, Internet Information Server activates a set of Performance Monitor counters to monitor the behavior of the Bandwidth Throttler. You can identify these counters by the presence of the phrase "Async I/O" in the counter name. These counters are active only when the Bandwidth Throttler is enabled. If the Bandwidth Throttler is not enabled, the counters appear in Performance Monitor, but they always have a value of zero.

The bandwidth set in the Bandwidth Throttler applies to the combined bandwidth used by all three IIS services. As such, the Async I/O counters are part of the Internet Information Services Global performance object. They represent totals for all of the IIS services. Bandwidth is not measured for each service.

The following table lists and describes the Async I/O counters.

Table 7.7   Performance Monitor Counters for Monitoring the Bandwidth Throttler

Counter	Indicates
Internet Information Services Global: Current Blocked Async I/O Requests	The number of requests blocked (that is, held in a buffer until the bandwidth clears) by the Bandwidth Throttler as reported during the most recent observation.
Internet Information Services Global: Total Allowed Async I/O Requests	The number of requests allowed by the Bandwidth Throttler since the service was last started.
Internet Information Services Global: Total Blocked Async I/O Requests	The number of requests blocked (that is, held in a buffer until the bandwidth clears) by the Bandwidth Throttler since the service was last started.
Internet Information Services Global: Total Rejected Async I/O Requests	The number of requests rejected by the Bandwidth Throttler since the service was last started.
Internet Information Services Global: Measured Async I/O Bandwidth Usage/Minute	The number of bytes sent per minute as indicated by a sample taken by the Bandwidth Throttler.

Analyzing Data About the Bandwidth Throttler

The Bandwidth Throttler determines whether to accept or reject a request based on the periodic samples of the rate at which bytes are sent on the server.

- If the bandwidth used (as indicated by the sample) approaches the maximum set by the user, the Bandwidth Throttler blocks read requests but allows write requests and transmission requests. Read requests are blocked first because they are likely to result in further requests.

- If the bandwidth used exceeds the maximum set by the user, the Bandwidth Throttler rejects read requests, blocks large write requests and transmission requests, and allows small write requests and transmission requests.

To determine how many requests are being blocked and rejected, monitor the Async I/O counters. These counters display cumulative totals, so it's best to use PerfLog to log the counter values. Alternatively, you can use a spreadsheet to calculate the rate over time. You can also set a Performance Monitor alert to notify administrators when the number of blocked or rejected requests exceeds a threshold.

No rule exists that sets a threshold or appropriate number of blocked and rejected requests. Tolerance for client delays and rejections is a business rule, not a performance measure. However, you can use the Async I/O counters to enforce your business's standards.

Suggestions for Maximizing Bandwidth

If the bandwidth on your server is not sufficient to support demand, you can solve the problem by increasing overall server bandwidth. For information on how this can be done, see Chapter 3, "Adding Bandwidth for Internet Connectivity."

You can also solve the problem by increasing the effective bandwidth of existing communication links. Some suggestions on how to do so follow. Many involve tuning parameters that can only be modified by editing the Registry. For more information about editing Registry entries, see Regentry.hlp, a Registry Help file on the *Supplement 1* CD. This newest version of Regentry.hlp includes an updated list of the Registry entries for Internet Information Server.

Adjusting the Length of the Connection Queues

You might effectively increase existing bandwidth by increasing the length of the connection queues. Requests for connections to the IIS services are held in queues until the service is available to respond to the request. A separate queue exists for each of the IIS services, but all queues have the same maximum size. By default, each queue can hold up to 15 connection requests. If the queue to a service is full, any new connection requests are rejected.

The default queue length of 15 connection requests is sufficient for most servers. However, if your server is rejecting many requests when the services are most active, you can increase the maximum number of items in the queue. If you change the queue length, be sure to monitor server processor use, server memory use, and the connection counters to avoid creating a system bottleneck.

To change the maximum number of connection requests in the queue for each IIS service, add the **ListenBackLog** value entry to the Registry. Set the value of **ListenBackLog** to the maximum number of connection requests you want the server to maintain. You must place **ListenBackLog** in the Registry at:

HKEY_LOCAL_MACHINE\System
   \CurrentControlSet
    \Services
     \Inetinfo
      \Parameters

Although there are separate queues for each IIS service, the maximum length for all three of the queues is identical and is determined by this value entry.

Using HTTP Keep-Alives

To ensure optimal bandwidth, you can also verify that HTTP keep-alives are enabled. *HTTP keep-alives* are an optimizing feature that maintain a connection even after its initial request is complete. HTTP keep-alives are enabled by default but can be disabled by adding the **AllowKeepAlives** value entry to the Registry and setting its value to 0.

Keep-alives are enabled if **AllowKeepAlives** does not appear in the Registry or if it appears and is set to 1. The only reason to disable keep-alives is for testing or debugging, or if the vast majority of connections involve only one data request.

AllowKeepAlives is an optional entry that appears in the Registry only if it is added. If it has been added, it is located in:

HKEY_LOCAL_MACHINE\System
   \CurrentControlSet
    \Services
     \Inetinfo
      \Parameters

Working with Black Hole Routers

Another way to add effective bandwidth is by detecting and properly responding to black hole routers. Black hole routers are a common cause of frequent connection resets.

Black hole routers are routers that do not send an "ICMP Destination Unreachable" message when they cannot forward an IP datagram. Instead, they ignore the datagram. Doing so causes the connection to be reset. Typically, the reason an IP datagram cannot be forwarded is because the datagram's maximum segment size is too large for the receiving server and the Don't-Fragment bit is set.

To respond effectively to black hole routers, you can enable the Path MTUBH Detect feature of TCP/IP. Path MTUBH Detect recognizes repeated unacknowledged transmission and responds by turning off the Don't-Fragment bit. After the datagram in question is transmitted successfully, it reduces the maximum segment size and turns the Don't-Fragment bit on again.

Path MTUBH Detect is disabled by default, but you can enable it by adding the **EnablePMTUBHDetect** value entry to the Registry and setting its value to 1. **EnablePMTUBHDetect** is an optional entry that does not appear in the Registry unless you add it. You must place it in:

```
HKEY_LOCAL_MACHINE\System
   \CurrentControlSet
      \Services
         \Tcpip
            \Parameters
```

You can disable Path MTUBH Detect by deleting **EnablePMTUBHDetect** from the Registry or by setting its value to 0.

Optimizing Graphics File Sizes

Graphics can consume significant bandwidth and result in noticeable network delay. You can increase effective bandwidth by changing your graphics format to reduce the size of graphics files. Different graphics formats use different methods of encoding the data. Try different formats for your graphics, and choose the format that produces the smallest file size.

For example, the Joint Photographic Experts Group (JPEG) format usually produces the smallest file for a photograph. Graphic Interchange Format (GIF) usually produces the smallest file for a computer-generated graphic.

In summary, maintaining adequate bandwidth is a primary concern on Internet Information Server. You can use Performance Monitor and Network Monitor to monitor different aspects of bandwidth. If your data analysis reveals that bandwidth is insufficient, you can increase the bandwidth available to the server or tune some of the parameters that affect bandwidth and network capacity. Also, if you are administering a multipurpose server, consider limiting the bandwidth available to the IIS services to maintain a minimum bandwidth for other services.

CHAPTER 8

Effects of IIS Security Features on Performance

Performance is not usually a primary consideration when designing a security strategy for servers running Internet Information Server (IIS), and it should not be. The intrinsic benefits of protecting your installation and its code and data from unwarranted access override performance concerns. Nonetheless, effective security features have performance overhead — sometimes quite significant overhead — so it is important to measure the overhead and provide enough excess capacity to accommodate it.

This chapter describes some techniques for measuring the effects on server performance of security strategies commonly used on Windows NT Internet servers. These techniques include controlling access by IP Address, basic client authentication, Windows NT Challenge/Response client authentication, and Secure Sockets Layer (SSL) protocol. The following topics are covered in this chapter:

- "The Challenge of Measuring Security Overhead."
- "Using Microsoft Web Capacity Analysis Tool (WCAT) to Measure Security Overhead."
- "Using Performance Monitor to Track Anonymous and Non-Anonymous Connections."
- "Using Performance Monitor to Count Not-Found Errors."
- "Capacity Planning to Support Security Features."

The Challenge of Measuring Security Overhead

Measuring the performance overhead of a security strategy is not simply a matter of monitoring a separate process or threads. The features of the Windows NT Security Model and other Internet Information Server security services run in the context of the IIS process and are integrated into several different operating system services. You cannot monitor security features separately from other aspects of the services.

Instead, the most common method of measuring security overhead is to run tests comparing the server performance with and without the security feature. The tests should be run with fixed workloads and a fixed server configuration so that the security feature is the only variable. During the tests, you probably want to measure:

- *Processor activity and the processor queue.* Authentication, IP address checking, SSL protocol, and encryption schemes are security features that require significant processing. You are likely to see increased processor activity, both in privileged and user mode, and an increase in the rate of context switches and interrupts. If the processors in the server are not sufficient to handle the increased load, queues are likely to develop.

- *Physical memory used.* Security requires that the system store and retrieve more user information. Also, the SSL protocol uses long keys — 40 bits to 1024 bits long — for encyrpting and decrypting the messages.

- *Network activity.* The most obvious performance degradation resulting from complex security features like SSL is increased latency. *Latency* is a measure of the time required to complete a task. Downloading files on servers using the SSL protocol can be 10 to 100 times slower than on servers that are not using SSL.

    You are also likely to see an increase in traffic between the IIS server and the domain controller used for authenticating logons and verifying IP addresses. If a server is used both for running Internet Information Server and used as a domain controller, the proportion of processor use, memory, and network and disk activity consumed by domain services is likely to increase significantly. The increased activity can be enough to prevent the IIS services from running efficiently.

You can run a test that monitors processor, memory, and network activity by using the Microsoft Web Capacity Analysis Toolkit (WCAT). You can run WCAT alone or in conjunction with other tools, such as Performance Monitor and Microsoft Internet Information Service Logging.

Using WCAT to Measure Security Overhead

WCAT is a script-driven, command-line–based application that tests your server configuration using a variety of predetermined, unvarying workloads. You can use WCAT to test how your server responds to different workloads or test the same workload on varying configurations of the server.

The WCAT toolkit includes a folder of prepared test workloads. You can also use WCAT to create your own workloads. WCAT also includes a special option, ssl.*testname*, that adds SSL protocol settings to any workload test.

WCAT is included on the *Windows NT Server Resource Kit Supplement 1* CD. Detailed instructions for using WCAT are in the WCAT folder accessible from Rktools.hlp.

Components of a WCAT Test

A WCAT test simulates clients and servers communicating over a network. WCAT requires at least three computers for each test:

- One computer simulating a client which runs one or more *virtual clients*
- One computer simulating a *server*
- One computer, called a *connector*, which initiates and monitors the test

To produce a realistic test, it is best to associate four or more client machines, each running several virtual clients, with each server.

The processors in the client computers should be at least as fast as the processors in the server computer. If the client processors are not as fast as the server processors, more client computers should be associated with each server computer. WCAT works best if the network that connects the computers has little or no traffic that is not related to the test. It is preferable to use a link dedicated only to the test. A 100MB network is recommended.

Designing a WCAT Test of Security Features

To test a security feature, first run a WCAT test with the feature, then run the same test without the feature. It is important to run the "with feature" and "without feature" versions of the test on varying workloads. WCAT includes prepared workloads ranging from 12 files to 1600 files (211MB). You can create additional tests of workloads with 2000 or more files.

WCAT has many options for collecting data on the tests:

- You can use WCAT's log of performance data. The WCAT log can be used as input to spreadsheet and charting applications. The WCAT user guide explains how to interpret a WCAT log.
- You can run Internet Information Server Logging in conjunction with WCAT to count logons and file accesses.
- You can run Performance Monitor with WCAT. The WCAT **run** command includes a **-p** switch that activates Performance Monitor. You can select Performance Monitor counters by entering the names of counters in a script file. WCAT even includes a sample Performance Monitor counter file, Server.pfc.

WCAT enables you to view test results in several formats. You can view the test results in a spreadsheet or charting program, or in Performance Monitor. You can use the same method to analyze the data of a WCAT test as you use to analyze other Performance Monitor data on processors, memory, disks, network, and applications. You should repeat each test several times and average the results to eliminate unintended variations of the test conditions. Then, compare the results of the "with feature" and "without feature" tests.

Consistent differences in the results of the tests are likely to indicate the overhead associated with the security feature. You can use these results to plan configuration changes to handle the security overhead.

WCAT is the primary tool used for monitoring security overhead. Performance Monitor also includes a set of counters you can use to monitor one specific aspect of security: authenticating users.

Using Performance Monitor to Track Anonymous and Non-Anonymous Connections

Performance Monitor includes counters that display the number of anonymous and non-anonymous connections to each IIS service. These counters are included in the HTTP Service, FTP Server, and Gopher Service performance objects. The term *non-anonymous* is used instead of *authenticated* to account for custom authentication schemes that require data from the client other than, or in addition to, the user name and password.

By themselves, these Performance Monitor counters help you determine the number and proportion of each type of connection. You can also use the counter values to project the estimated effect of changing how you handle anonymous and non-anonymous users. For example, if the vast majority of connections are anonymous, prohibiting anonymous connections has a more significant impact than if most connections are non-anonymous.

Combining data from these counters with general measures of server performance, such as data on processor time, the processor queue, memory, disk reads and writes, and throughput, is even more useful. Using the combined data, you can associate varying numbers and proportions of anonymous and non-anonymous users with their effect on the performance of system components.

Anonymous and Non-Anonymous Connection Counters

The Performance Monitor counters that display the numbers of anonymous and non-anonymous connections are called Current Anonymous Users and Current Non-anonymous Users. These counters display connections, not users. Users who connect more than once are counted once for each time they connect.

The following table lists the Performance Monitor counters for anonymous and non-anonymous connections. These counters are part of the HTTP Service, FTP Server, and Gopher Service performance objects.

Table 8.1   Performance Monitor Counters for Anonymous and Non-Anonymous Connections

Counter	Indicates
HTTP Service: Current Anonymous Users	How many anonymous and non-anonymous users are currently connected to the IIS service.
Gopher Service: Current Anonymous Users	
FTP Server: Current Anonymous Users	
HTTP Service: Current NonAnonymous Users	
Gopher Service: Current NonAnonymous Users	
FTP Server: Current NonAnonymous Users	
HTTP Service: Maximum Anonymous Users	The maximum number of anonymous and non-anonymous users that have been connected simultaneously to the IIS service since the service was last started.
Gopher Service: Maximum Anonymous Users	
FTP Server: Maximum Anonymous Users	
HTTP Service: Maximum NonAnonymous Users	
Gopher Service: Maximum NonAnonymous Users	
FTP Server: Maximum NonAnonymous Users	

Table 8.1   Performance Monitor Counters for Anonymous and Non-Anonymous Connections *(Continued)*

Counter	Indicates
HTTP Service: Total Anonymous Users	A running total of anonymous and non-anonymous connections to the IIS service since the service was last started.
Gopher Service: Total Anonymous Users	
FTP Server: Total Anonymous Users	
HTTP Service: Total NonAnonymous Users	
Gopher Service: Total NonAnonymous Users	
FTP Server: Total NonAnonymous Users	

The anonymous and non-anonymous user counters display the number of anonymous and non-anonymous connections to the IIS service when the values were last observed. They do not report averages or rates. These counters might exaggerate the number of connections because closed connections might not yet be deleted when the counter is displayed.

The Current Anonymous Users and Current Non-anonymous Users counters operate based on the following definitions:

- The *anonymous user* counters display the number of connections whose requests either did not contain a user name and password or whose user name and password were ignored because authentication is not permitted on the server. If anonymous connections are not permitted on the server, the value of all *anonymous user* counters is always zero.

- The *non-anonymous user* counters display the number of connections whose requests contained a valid user name and password, or whatever authentication is required by a custom authentication scheme. If authentication is not enabled on the server, and none of the applications that run on the server request or require authentication, then the value of all *non-anonymous user* counters is always zero.

The *anonymous user* and *non-anonymous user* counters count successful connections only. If a client request for an anonymous connection is rejected and the client responds with valid authenticating data, the connection is counted as non-anonymous.

Using Performance Monitor to Count Not-Found Errors

The HTTP Service performance object in Performance Monitor includes a counter that displays not-found errors. *Not-found errors* are client requests that could not be satisfied because they included a reference to a Web page or a file that did not exist.

Many not-found errors occur because Web pages and files are deleted or moved to another location. However, some might result from user attempts to access documents that they are not authorized to have.

You can use the HTTP Service: Not Found Errors counter to track the number of not-found errors on your server. You can also set a Performance Monitor alert to notify the Administrator when the number of not-found errors exceeds a threshold.

Following is a brief description of the HTTP Service: Not Found Errors counter.

Table 8.2   Performance Monitor Counter for Not-Found Errors

Counter	Indicates
HTTP Service: Not Found Errors	The number of client read requests that could not be satisfied because the URL did not point to a valid file. Increases in not-found errors might indicate that a file has been moved without its link being updated. However, it might also indicate failed attempts to access protected documents, such as user lists and file directories.

Capacity Planning to Support Security Features

After you have collected data on the effect of adding security features to your server configuration, you can use the results to plan configuration changes to handle the addition workload required to support security features. The following approaches are recommended:

- *Upgrade or add processors.* Security features are often very processor-intensive. In particular, the SSL protocol consumes a significant amount of processor time. Because the Windows NT security features are multithreaded, they can run simultaneously on multiple processors. Thus, adding processors improves performance significantly and prevents the processors from becoming a bottleneck.

- *Upgrade the processor cache.* For best results, you should choose a processor with a large (up to 2 MB) secondary (L2) cache. When encrypting and decrypting data, the processor spends much of its time reading and writing small units of data to and from the main memory. If this data can be stored in the processor cache instead, the data can be retrieved much faster.

- *Add memory.* If the security features cause increased paging or shortages in virtual memory, adding more memory will help. The physical memory used to support the security service consumes space that can be used otherwise to cache files. To accommodate peak use, you should allow for twice as much memory as is required during times of average use while still maintaining 10MB of available memory.

- *Do not add disk space.* Any increased disk activity associated with security features is likely to be the result of a shortage of physical memory, not a need for more disk space. Security features, such as the SSL protocol, rely primarily on processors and physical memory, as opposed to the disks.

Security is an integral feature of the IIS services. You can protect your vital data without sacrificing the performance of your server by planning carefully.

C H A P T E R   9

Monitoring Dynamic Page Generation

One of the most exciting recent developments in Web page technology is the ability to develop dynamic pages — Web pages that are not assembled until the client requests them. Dynamic pages can display the most current data available and can be tailored to clients' preferences. The power of dynamic pages is likely to increase their use on intranets and on the Internet.

Recent experience has shown that applications written for the Common Gateway Interface (CGI), the most popular dynamic Web page interface, severely degrade performance on Windows NT servers. The performance overhead of some CGI applications can cause both memory and processor bottlenecks. These bottlenecks are far less likely on applications written for the Internet Server Application Programming Interface (ISAPI). Therefore, it is important to understand how CGI and ISAPI applications generate dynamic pages, and how to measure and minimize their overhead.

This chapter covers the following sections:

- "CGI and ISAPI Interfaces." An overview of the supported interfaces for generating dynamic pages on Windows NT. This section explains how CGI and ISAPI run on Windows NT and why they perform differently.

- "Monitoring Client Requests for Dynamic Pages." Guidelines for using Performance Monitor to monitor client requests for pages generated by CGI and ISAPI. Requests are the primary measure of activity of applications that generate dynamic pages.

- "Monitoring Servers Running CGI and ISAPI Applications." Suggests methods of monitoring the overall performance of servers running CGI and ISAPI applications using Performance Monitor and Microsoft Web Capacity Analysis Tool (WCAT).

- "Tracking CGI Processes." Guidelines for using Process Monitor and the Processes Tab in Task Manager to track CGI request processes.

- "Capacity Planning to Support CGI Applications." Suggests additions to an Internet Information Server (IIS) server configuration to enable you to support CGI applications and minimize their performance overhead.

These topics build on information presented in Chapter 5, "Monitoring Virtual Memory" and Chapter 6, "Preventing Processor Bottlenecks." For more information about CGI and ISAPI interfaces, see the online *Windows NT Microsoft Internet Information Server Installation and Administration Guide*.

CGI and ISAPI Interfaces

The supported interfaces for dynamic page generation on Windows NT are:

- *Common Gateway Interface (CGI).* An accepted standard for sharing data between browsers and servers. CGI allows interactive applications, such as database query applications, to be run over the Internet. The primary advantage of CGI is that it is *common.* CGI applications can be run on all popular Web servers and can be written in all common scripting languages, such as Perl and the Visual Basic® programming system.

- *Microsoft Internet Server Application Programming Interface (ISAPI).* The newcomer to the field of dynamic interfaces. This API is designed to optimize the performance of applications that generate dynamic pages on intranet and Internet servers. ISAPI can be run on Windows NT 3.51 and later.

CGI and ISAPI have similar functions, and the technique for coding scripts and applications for CGI and ISAPI is also quite similar. However, CGI and ISAPI applications run very differently on Windows NT.

How CGI Applications Operate

CGI applications are compiled as stand-alone executables. When these executables run, Windows NT creates a new, separate process for every client request handled by the application, even if a single client submits more than one request. At any given time, the server is supporting a separate process for every ongoing request. When a request is complete, the server must perform a series of steps to delete the process.

CGI was created for a UNIX environment where processes are the basic unit of operation and have less overhead than processes in Windows NT. In Windows NT, where threads are the basic unit of operation, processes have substantial overhead. Each process receives a private physical memory allocation, is granted space in the paged and nonpaged memory pools, and is protected by the features of the Windows NT security model. In fact, every attribute that makes processes in Windows NT robust also makes them costly. Because CGI requests each executable to run in a separate process, CGI applications have much higher overhead than the alternative, ISAPI extensions.

How ISAPI Extensions Operate

ISAPI applications are compiled as dynamic link libraries (DLLs) that are loaded into the HTTP service when the service starts. ISAPI applications are actually extensions of the HTTP service. ISAPI applications remain in physical memory; run as threads within the IIS service process, Inetinfo.exe; and share the Inetinfo.exe memory space. When a client requests a page generated by an ISAPI extension, a waiting thread processes the request. When the request is complete, the thread returns to the thread pool until another request arrives. No further processing time or memory is required.

CGI and ISAPI Overhead

The effect of running requests as processes rather than as shared threads is significant. CGI applications have been demonstrated to use three to five times more processor time and memory space. CGI applications have also been demonstrated to be three to five times slower than equivalent ISAPI DLLs on the same server and network.

If you run CGI or ISAPI applications, or plan to, you need to know how to monitor their overhead. You must also build in sufficient excess capacity to accommodate their use. The following sections explain how to monitor CGI and ISAPI applications, and how to use simulation tools to help predict processor and memory requirements for CGI and ISAPI.

Monitoring Client Requests for Dynamic Pages

The first step you should use to measure the effect of an application on a computer configuration is to determine how the computer responds to different levels of application activity.

The most common indicator of the activity of an application that generates dynamic pages is rate of requests to the application. CGI and ISAPI applications become active when they respond to requests and are generally inactive between requests. The more requests the application responds to, the more active it is judged to be.

First, you measure the activity level of an application. Then you can compare the effect of different levels of activity of a single application on the computer. You can also compare the effect of the same activity levels of different applications.

Using Performance Monitor to Monitor Client Requests

Performance Monitor includes a set of counters that measure the rate of requests to CGI and ISAPI applications running under each IIS service. These counters are included in the HTTP Service, FTP Server, and Gopher Service performance objects. However, Internet Information Server 2.0 supports ISAPI only on the HTTP service. The ISAPI counters on other services always display a value of zero.

The following table lists the counters that count requests to ISAPI and CGI applications. Please note that these counters display the last observed value, not an average. It is important to log these counters over time and to display the results in a chart, as opposed to a report.

Table 9.1   Performance Monitor Counters for ISAPI and CGI Requests

Counter	Indicates
HTTP Service: Current CGI Requests	How many requests for pages generated by CGI applications are being processed simulataneously.
HTTP Service: Maximum CGI Requests	The maximum number of requests for pages generated by CGI applications that were processed simultaneously since the service started.
HTTP Service: CGI Requests	The total number of requests for pages generated by CGI applications since the service started. The value of this counter includes successful and failed requests.
HTTP Service: Current ISAPI Extension Requests	How many requests for pages generated by ISAPI DLLs are being processed simultaneously.
HTTP Service: Maximum ISAPI Extension Requests	The maximum number of requests for pages generated by ISAPI DLLs that were processed simultaneously since the service started.
HTTP Service: ISAPI Extension Requests	The total number of requests for pages generated by ISAPI DLLs since the service started. The value of this counter includes successful and failed requests.

These counters are also included in IISDyn.pmw, a Performance Monitor workspace settings file on the *Windows NT Server Resource Kit Supplement 1* CD.

By themselves, these counters are indirect indicators of processor activity. When combined with information about server performance, however, these counters can help you judge the effects of different levels of activity on the performance and efficiency of your server.

Monitoring Servers Running ISAPI and CGI Applications

You can monitor the effect of ISAPI and CGI applications on the overall performance of your server. In general, CGI applications use significantly more processor time and memory than equivalent ISAPI DLLs. You can measure this disparity on your servers by using the general server monitoring techniques developed in Chapter 5, "Monitoring Virtual Memory" and Chapter 6, "Preventing Processor Bottlenecks."

This section suggests two approaches to monitoring the effects of dynamic page-generating applications on general server performance:

- Using Performance Monitor to monitor server performance while running ISAPI extensions and CGI applications on your server.
- Using WCAT, the Web Capacity Analysis Toolkit, to simulate the effects of CGI and ISAPI applications on your server.

You can also use Performance Monitor to monitor your WCAT tests. The following sections explain these monitoring techniques in more detail.

Monitoring the Effect of CGI and ISAPI Applications on Overall Server Performance

If you are running CGI applications or ISAPI extensions, you can use Performance Monitor to monitor the effect of these processes on your server.

Use the Performance Monitor counters in IISProc.pmw, IISMem.pmw, and IISDyn.pmw to measure processor and memory use on the server during periods of very high or very low CGI or ISAPI application activity. Log these counters while running one of the following tests:

- Monitor the effect of a CGI application or an ISAPI extension on overall server performance.

  Monitor the server while running with, and then, without the CGI or ISAPI application. Log the counters for several days under similar conditions. Next, compare the rates of processor use, the average length of the processor queue, the number of available bytes, and the rate of page faults of the "with application" and "without application" tests. The difference between the values should be due to performance and memory overhead of the application.

- Compare the effect on your server of equivalent ISAPI and CGI applications.

  If you have ISAPI and CGI scripts that generate the same pages, you can use IISProc.pmw, IISMem.pmw, and IISDyn.pmw to compare ISAPI and CGI performance. Log server performance while the server is running one application and then log server performance while the server is running the other application. Classify the data based on the average number of requests to the application during each period. Then, compare the values of the counters during periods when the rates of CGI and ISAPI requests were similar.

Using WCAT to Simulate ISAPI and CGI Applications

Even if you do not have any available ISAPI or CGI applications, you can still test the effect of such applications on your server configuration by using WCAT. WCAT comes with several prepared tests designed for simulating the effects of CGI and ISAPI applications on your server. The following table lists these tests and provides a brief explanation of each test.

Table 9.2   WCAT Tests of ISAPI and CGI Applications

Test	Description
CGI25	25% of the workload consists of CGI requests; the remaining 75% represents requests for static files based on an average workload.
CGI50	50% of the workload consists of CGI requests; the remaining 50% represents requests for static files based on an average workload.
CGI75	75% of the workload consists of CGI requests; the remaining 25% represents requests for static files based on an average workload.
ISAPI25	25% of the workload consists of ISAPI requests; the remaining 75% represents requests for static files based on an average workload.
ISAPI50	50% of the workload consists of ISAPI requests; the remaining 50% represents requests for static files based on an average workload.
ISAPI75	75% of the workload consists of ISAPI requests; the remaining 25% represents requests for static files based on an average workload.

Using Performance Monitor to Monitor WCAT Tests

You also can use Performance Monitor to monitor server performance during WCAT tests. The method for activating Performance Monitor during a WCAT test is described in detail in the WCAT user guide on the *Supplement 1* CD.

The WCAT **run** command includes a **-p** switch that activates Performance Monitor during a WCAT test. When you include the **-p** option in the WCAT **run** command, the WCAT controller samples and averages selected Performance Monitor counters during the WCAT test. You can specify the Performance Monitor counters that you want WCAT to sample by including them in a script file with a filename extension of .pfc. The name of your .pfc file is part of the syntax of the **-p** switch.

The *Supplement 1* CD includes IISDyn.pfc, a WCAT file of Performance Monitor counters, designed for use with the ISAPI and CGI tests. This file consists of the counters in IISProc.pmw, IISMem.pmw, and IISDyn.pmw.

The following experiments involve running different WCAT tests in sequence and monitoring the effect of the test on your server, using Performance Monitor. When the tests are complete, you can compare the relative effect of each test on server performance.

The suggestions for using WCAT and Performance Monitor to test server performance are:

- To determine the effect of a CGI application on your server, run the CGI25, CGI50, and CGI75 tests sequentially while logging the Performance Monitor counters in Dyn.pmc.

- To determine the effect of an ISAPI application on your server, run the ISAPI25, ISAPI50, and ISAPI75 tests sequentially while logging the Performance Monitor counters in Dyn.pmc.

- To compare the effects of CGI to those of ISAPI, run the CGI75 and ISAPI75 tests sequentially while logging the Performance Monitor counters in Dyn.pmc.

To analyze the data from these tests, note any change in processor and memory use as the proportion of CGI or ISAPI requests increases, or between CGI and ISAPI. The effect of the change in workload varies substantially between server configurations. You can use this data to determine whether your server is prepared to handle this workload efficiently. You can vary the workload or vary the server configuration by adding processors or memory between test trials.

The next section introduces another aspect of monitoring CGI and ISAPI applications. In addition to monitoring general server performance, you can also monitor the processes in which the applications run.

Tracking CGI and ISAPI Processes

The most common way to monitor the overhead of ISAPI and CGI applications is to monitor general server performance under varying levels of application activity. This technique is described in the preceding sections.

In addition to monitoring changes in overall server performance, you can also monitor the processes in which the applications run. This section suggests some tools and methods for monitoring the processes in which ISAPI extensions and CGI applications run.

Monitoring ISAPI Extensions

ISAPI scripts are compiled into DLLs that run in the Internet Information Server process, Inetinfo.exe. You can monitor the processor and memory use of the Inetinfo process, but it is difficult to distinguish the resource use attributable to ISAPI from that of the rest of the services running under Inetinfo. It is also extremely difficult, though technically possible, to associate individual threads in Inetinfo with ISAPI requests.

Monitoring CGI Requests

CGI applications are not as difficult to monitor as ISAPI extensions. In Windows NT, CGI applications are stored and run as separate executables. Requests for pages generated by CGI run as separate processes. You can use most process-monitoring tools to view the processes in which the CGI requests run. However, the request processes often are so ephemeral that it is hard to track them effectively with any tool that isn't updated frequently or that requires that you choose the process before monitoring it.

Process Monitor and Task Manager provide a continually updated running list of processes. You can use Process Monitor and Task Manager to monitor the processes in which CGI requests run.

Using Process Monitor and Task Manager to Monitor CGI Processes

Process Monitor (Pmon.exe) and the Task Manager **Process** tab are both useful for monitoring CGI processes. Although these tools do not log process-specific data over time and cannot export data for other uses, they are particularly effective for monitoring short-lived processes. Both tools display a list of all processes running on the computer, along with different measures of processor and memory use.

Process Monitor is included on the *Windows NT Workstation Resource Kit* CD in the Performance Tools group (\Perftool\Meastool). Process Monitor is updated automatically every five seconds.

Task Manager is integrated into Windows NT. To start Task Manager, press CTRL+SHIFT+ESC. Click the **Processes** tab on Task Manager to see a list of processes running on the server, including the processes in which CGI requests run. You can set the rate at which Task Manager is updated by clicking **Update Speed** on the **View** menu.

The Task Manager **Processes** tab displays a table listing the running processes along with performance information about each process. By default, Task Manager displays the **Process Identifier**, **CPU Usage**, **CPU Time**, and **Memory Usage** of each process. You can change the type of performance information listed about each process. To add or remove a Task performance measure, from the **View** menu, click **Select Columns**, then click a performance measure.

Note Please note that the Process Monitor and Task Manager **CPU Time**, **Page Faults** and **Mem Usage** counts are cumulative. These performance measures show how much of a resource the process has used since the process started. A high value might indicate that a process has been running for a long time, not that the process is using the resource at a high rate.

Warning You should be careful when running any monitoring tool for an extended period of time at a very high refresh rate. The overhead of the tool is directly proportional to the frequency at which it is updated. When using Process Monitor and Task Manager, monitor the overhead of the processes in which the tools run and subtract the overhead from your test results.

Monitoring CGI and ISAPI processes provide another view of the performance of CGI and ISAPI applications. This additional information can help you plan your server capacity.

Capacity Planning to Support ISAPI and CGI Applications

Although the data values vary widely among different servers, CGI applications and, to a lesser extent, ISAPI extensions, have much higher overhead than standard "static" pages. But the overhead of dynamic page-generating applications should not deter you from adding dynamic pages to your published files. The ability to monitor these applications and estimate their overhead during periods of varying activity allows you to prepare your server for the increased workload.

Some suggestions for optimizing your configuration to run applications that generate dynamic pages are:

- *Upgrading processors.* CGI and ISAPI applications both benefit from faster processors. Fast processors are especially important to CGI applications in which each request runs in a separate, single-threaded process.

- *Adding processors.* ISAPI extensions are multithreaded and can run simultaneously on multiple processors. Adding processors is probably the easiest way to improve the efficiency of ISAPI applications. CGI applications benefit from multiple processors, too. Even though CGI requests run in separate single-threaded processes, multiple CGI requests can each run on different processors simultaneously.

- *Adding memory.* CGI applications typically use three to five times more physical memory than equivalent ISAPI applications.

- *Defragmenting your disks.* If your cache performance declines over time, defragment the disk. Your files might have become fragmented over time.

- *Redesigning your static pages.* Using current technology, even ISAPI, which is optimized for Windows NT, is far slower and less efficient than serving static pages. If you are generating pages dynamically to satisfy user preferences, consider substituting ten or twenty different static variations for a single dynamically generated page. If you are generating pages dynamically to provide frequently updated data, consider redesigning your application so that it generates a single dynamic page on a fixed schedule and then stores that page for repeated static retrieval until the next update.

- *Converting CGI Scripts to ISAPI Scripts.* ISAPI is optimized to run on Windows NT. Converting CGI applications to ISAPI extensions can improve performance significantly in a small or large installation. (To see the magnitude of the difference on your server, run the WCAT CGI75 and ISAPI75 tests, and compare the results.) For instructions on converting CGI scripts to ISAPI DLLs, see the *ISAPI Programmer's Reference* in the Win32 Software Development Kit.

- *Incorporate logging in CGI and ISAPI routines.* Add transaction logging functions to your CGI and/or ISAPI code. The transaction-logging function should record the time each incoming request was received and the time it was completed. Or, you can add extensible Performance Monitor counters to the code and use Performance Monitor to create the transaction log or monitor the routines. When delays arise, the transaction log will help you determine the source of the delay.

Despite their performance cost, dynamic Web pages are likely to increase in popularity and constitute a larger proportion of the average Web server file base as the technology progresses. The challenge for administrators is to preserve speed and efficiency while publishing ever more complex pages.

On Windows NT, CGI and ISAPI both have higher overhead than serving static pages from memory. But the difference between CGI and ISAPI performance is significant. In general, CGI applications are much slower and use more processor time and memory space than equivalent ISAPI extensions. Fortunately, you can measure the effect of CGI and ISAPI applications on the performance of your servers and upgrade your configuration to meet the challenges CGI and ISAPI pose.

PART III

Interoperability With Additional Enterprise-Level Services

C H A P T E R   1 0

Additional Network Services: Enterprise Level

Terra Flora was introduced in the *Microsoft Windows NT Server version 4.0 Resource Kit: Windows NT Server Networking Guide* as a case study in interoperability of heterogeneous networks. Chapter 4, "Terra Flora: A Fictitious Case Study," in the *Windows NT Server Networking Guide,* provided the history of the corporation and presented a plan for interoperability. Chapter 5, "Network Services: Enterprise Level," provided the business justification for selecting Windows NT Server services to interoperate the heterogeneous networks. It also presented specific information on the installation and configuration of Enterprise level services that support the network itself and keep the corporation-wide information synchronized.

Terra Flora is a totally fictitious company whose business operations and networking environment are being examined and used to demonstrate the functionality of Windows NT Server products. The names of companies, products, people, characters, and data mentioned herein are fictitious and are in no way intended to represent any real individual, company, product, or event, unless otherwise noted.

This chapter will present information on some of the additional Enterprise services that were not covered earlier. The services that will be discussed include:

- Directory Service Manager for NetWare (DSMN)
- Web Administration for Windows NT Server

Information about each service will include the business reasons for selecting the service and instructions on how to install and configure the service.

Located inside the back cover of the *Windows NT Server Resource Kit Supplement 1* is a network diagram that represents the hardware and software now interoperating at Terra Flora. Frequent references will be made to the diagram.

Directory Service Manager for NetWare

Microsoft Directory Service Manager for NetWare (DSMN), a Microsoft Windows NT Server utility, enables synchronization of user accounts between Windows NT Server domains and servers running Novell NetWare version 2.*x,* 3.*x,* and 4.*x,* running in the bindery emulation mode. DSMN extends the Windows NT Server directory database service features for user and group account management to NetWare servers. By using DSMN, the NetWare server can be managed as part of the Windows NT domain, using the Windows NT Directory Services to manage the NetWare-based servers.

DSMN is a utility offered as part of the Microsoft product called Services for NetWare. For details on the use of DSMN, see the *Services for NetWare Administrator's Guide.*

Chapter 5 of the *Windows NT Server Networking Guide* described how centralized network logon was installed and configured. Terra Flora chose the network logon services provided by the Windows NT operating system because Windows NT Server is the only product that allows users to log on to all of the Terra Flora heterogeneous networks with a single user account and password. The benefit of using a single user account and password is that users only have to remember one account and password to log on and then be able to access any application they need.

One of the challenges with the use of a single logon is the synchronization of the user accounts and passwords on all servers that the users access. Currently, to synchronize user accounts and passwords at Terra Flora, network administrators must grant permissions to each user on each individual NetWare server by creating a user account. In addition to adding the users to each NetWare server, users must be added to the Windows NT domain. Thus, although the Windows NT Server network logon service provides single-account logon to all servers, administrators must still add the users to several servers.

If a user changes the password for the logon, the password must be changed on all servers that the user accesses. If the administrator forgets to change the password on a single server, the user accounts and passwords are out of sync and the user cannot access the server.

For each Windows NT domain, the directory database of the primary domain controller (PDC) contains all users of all services. Therefore, any user with permissions who is added to the domain's directory database can access any server that is part of that domain.

The Decision to Use DSMN

Terra Flora will use DSMN to synchronize the user accounts and passwords on both the Windows NT and NetWare servers. Because DSMN simplifies network administration tasks, Terra Flora can save time and money.

By using DSMN, NetWare servers can be added to the Windows NT domain and then be administered as part of that domain. The NetWare users are added to the directory database residing on the Windows NT PDC. All permissions granted to users on the NetWare servers can be granted on servers running Windows NT Server. Similarly, all permissions granted to users in the Windows NT domain can be granted on servers running NetWare. Administrators no longer need to add individual users to each individual server.

Simplifying Administrative Tasks

By using DSMN, administrators can centrally manage their Windows NT Server and NetWare account information from Windows NT Directory Services.

- Administrators set up only one user account and password for each user on the network.

- Administrators use a point-and-click interface to *propagate*, or copy, user accounts to and from servers running Windows NT version 3.51 or higher and servers running NetWare version 2.*x* and 3.*x*.

- Administrators have multiple options for setting up initial passwords, selecting which user accounts are to be propagated, and performing account deletions. A trial run option is included to test a propagation strategy.

DSMN Provides Benefits to Network Users

In addition to simplifying administrative tasks, DSMN provides the following benefits to network users:

- New users are added to the network quickly. The administrator adds the user to the Windows NT Server Directory Services, and the user account is automatically propagated back to all authorized NetWare servers.

- Each user's account name and password are identical on all NetWare and Windows NT servers, so the same name and password are used regardless of where a user logs on.

- Users who use Windows NT Server Remote Access Service (RAS) can log on through RAS by using the same user account and password.

- Windows NT Directory Services can authenticate users to business applications that are running on the Windows NT and NetWare servers.

Synchronizing User Accounts at Terra Flora

The primary benefit that Terra Flora receives by using DSMN is that user accounts are synchronized between Windows NT and NetWare servers. (Please refer to the network diagram located inside the back cover of the *Windows NT Server Resource Kit Supplement 1*. There are two NetWare servers represented on the Terra Flora network diagram in the California domain, named CANW410DIV01 and CANW312DPT01.)

Deciding Which NetWare Servers to Add to the Domain

CANW312DPT01 is a NetWare server that houses front-end applications to the Oracle databases running on the DEC UNIX server in the Nursery division. The Nursery division users require access to the business applications housed on the DEC UNIX server through the NetWare servers. The users also need access to the Enterprise services on the Windows NT servers. For this reason, Terra Flora will add CANW312DPT01 to the Windows NT California domain.

The NetWare server CANW410DIV01 runs NetWare 4.10. This server is set up exclusively to pilot the Network Directory Services (NDS) product in the NetWare operating system. DSMN does not function on NetWare 4.10 servers unless they are operating bindery emulation. Because this NetWare server is using NDS and not bindery emulation, this server will not be added to the Windows NT California domain.

Terra Flora wants to add all of its NetWare servers running version 3.*x* and 2.*x* to the Windows NT California domain. A NetWare server in the California domain that runs version 3.12 is not represented on the network diagram. CANW312DPT02 is a department-level server that runs customized business applications for the sales department.

After adding the DSMN software, the administrators will use DSMN to select CANW312DPT01 and CANW312DPT02 as the two NetWare servers to be added to the Windows NT California domain. After they are added, the NetWare servers will be administered in the same way as any other server in the domain.

Deciding Which Accounts to Administer with DSMN

Different groups within the Nursery division, including accounting, sales, and administrators, require access to the CANW312DPT01 NetWare server. Administrators need access to perform administrative tasks on the server itself. Accounting and sales need access to the Nursery business applications housed on the DEC UNIX machine. Additionally, all three groups need access to the Windows NT servers, such as CANTS40ENT03, which houses Enterprise services of DHCP, DNS and WINS.

CANW312DPT02 is a NetWare server that stores the customized sales business applications. The sales and administrators groups will, therefore, need access to CANW312DPT02 to perform sales and administrative tasks. The accounting group will not need access to CANW312DPT02.

After the servers are added to the domain, the administrators will select which of the NetWare server user and group accounts the domain will manage. All user and group accounts can be moved to the Windows NT directory database, or only some of them. The selected accounts will be copied to the directory database of the Windows NT PDC.

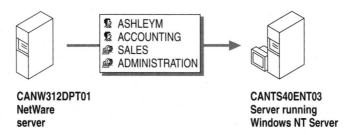

CANW312DPT01
NetWare
server

CANTS40ENT03
Server running
Windows NT Server

Figure 10.1   When a NetWare server is added to a domain for management, NetWare user and group accounts are moved to the domain.

Maintain or Delete Remaining Accounts

If some of the users and groups are moved to the directory database, the Terra Flora administrators will choose whether to delete or retain the remaining users and groups on the NetWare server. If they are retained, the accounts will be administered by using the NetWare administrative tools.

Note Do not use NetWare administrative tools on accounts managed by Directory Service Manager for NetWare. If you do, the accounts on that NetWare server become unsynchronized with the accounts in the domain.

After selecting which accounts will be retained and added to the Windows NT directory database, the administrators will specify how the Windows NT Server domain is to propagate user and group accounts back to the CANW312DPT01 and CANW312DPT02 NetWare servers. All accounts, or a subset of the accounts, can be copied to the NetWare servers. When the Terra Flora administrators select which Windows NT Server groups to copy, user accounts that are members of any of the groups selected will also be copied.

The list of users and groups being copied will differ for each of the two NetWare servers in the domain. If a NetWare user needs access only to specific NetWare servers, the user's account will be copied to only those servers, which minimizes network traffic and makes DSMN run more efficiently.

For example, the sales and administrators groups at Terra Flora need access to both of the NetWare servers, CANW312DPT01 and CANW312DPT02, while members of the accounting group need access to only CANW312DPT01. When specifying which groups to copy to CANW312DPT02, Terra Flora administrators select both administrators and sales; but when specifying the users to propagate to CANW312DPT01, they select all three groups.

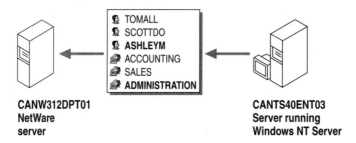

CANW312DPT01
NetWare
server

CANTS40ENT03
Server running
Windows NT Server

Figure 10.2   The NetWare user accounts, along with Windows NT Server accounts, are copied back to the NetWare server.

Note The list of groups that the Windows NT Server domain copies to the NetWare server can be modified any time after adding the NetWare server to the domain.

Identical User Names Are Merged

Terra Flora is adding multiple NetWare servers to be managed by the same California domain. Because each server has a user or group account with identical names, the accounts will be merged in the California domain.

For example, AshleyM has an administrator's account on both of Terra Flora's NetWare servers. When CANW312DPT01 is added for management to the domain, the AshleyM account is created in the Windows NT Server domain. That Windows NT Server account is also given the same rights and permissions that the AshleyM NetWare account had.

When CANW312DPT02 is added to the domain, DSMN recognizes that AshleyM already has an account in the domain. DSMN gives the account the rights and permissions of the CANW312DPT02 AshleyM account. The domain's AshleyM account then has the same rights and permissions that were previously assigned to both the NetWare server's AshleyM accounts.

DSMN can also merge accounts with different user names on multiple NetWare servers. For example, if AshleyM had an account on the CANW312DPT02 server with a user name of AshleyMe, this account can be merged into the domain's AshleyM account. This account would then have the same rights previously held by both AshleyM and AshleyMe.

For more information about renaming accounts, see the section "Using a Mapping File to Rename User Accounts" in Chapter 7, "Administering Directory Service Manager for NetWare," in the *Services for NetWare Administrator's Guide.*

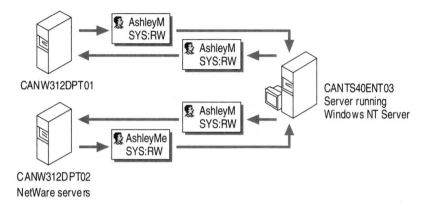

CANW312DPT01

CANTS40ENT03
Server running
Windows NT Server

CANW312DPT02
NetWare servers

Figure 10. 3   User accounts on separate NetWare servers can be merged into a single account in the domain, with all of the rights previously held by both accounts.

Note If there is an account on a NetWare server that has the same name as an account on the Windows NT Server domain, the rights and permissions of the NetWare account are given to the existing Windows NT Server account. If the existing Windows NT Server account is NetWare-enabled, then the account's existing password is used. If the account is not NetWare-enabled, the account is given a new password to enable it to be copied to NetWare servers.

Installing DSMN

While you can install DSMN on any Windows NT domain server, the service runs only on PDCs. The server on which you are installing DSMN must:

- Be running Windows NT Server version 4.0 or version 3.51. If the computer runs Windows NT Server 3.51, it must also run Windows NT Server Service Pack 2 or later. Only instructions for installing on Windows NT Server 4.0 are included in this supplement. For details about installing on Windows NT Server 3.51, see Chapter 1, "Understanding and Installing Directory Service Manager for NetWare," in the *Microsoft Directory Service Manager for NetWare Administrator's Guide* for Windows NT Server 3.51.

- Have Gateway Service for NetWare installed. This service is included with Windows NT Server. For installation instructions, see the *Windows NT Server Networking Guide*, Chapter 5, "Network Services: Enterprise Level."

Note You may want to install DSMN on one or more backup domain controllers to speed up recovery in the event of a failure of the PDC.

Instructions in this section include those for:

- Installing DSMN from a CD-ROM.
- Creating disks from the CD-ROM and installing DSMN from those disks.
- Installing only the DSMN administrative tools, which can be used to remotely run DSMN on any domain server on the network.

Installing DSMN from a CD-ROM

DSMN is shipped as a separate Microsoft product and is included on the compact disc titled *Services for NetWare*.

▶ **To install DSMN on a Windows NT Server 4.0 computer from a CD-ROM**

1. Double-click My Computer.
2. Double-click Control Panel.
3. Double-click **Network**.
4. Click the **Services** tab, and then click **Add**.
5. Click **Have Disk** even if **Directory Service Manager for NetWare** appears in the **Network Service** list.
6. Insert the *Services for NetWare* CD in the CD-ROM drive.
7. Type the path, and then click **OK**.

   The path is *drive***:\DSMN\NT40***processor*, where *drive* is the drive letter of the CD-ROM drive and *processor* is the server's processor type. For example, type **d:\dsmn\nt40\i386** to install on an *x*86-based computer with a CD-ROM drive at drive D. The possible values for *processor* are **i386**, **MIPS**, **ALPHA**, and **PPC**.
8. Select **Directory Service Manager for NetWare**, and then click **OK**.
9. In both the **Password** and **Confirm Password** boxes, type a password for the DSMN user account, and then click **OK**.

   This account is used by the service to perform tasks.

When you restart the computer, the DSMN service will automatically start. To configure how this service starts and stops, use the **Services** option in Control Panel or the **net start mssync** and **net stop mssync** commands.

Note On computers that have multiple network cards and that run DSMN but not File and Print Services for NetWare, the computer itself must have a *network number* defined for the NWLink IPX/SPX Compatible Transport running on the Windows NT PDC. This *network number* is a NetWare concept (see your NetWare documentation), and the number you define must be unique. It must be different from all other network numbers on your NetWare network. To configure a network number, go to Control Panel, click **Network**, click **Protocols**, click **NWLink IPX/SPX Compatible Transport**, and then type your network number in the **Internal Network Number** box.

Installing DSMN from a Floppy Disk

Even if a computer does not have a CD-ROM drive, DSMN can be installed by creating floppy disks from the *Services for NetWare* CD.

▶ **To install DSMN on a Windows NT Server 4.0 computer from a floppy disk**

1. Insert the *Services for NetWare* CD into the CD-ROM drive.

2. Format two blank, high-density, 3.5-inch floppy disks. Insert one disk into the floppy disk drive, usually drive A.

3. Switch to the \Dsmn\Nt40\Disks directory.

4. Switch to the subdirectory for the platform that you want to create installation disks for. For example, switch to Disks\i386 to create installation disks for an x86-based computer.

5. Copy the contents of the Disk1 subdirectory to the disk, and then copy the contents of the Disk2 subdirectory to the other disk.

6. Follow the steps in the previous procedure, with the following exception. In the **Insert Disk** dialog box, specify the drive that contains Disk 1. You will be prompted to insert Disk 2.

Installing DSMN Administrative Tools

Terra Flora will install just the administrative tools for DSMN on computers running Windows NT Workstation or Windows NT Server that will be used to administer domain servers remotely.

For instructions on how to install the DSMN administrative tools, follow the steps in the earlier procedure for installing DSMN from a CD-ROM. In step 8, however, select **Directory Service Manager for NetWare Administrative Tools Only** instead of **Directory Service Manager for NetWare**.

> **Note** To administer a domain other than the domain containing your computer, that domain must be trusted by the domain containing your computer.

Synchronizing Accounts on Servers

Synchronization Manager is the tool used to add NetWare servers for management within Windows NT Server domains and to manage other aspects of DSMN. The main screen of Synchronization Manager appears below.

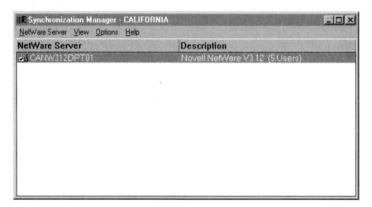

The **NetWare Server** column lists the names of servers that have been added to this domain for management. The **Description** column shows the version and type of each server. To the left of the server name is an icon that indicates the current synchronization status of the server, as shown in the following table.

Table 10.1   Icon Representation of Synchronization Status

Icon	Status
🖫	The server is currently synchronized with the domain.
🖫	The server is not currently synchronized. Directory Service Manager for NetWare will soon synchronize it.

When DSMN is installed, it is added to the **Administrative Tools** menu of Windows NT Server. When you click DSMN to start it, Synchronization Manager is displayed.

▶ **To start Synchronization Manager**

1. Click **Start**.

2. Point to **Programs**.

3. Point to **Administrative Tools**.

4. Click **Directory Service Manager for NetWare**.

Adding a NetWare Server for Management

At Terra Flora, the NetWare servers in the California domain named CANW312DPT01 and CANW312DPT02 will be added to the Windows NT California domain. In this way, users set up in the Windows NT directory database can be copied to the NetWare servers and will remain synchronized.

When a NetWare server is added to a Windows NT domain, user and group accounts are copied from the server to the domain. Those accounts, along with original Windows NT Server accounts, are then copied back to the NetWare server. From then on, the accounts are maintained on the domain, and account changes are automatically copied to the NetWare servers in the domain.

Note   For compatibility, Directory Service Manager for NetWare cannot propagate more than 2,000 accounts to a NetWare server. If you try to propagate too many accounts to a NetWare server, you will be prompted to propagate fewer groups.

Before Adding a NetWare Server to a Domain

To ensure that the addition of a NetWare server to a domain for management goes smoothly, do the following before adding the server:

- Use NetWare utilities to back up the NetWare server's bindery.

- Check user names on the NetWare server and the Windows NT Server domain. If any are identical, unless you rename the NetWare user account, the rights and permissions of the NetWare user account will be granted to the existing Windows NT Server account. For more information about renaming user accounts, see the section "Using a Mapping File to Rename User Accounts" in Chapter 7, "Administering Directory Service Manager for NetWare," in the *Services for NetWare Administrator's Guide*.

- If multiple NetWare servers are being added to the domain, check whether any users have accounts on multiple NetWare servers with different user names. If so, choose the name you want the user to have on the domain, and then transfer the other accounts to that user name. For more information, see the section "Using a Mapping File to Rename User Accounts" in Chapter 7, "Administering Directory Service Manager for NetWare," in the *Services for NetWare Administrator's Guide*.

- Check the account policies of the domain to make sure they are acceptable. After a NetWare server is added, these policies will affect user logons to the NetWare server.

Note To maintain password history, set the domain's password uniqueness to remember passwords, and then set the number of passwords to eight or more. If the limit is less than eight, password history affects only logons to servers running Windows NT Server, not to NetWare servers.

- If the File and Print Services for NetWare product was previously installed on the primary domain controller, reset the passwords of any user accounts that were NetWare-enabled before DSMN was installed. DSMN cannot read these existing passwords.

  To enable previously NetWare-enabled users to be copied to NetWare servers, create a batch file that calls the **net user** command for each user and resets the password. For the most security, you can use the **/rand** option to randomly generate new passwords for these users.

- Perform a trial run of the addition, and then carefully examine the report it generates to make sure that the results are what you want.

For details on any of the preceding steps, see Chapter 7, "Administering Directory Service Manager for NetWare," in the *Services for NetWare Administrator's Guide*.

After the preceding steps are complete, you are ready to add the NetWare server to the Windows NT domain, where it will be managed by using Windows NT Server administrative tools.

▶ **To add a NetWare server to be managed in a domain**

1. In Synchronization Manager, click **Add Server to Manage** on the **NetWare Server** menu.

2. Enter the name of the NetWare server, and then click **OK**.

3. Type the user name and password to be used to connect to the NetWare server, and then click **OK**.
   The user name must have Supervisor privileges on the NetWare server.

4. Select options in the **Propagate NetWare Accounts to Windows NT Domain** dialog box to specify how you want NetWare user accounts copied to the domain.

   - To use a mapping file, click **Use Mapping File**. To create the mapping file, type a new file name in the **File** box, and then click **Edit**. For details on how to use a mapping file, see Chapter 7, "Administering Directory Service Manager for NetWare" in the *Services for NetWare Administrator's Guide*.

   - To specify users, groups, and passwords, click **Ignore Mapping File**.

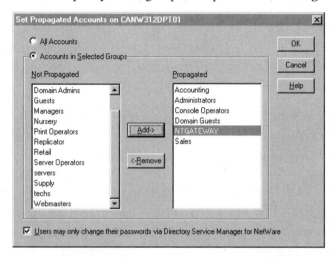

5. Click **Trial Run**.

   This optional but recommended step generates a report that shows which user and group accounts will be successfully propagated, as well as new user passwords.

6. Click **OK** to add the server.

7. Click **Yes** to continue if you have already backed up the bindery of the NetWare server. Otherwise, click **No** and then back up the bindery before adding the server.

8. In the **Set Propagated Accounts on** [*Server*] dialog box, click the option to propagate either all groups (and their members) or only some groups back to the NetWare server.

   For help with an option in this dialog box, click **Help**.

9. Click **Yes** to delete the NetWare user and group accounts that you are not propagating to the Windows NT Server domain. Click **No** to keep these accounts and continue managing them on the NetWare server using NetWare administrative tools.

Accounts left behind on the NetWare server cannot use **chgpass**; they must use NetWare utilities to change their passwords.

Note When a NetWare server is added to a domain for management, a user account named WINNT_SYNC_AGENT appears in that server's bindery. This account is used by DSMN to access the NetWare server's bindery and should not be deleted.

You can remove a NetWare server from management with a domain at any time. You can then use NetWare administrative tools to administer the server and its current bindery. Or you can restore the bindery if you want to return the server to how it was before you added it to the domain. You can add the server back to a domain at any time.

Administering NetWare Servers as Part of a Domain

After NetWare servers are added to a domain for management and NetWare accounts are specified, Terra Flora will use the Windows NT Server tool, User Manager for Domains, to administer those accounts. Any changes are automatically copied to the NetWare server.

The following table indicates which tools are used to perform administrative tasks.

Table 10.2   Administrative Tools Used to Perform Administration Tasks

Task	Administrative tool
Add NetWare servers to domains	Synchronization Manager
Specify which Windows NT Server groups to copy to NetWare servers	Synchronization Manager
Administer the association of NetWare servers and Windows NT Server domains	Synchronization Manager
Manage account properties of users and groups	User Manager for Domains

For more information, see Chapter 7, "Administering Directory Service Manager for NetWare," in the *Services for NetWare Administrator's Guide*

Note After adding a NetWare server to a domain, you continue to use NetWare administrative tools to manage NetWare server functions other than user account management. These functions include shared volumes, file permissions and trustee rights, accounting, and printing.

A NetWare server can participate in only one Windows NT Server domain. After a NetWare server has been added to a domain for management, you cannot add it to another domain without removing it from the first one.

Web Administration for Microsoft Windows NT

Terra Flora administrators often perform network administrative duties at locations other than their desks—for example, when they need to replace a server at another location. Because replacing a server can take several hours, the administrators would like to remotely administer any Windows NT Server from any computer anywhere on the network. Web Administration for Microsoft Windows NT Server provides this capability.

The Web Administration software can be installed on any server that runs Windows NT Server 4.0 and Microsoft Internet Information Server 2.0 (IIS). Installing the Web Administration software on the server enables the server to *publish* or display Web pages that include forms you can use to administer that particular server.

For information about using Web Administration for Windows NT, see: **http://www.microsoft.com/ntserver/webadmin/webadminfaq.htm**.

The Decision to Use Web Administration

Web Administration for Microsoft Windows NT Server was chosen by Terra Flora because it is a centralized administration tool that enables remote administration of Windows NT servers from any computer that has a Web browser installed.

Most Terra Flora administrators work primarily at corporate headquarters in Sacramento, California. They travel to various locations within corporate headquarters to perform their work. When administrators are away from their computers, they also need to be able to administer the company's computers that run Windows NT Server.

For example, Terra Flora administrator AshleyM has an office and desktop client computer in the administrator's bull pen, which is located in the area of Building 1 that houses all the main Enterprise servers. On Tuesday, one of the payroll department servers in Building 4 failed. AshleyM went to Building 4 to reload and configure the payroll server.

While in Building 4, AshleyM received a call from a retail store manager stating that a recently hired employee did not have access to the retail store's software.

To better understand this scenario, refer to the Terra Flora network diagram inside the back cover of this supplement. The new employee would authenticate to the network through the server named NENTS40ENT01. AshleyM needs the ability to log on to the Web and set up the user account in the northeast domain from the client she was using in the Building 4 site. Without the Web Administration tool, AshleyM needs to contact another administrator to perform the task.

Web Browsers Are Required

To use the Web Administration tool, administrators need access to a computer that has a Web browser installed. A *Web browser* is a software tool that retrieves a document from a Web server, interprets the hypertext markup language (HTML) codes, and displays the document to the user with as much graphical content as the software can supply. The client's Web browser will display the graphical interface needed to administer the Windows NT servers. After Web browsers are installed, the Terra Flora administrators will be able to administer any Windows NT Server.

Security

Web Administration for Windows NT Server provides the capability to administer remote Windows NT servers anywhere on an intranet and from the Internet. Terra Flora recognized that they could communicate on the Internet with thousands of potential customers. Conversely, this means that they could be opening their corporate intranet to these same thousands, creating a certain degree of risk. Terra Flora management realized that they need to implement a security configuration that would reduce some of this risk.

Web Administration for Windows NT Server supports several modes of security. Each server administered must support Basic authentication, Windows NT Challenge Response security, or both. Also, the Secure Sockets Layer (SSL) protocol can be used with either or both of these modes for encryption. With *encryption* turned on, the information in a session is not displayed in readable format by the user.

Basic authentication simply prompts the user for a name and password when the administrator accesses the server. The name supplied is checked against the members of the administrators group on the server. Passwords are transmitted in *clear text*, which means that they can be viewed.

Windows NT Challenge Response is more sophisticated, and passwords are not transmitted over the network. With this security, the administrator must be logged on to the computer with a user name that is recognized as a member of the Administrator group on the computer they want to administer.

When choosing between Basic authentication and Windows NT Challenge Response, the administrator must consider what the Web browser used to administer the server supports. For more information about what security is supported by different browsers, see the "Browser/Password Authentication Matrix" at **http://www.microsoft.com/ntserver/webadmin/webadminfaq.htm**.

Terra Flora will also configure Web Administration for Microsoft Windows NT to use the Secure Sockets Layer (SSL) protocol. SSL supports authentication of users and encryption of session data. To use SSL, Terra Flora administrators must obtain a certificate from a certificate authority such as VeriSign. For more information on SSL, see Chapter 5, "Securing Your Site Against Intruders," in the online *Windows NT Server Microsoft Internet Information Server Installation and Administration Guide.*

Because the Web browsers at Terra Flora support only Basic authentication, Terra Flora decided to use SSL. Even if additional clients supporting Windows NT Challenge Response are supplied with Web browsers, SSL will still be used because SSL encrypts all data in the session. See the section "Adding SSL to Provide Additional Security" later in this chapter for details.

If you are not familiar with Internet security, see the following sources to learn more about it:

- Chapter 3, "Configuring and Managing Your Internet Information Server," in the online *Microsoft Internet Information Server Installation and Administration Guide.*
- Chapter 5, "Securing Your Site Against Intruders," in the online *Microsoft Internet Information Server Installation and Administration Guide.*
- Chapter 3, "Server Security on the Internet," in the *Microsoft Windows NT Server Resource Kit: Windows NT Server Internet Guide.*

For more information about general Windows NT Server security, see the following:

- *Windows NT Server Concepts and Planning.*
- Chapter 2, "Network Security and Domain Planning," in the *Microsoft Windows NT Server Resource Kit: Windows NT Server Networking Guide.*

Why Terra Flora Will Use Web Administration

The benefit to Terra Flora in using the Web Administration for Windows NT is that limited administrative tasks can be performed remotely to any Windows NT Server from any computer with a Web browser installed. Web Administration for Windows NT assumes that the administrator is familiar with the use of the Windows NT administration tools. For information on use of the Windows NT Server administration tools, see Help.

The following table lists some of the Windows NT Server administration tasks you can accomplish with Web Administration for Microsoft Windows NT Server.

Table 10.3   Tasks You Can Perform with Web Administration for Microsoft Windows NT Server

Category	Tasks
Account Management	Create and delete user accounts (including FPNW user accounts)
	View and change user information (properties)
	Change user passwords
	Disable user accounts
	Create and remove groups
	Add and remove users to and from groups
	Add workstations to the domain
Share Management	View shares for all installed file services (Microsoft, Macintosh, and NetWare compatible file services)
	Change permissions on shares
	Create new shares for all installed file services
Session Management	View current sessions
	Delete one or all sessions
	Send message to current users of the server
Server Management	Shutdown (reboot) server
	Change services/driver configuration
	View System, Application, and Security Log events
	Server configuration data dump
Printer Management	List print queues and jobs in each queue
	Pause queue or specific print job
	Flush queue or specific print job

Remote Administration Using Web Administration

As stated earlier, to use the Web Administration tool, you must be familiar with the Windows NT Server Administrative tools. For example, setting up user accounts using the Web Administration tool is visually different to the administrator than if the administrator uses the Windows NT Server Administrative tool, User Manager for Domains. The differences are not significant if you are familiar with what is required to set up user accounts using the Windows NT Server Administrative tool, User Manager for Domains. For details about using Windows NT Server Administrative tools, see Help.

This section demonstrates how AshleyM, the Terra Flora administrator was able to set up a user remotely from a client located in Building 4 using the Web Administrator.

Adding a User Account with Web Administration

For details on installing the Web Administration for Microsoft Windows NT Server, see the next section, "Web Administration Installation at Terra Flora." Once the software is installed, Ashley M can remotely set up user accounts with Web Administration.

▶ **To add a user account using Web Administration:**

1. From the Web page titled **Web Administration of Microsoft Windows NT Server**, click **Accounts**. The Account Management on Server CANTS40ENT02 Web page is displayed. The Web page will display the name of the server you are administering; in the following example, CANTS40ENT02 is displayed.

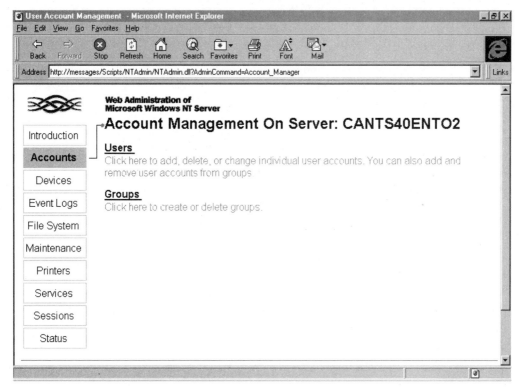

2. Click **Users**. A **User Accounts** dialog box is displayed on the Web page, as shown following.

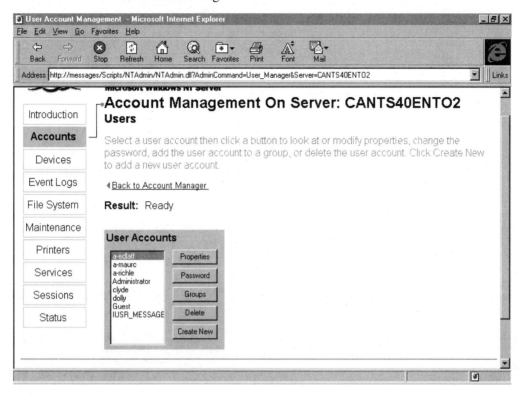

3. Click **Create New**. The **Create New User Account** dialog box is displayed on the Web page, as shown following.

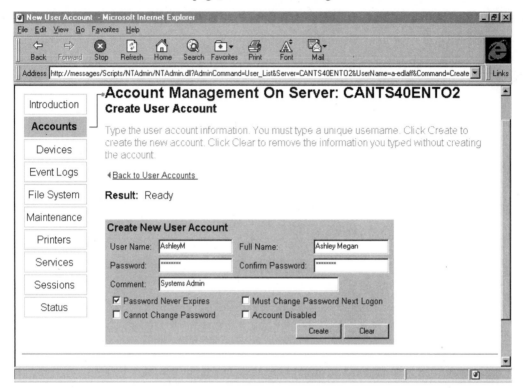

4. Supply the information as illustrated in the Web page displayed directly preceding. Click **Create**. The user account is added to the domain.

Web Administration Installation at Terra Flora

At Terra Flora, installing Web Administration will involve three steps.

- Installing Web Administration
- Adding SSL to provide additional security
- Configuring Password Authentication

You can install the Web Administration for Microsoft Windows NT Server software on any server that runs both of the following:

- Windows NT Server 4.0
- Internet Information Server 2.0 (included on the Windows NT Server CD)

The actual Web Administration interface is a series of HTML pages that the Administrator navigates through using the client's Web browser. Administrative tasks can be performed using the pages, which include some Wizard-like explanations to assist the user.

You will also need to use a Web Browser. The browser can be located on the server itself or on any other computer that has network access to your server.

Installing Web Administration

Before installing Web Administration, check to see if a previous version of Web Administration of Microsoft Windows has been installed on the server. If so, complete the following steps. Once the steps are completed, you can re-install Web Administration on the server.

1. If you have a previous version of Web Administration of Microsoft Windows NT Server tool installed on this server, stop **all** Microsoft Internet Information Server services you have running.

2. Delete the following two directories and their contents: *inetsrv_root*\scripts\NTAdmin and *inetsrv_root*\wwwroot\NTAdmin

▶ **To install Web Administration on the server**

Install the software by clicking **Web Administration** on the Resource Kit Master Setup Screen.

1. The **Master setup program** auto-launches when the Resource Kit CD is installed, or you can run **MSETUP.EXE** from the CD root directory.

   Or with the Resource Kit CD in the CD ROM, from the **Start** menu, click **Run**. Under **Open**, type

   drive:**\apps\webadmin**

   and click **OK**.

2. Restart the Microsoft Internet Information Server services if necessary.

3. Configure password authentication in Microsoft Internet Information Server. For more information, see the section "Configuring Password Authentication."

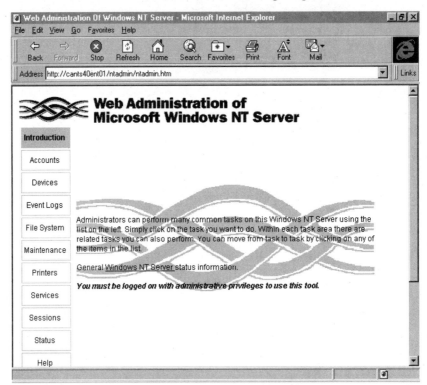

Note This self-extracting setup program will install all the files needed into two directories on your server (*inetsrv_root*\scripts\NTAdmin and *inetsrv_root*\wwwroot\NTAdmin) and make the required Registry entries.

Adding SSL to Provide Additional Security

As mentioned in the section "Security," if your browser supports only Basic password authentication, it is recommended that you also use SSL. You may also want to use SSL even if you use Windows NT Challenge Response because SSL encrypts all data in the session.

Using the Web Administration tools, you can set up a server to require the use of SSL for administration. To do so, after installing Web Administration on the server, use a Web browser to connect to the server over the Web to administer it.

▶ **To require the use of SSL for administration**

1. Click **Maintenance**.

2. Click **Web Admin Preferences**.

3. Select the **Ensure use of SSL** secure channel check box and click **OK**.

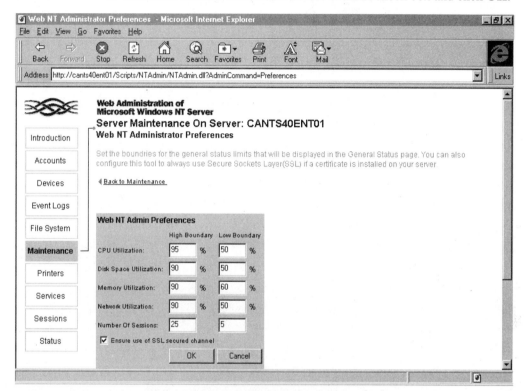

This sets the Registry entry **SSLRequired** to 1. **SSLRequired** is in the Registry key:

HKEY_LOCAL_MACHINE\Software
    \Microsoft
        \Inetsrv_NTAdmin.

Note To find which type of password authentication works for the Web browser you will be using, see "Troubleshooting and Common Issues" in the paper titled Web Administration of Microsoft Windows NT Server located at:
http://www.microsoft.com/NTServer/webadmin/webadmin.htm.

Configuring Password Authentication

When configuring password authentication, you indicate which authentication type you are going to use. As stated previously in the section "Security," the type of authentication you select depends on what is supported by your Web browser.

To see what authentication methods work with your browser, see "Troubleshooting and Common Issues" on the Web page titled Web Administration of Microsoft Windows NT Server located at: **http://www.microsoft.com/ntserver/webadmin/webadmin.htm**.

▶ **To configure password authentication on the server**

1. To start the tool, click **Start**.

2. Point to and click **Programs**.

3. Point to and click **Microsoft Internet Server**.

4. Point to and click **Internet Service Manager**.

    You should see a list of services running on your machine.

5. Double-click the server name on the WWW Service line to open the property page and to start the WWW service if it isn't already started.

6. On the property page, in the **Password Authentication** group box, select the authentication method you wish to use.

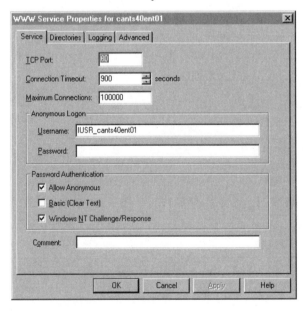

If you need additional information on how to configure the service, see your Microsoft Internet Information Server version 2.0 documentation.

PART IV

Appendixes

APPENDIX A

Major Revisions to Existing Resource Kit Books

Supplemental or updated information for both the *Microsoft Windows NT Workstation Resource Kit: Windows NT Workstation Resource Guide* and the *Microsoft Windows NT Server Resource Kit: Windows NT Server Networking Guide* is included here as follows:

- For *Windows NT Workstation Resource Guide*, Part V, "Windows NT Registry," this appendix adds a supplemental section titled "Remote Access to the Registry." This supplemental section also contains a correction to an error in *Windows NT Workstation Resource Guide* Chapter 6, "Windows NT Security," and information on a related topic, "Remote Performance Monitoring."

- For *Windows NT Server Networking Guide*, Chapter 9, "Managing Microsoft DNS Servers," this appendix updates the section titled "Porting Data Files from Other DNS Servers."

- For *Windows NT Server Networking Guide*, Chapter 1, "Windows NT Networking Architecture," this appendix replaces the former section titled "Server Message Blocks" with a new version, titled "Server Message Blocks and the Common Internet File System."

Windows NT Workstation Resource Guide, Part V, "Windows NT Registry"

The following section contains supplemental information on the Windows NT Registry.

Remote Access to the Registry

Windows NT includes a number of security features that protect the Registry from inadvertent or unwarranted access. Windows NT establishes an access control list (ACL) for each Registry subtree, key, and subkey that determines who has access to a Registry element and what a user is permitted to do to that element.

In addition, Windows NT version 4.0 includes an optional security check that controls remote access to the Registry. This check determines which users can connect to the Registry from another computer. After a user is connected, the ACLs for each Registry element govern the user's access to the Registry.

This section explains how Windows NT controls who can connect to the Registry of a remote computer, and it describes:

- How the system determines who can connect to the Registry.
- The **winreg** subkey, whose ACL determines who can connect to the Registry.
- The default values for the **winreg** ACL and how to change them.
- The **AllowedPaths** subkey of **winreg**, which stores a list of commonly used Registry paths. Users who are not included in the **winreg** ACL can connect to the Registry by using access keys listed in these exception paths.

This material is intended for users who are familiar with both the basic structure of the Windows NT Registry and the basic security features of Windows NT. It is a supplement to *Windows NT Workstation Resource Guide,* Part V, "Windows NT Registry," and it corrects an error in *Windows NT Workstation Resource Guide* Chapter 6, "Windows NT Security."

This material also contains a related topic, "Remote Performance Monitoring," which explains the **winreg** permissions that must be granted to anyone who uses Performance Monitor to monitor Windows NT computers remotely.

Warning To add or modify a Registry value entry, use admininstrative tools such as Control Panel or System Policy Editor whenever possible. Using a Registry editor (Regedit or Regedt32) to change a value can have unforeseen effects, including changes that can prevent you from starting your system.

---

winreg: Connecting to the Windows NT Registry

Windows NT 4.0 uses the ACL for **winreg**, an optional Registry subkey, to determine who can connect to the Registry from another computer. This section explains how to use the **winreg** subkey ACL to control remote access to the Registry.

Note The ACL for **winreg**, not a Boolean value stored in **winreg**, controls remote access to the Registry. The information in *Windows NT Workstation Resource Guide*, Chapter 6, "Windows NT Security," is incorrect in this regard.

When a user tries to connect to the Registry remotely, Windows NT looks for the **winreg** subkey.

- If **winreg** is in the Registry, the ACL for **winreg** determines which users can connect to the Registry remotely. To connect to the Registry, users must have at least read/write permission, including permission to create subkeys and set values.

- If **winreg** does not appear in the Registry, all users can connect to the Registry remotely.

After a user is connected to the Registry, the ACL for each Registry key or subkey determines whether the user can read, edit, add, and/or delete Registry contents.

The **winreg** subkey must be located in the following Registry path:

```
HKEY_LOCAL_MACHINE\System
    \CurrentControlSet
        \Control
            \SecurePipeServers
                \winreg
```

By default, **winreg** is included in the Registry of Windows NT 4.0 servers only. Administrators can add **winreg** to the Registry of Windows NT workstations and to the Registry of workstations and servers running Windows NT 3.51 Service Pack 2.

Note If you add a **winreg** subkey to the Registry, be sure to add an **AllowedPaths** subkey under it. Failure to do so can disable some system services. The **AllowedPaths** subkey is described in the following sections.

The default ACL for **winreg** is as follows:

Operating system	Default ACL
Windows NT Server	Administrators: Full Control
Windows NT Workstation	(Not in the Registry)

▶ **To give a user permission to connect to the Registry remotely**

1. Start Regedt32.
2. Click the **winreg** subkey to select it.
3. On the **Security** menu, click **Permissions**.

   The ACL for **winreg** appears in the **Registry Key Permissions** dialog box.
4. Click the **Add** button in the **Registry Key Permissions** dialog box.
5. Add the user to the **winreg** ACL and give the user read access. For detailed instructions, click the **Help** button in the **Registry Key Permissions** dialog box.
6. Double-click the name of the user you just added.
7. In the **Special Access** dialog box, select the **Set Value** and **Create Subkey**check boxes.
8. Click **OK**, and then click **OK** again to close the dialog boxes.

If a user does not have sufficient access to **winreg**, that user may still be able to connect to the Registry. The **winreg** subkey contains the **AllowedPaths** subkey, which stores exceptions to the permissions set in **winreg**.

AllowedPaths: Exceptions to winreg

The **AllowedPaths** subkey in **winreg** contains a single value entry, **Machine**, which stores a list of paths from the **HKEY_LOCAL_MACHINE** subtree. The paths named in **AllowedPaths** are known as *exception paths*. Users who are not included in the **winreg** ACL can connect to the Registry to access one of these exception paths.

AllowedPaths was added to enable users to use system services that require that they connect to the Registry. Users must have permission to access the final subkey in an exception path before they can view or edit the Registry remotely.

Note The exception paths in **AllowedPaths** are necessary to maintain backward compatibility with system components that need remote Registry access. If you add a **winreg** subkey to the Registry, be sure to also add an **AllowedPaths** subkey under it, and then add the default values for the **Machine** value entry, as described following.

The allowed paths are stored in the **Machine** value entry in the **AllowedPaths** subkey. **AllowedPaths** must appear in the following Registry path:

HKEY_LOCAL_MACHINE\System
   \CurrentControlSet
     \Services
       \SecurePipeServers
        \winreg
          \AllowedPaths

The **Machine** value entry appears as follows:

Machine REG_MULTI_SZ
Range: *HKEY_LOCAL_MACHINE registry paths*
Default: System\CurrentControlSet\Control\ProductOptions
            System\CurrentControlSet\Control\Print\Printers
            System\CurrentControlSet\Services\EventLog
            Software\Microsoft\Windows NT\CurrentVersion

Administrators can add paths to this list. However, if you delete a path, you might disable an essential system service.

The exception granted to paths listed in **Machine** applies to the last subkey listed in the path and to all subkeys it contains. For example, if **Machine** includes **System\CurrentControlSet\Services\EventLog**, any user could connect remotely to the **EventLog** subkey or to any of its subkeys (or to the subkeys of its subkeys), but not to any other subkey directly under **Services,** unless that other subkey was specifically listed in **Machine**.

Remote Performance Monitoring

Windows NT 4.0 includes increased security features to protect the Registry from unwarranted remote access. These new features can prevent users who are not administrators from using Performance Monitor to monitor a Windows NT 4.0 Server from another computer.

This section includes recommended changes to your configuration to allow remote performance monitoring without compromising the security of Registry data. It assumes that you are familiar with the Windows NT Registry structure and with the basic security features of Windows NT.

For general information about security for remote Registry access, see "Remote Access to the Registry," earlier in this appendix.

Enabling Remote Monitoring

Users who monitor another computer remotely by using Performance Monitor require the following permissions:

- At least read access to the Perfc*.dat and Perfh*.dat files on the remote computer. These files are installed with Windows NT.

  The asterisk in the preceding filenames represents the numeric ID of the spoken language installed with Windows NT. For example, on systems using the English language, the files are called Perfc009.dat and Perfh009.dat.

- Permission to connect to the Registry of the computer they are monitoring.

- At least read access to the **Perflib***LanguageID*** subkey in the Registry of the remote computer.

  The *LanguageID* subkey noted earlier is named for the numeric ID of the spoken language installed with Windows NT. For example, on systems using the English language, the subkey is **Perflib\009**.

The following sections explain how to display and change these permissions. It recommends settings that enable a Performance Monitor user to remotely monitor another computer.

Access to Performance Monitor Files on Disk

To monitor a computer remotely by using Performance Monitor, you must have access to Perfc*.dat and Perfh*.dat files, as described previously. By default, these files are installed in *Systemroot*\System32. If these files are stored on a Windows NT file system (NTFS) partition on the computer being monitored, make certain that the user who is monitoring the remote computer has at least read access to both of the files.

You can use Windows Explorer to view or change the ACL for the Perfc*.dat and Perfh*.dat files. The ACL controls security for these files.

Remote Access to the Registry for Performance Monitor Users

Performance Monitor extracts counter data from the Registry. A Performance Monitor user who monitors another computer remotely must have permission to connect to the Registry of the remote computer.

Permission to connect is set on the remote computer. Users who have permission to connect to a remote computer's Registry can do so from any computer. By default, only the administrators of a Windows NT Server are permitted to connect to its Registry from another computer. This section explains how to give other users this permission.

On computers running Windows NT 4.0 (and Windows NT 3.51 Service Pack 2), the system uses the ACL for **winreg**, an optional Registry subkey, to determine who can connect to the Registry from another computer. When a user tries to connect to the Registry remotely, the system looks for this **winreg** subkey, as described previously in the section "winreg: Connecting to the Windows NT Registry." **winreg** is located in the following Registry path:

HKEY_LOCAL_MACHINE\System
    \CurrentControlSet
       \Control
          \SecurePipeServers
             \winreg

When a user tries to connect to the Registry remotely, the system looks for the **winreg** subkey.

On Windows NT servers, **winreg** is included in the Registry by default. The default ACL for **winreg** gives full control to administrators, allowing them to connect to the Registry. No other users have permission by default. If the Performance Monitor user who is monitoring the server remotely is not an administrator, you must add that user to the ACL for **winreg** and then give him or her at least read/write permission.

On Windows NT workstations, and computers running Windows NT 3.51 Service Pack 2, **winreg** is not included in the Registry by default. However, administrators can add **winreg** to the Registry of these computers to control remote access. If **winreg** appears in the Registry, the Performance Monitor user must be listed in the ACL for **winreg** and have at least read/write permission to **winreg**.

▶ **To display the ACL for winreg**

1. Start Regedt32 on the computer to be monitored.

2. Click the **winreg** subkey in the following Registry path:

   HKEY_LOCAL_MACHINE\System
       \CurrentControlSet
          \Control
             \SecurePipeServers
                \winreg

   If **winreg** does not appear in the Registry, all users can connect to the Registry remotely. In that case, you can skip both this procedure and the following one and go to the next section, "Access to the Perflib Subkeys."

3. On the **Security** menu, click **Permissions**.

   The ACL for **winreg** appears in the **Registry Key Permissions** dialog box.

4. Double-click the ACL entry for a user or user group to display its permissions.

Users must have at least read/write permission (that is, they must have special access permission to create subkeys and set values) to use **winreg** to monitor a computer from another computer. Full control is not required. If those people listed as Administrators for your computer have read/write permission to **winreg**, you can add a user to the list of Administrators. However, you can also give users just the permissions they need to monitor computers remotely.

▶ **To give a user permission to monitor a computer remotely**

1. Display the ACL for the **winreg** subkey.

2. Click the **Add** button in the **Registry Key Permissions** dialog box for **winreg**.

3. Add the user to the **winreg** ACL and give the user read access. For detailed instructions, click the **Help** button in the **Registry Key Permissions** dialog box.

4. Double-click the name of the user you just added.

5. In the **Special Access** dialog box, select the **Set Value** and **Create Subkey** check boxes.

6. Click **OK**, and then click **OK** again to close the dialog boxes.

When you have set the access to **winreg**, verify that the user has at least read access to all subkeys in the path to **winreg**. (By default, the Everyone group has permission to read all **winreg** subkeys and the subkeys in its path.) To check the ACL for each subkey in the path, click **Permissions** on the **Security** menu, and then grant the user read access to any ACLs that do not otherwise permit it.

Access to the Perflib Subkeys .

After a Performance Monitor user is connected to the Registry of the computer to be monitored, that user needs at least read access to the subkeys that Performance Monitor uses on the remote computer.

The system uses the ACL for the **Perflib/**_LanguageID_ subkey to determine who has access to Performance Monitor data in the Registry, where _Language ID_ is the numeric code for the spoken language installed with Windows NT. The **Perflib**_LanguageID_ subkey is located in the following Registry path:

```
HKEY_LOCAL_MACHINE\Software
    \Microsoft
        \Windows NT
            \CurrentVersion
                \Perflib
                    \LanguageID
```

By default, the Everyone group has read access to the **Perflib/**_LanguageID_ subkey. However, you might need to give a user permission to read the **Perflib**_LanguageID_ subkey permissions if default permissions on the computer being monitored have been changed.

▶ **To give a user permission to read the Perflib**_LanguageID_ **subkey**

1. Start Regedt32 on the computer to be monitored.

2. Click the _LanguageID_ subkey to select it.

3. On the **Security** menu, click **Permissions**.

   The ACL for the subkey appears in the **Registry Key Permissions** dialog box.

4. If necessary, click **Add** to add the user to the ACL and grant read access. For detailed instructions, click the **Help** button in the **Registry Key Permissions** dialog box.

5. To check the ACL for each subkey in the path to the _LanguageID_ subkey, click **Permissions** on the **Security** menu. Verify that the user has read access to all subkeys in the path. Add read access to any ACLs that do not otherwise permit it.

Windows NT Server Networking Guide, Chapter 9, "Managing Microsoft DNS Servers"

The following section has been updated in this chapter.

Porting Data Files from Other DNS Servers

You can use the boot, zone, cache, and other files from non-Microsoft RFC-compliant DNS servers on a Microsoft DNS server. (_RFCs,_ or _Requests for Comments,_ are the official documents of the Internet Engineering Task Force specifying the details for Transmission Control Protocol/Internet Protocol, or TCP/IP, protocols.) To do this, you must install these files in the _Systemroot_\\System32\\DNS directory, and then stop and restart the DNS server.

Before installing files from other DNS servers on a Microsoft DNS server, you must edit the filename and directory location text in the ported files and make additional changes as described in this section.

The boot file is used to load the data files you want to port into a Microsoft DNS server. A _boot file_ is actually a file that controls the startup behavior of DNS servers running under a Berkeley Internet Name Domain (BIND) implementation of DNS. It is a BIND-specific feature and not a requirement of the DNS RFCs. The Microsoft DNS server ability to use a boot file on initial startup is provided to support migration of data from BIND-based DNS servers to Microsoft DNS servers.

Although Microsoft DNS server supports boot files, you must install the edited boot file before using DNS Manager. Starting DNS Manager configures the Microsoft DNS server to use the Windows NT Server Registry instead of the boot file.

If you need to port data files after starting DNS Manager, you must change the value of the **EnableRegistryBoot** Registry parameter from 1 to 0. The **EnableRegistryBoot** parameter is located in the following key:

```
\HKEY_LOCAL_MACHINE\System
    \CurrentControlSet
      \Services
        \DNS
          \Parameters
```

▶ **To change the value of the EnableRegistryBoot parameter**

1. Click the **Start** button, and then click **Run**.

2. In the **Open** box, type **regedit**, and then press ENTER.

3. Open the following key folder:

```
\HKEY_LOCAL_MACHINE\System
    \CurrentControlSet
      \Services
        \DNS
          \Parameters
```

4. Select the **EnableRegistryBoot** parameter in the right pane of the Registry Editor, and then on the **Edit** menu click **Modify**.

5. In the **Value Data** box, type **0**.

6. Click **OK**.

7. On the **Edit** menu, click **New**, and then click **DWORD Value**.

8. Type **0** in the value box, and press ENTER.

9. Stop and restart the Microsoft DNS server by using Services in Control Panel.

The following table describes the format of boot file commands. You can use any text editor to edit or create a boot file. Commands must start at the beginning of a line, and no spaces may precede the commands.

Table A.1   BIND Boot File Commands (Replaces Table 9.4 in Windows NT Server 4.0 Networking Guide)

Command	Description	Syntax
Directory	Specifies a directory where other files referred to in the boot file can be found.	**directory** *directory*
Cache	Specifies a file used to help the DNS service contact DNS servers for the root domain. This command and the file it refers to must be present.	**cache** *filename*
Primary	Specifies a domain for which this DNS server is authoritative, and a database file that contains the resource records for that domain in the zone file. Multiple primary command records can be entered in the boot file.	**primary** *domain filename*
Secondary	Specifies a domain for which this DNS server is authoritative, and a list of master server Internet Protocol (IP) addresses from which to attempt downloading the zone information.	**secondary** *domain hostlist local filename*
Forwarder	Identifies other DNS servers to which the local DNS server can send recursive queries when the local DNS server cannot resolve the queries itself.	**forwarders** *hostlist*
Slave	Specifies that the local DNS server cannot resolve queries and must send the queries to DNS servers identified in the forwarders host list. This command can only be used directly following the forwarder command.	**slave**

Windows NT Server Networking Guide, Chapter 1, "Windows NT Networking Architecture"

The following section replaces the existing section titled "Server Message Blocks."

Server Message Blocks and the Common Internet File System

The Server Message Blocks (SMB) protocol, developed jointly by Microsoft, Intel, and IBM, defines a series of commands used to pass information between networked computers. The SMB redirector packages requests meant for remote servers in an SMB structure.

SMB uses four message types, which are listed following:

- Session control messages, which consist of commands that start and end a redirector connection to a shared resource at the server.
- File messages, which the redirector uses to gain access to files at the server.
- Printer messages, which the redirector uses to send data to a print queue at a server and to get status information about the print queue.
- Message messages, which allow an application to exchange messages with another workstation.

The Common Internet File System (CIFS) is a subset of the SMB protocol tuned for use on the Internet. CIFS has been submitted by Microsoft to the Internet Engineering Task Force as an Internet Draft.

SMBs and CIFS provide interoperability between different versions of the Microsoft family of networking products and other networks that use SMBs. SMB and CIFS clients and servers are available for the following operating systems and products:

- Windows NT Server
- Windows NT Workstation
- Microsoft Windows 95
- Microsoft Windows for Workgroups
- Microsoft LAN Manager for Microsoft Operating System/2 (MS OS/2)
- LAN Manager for MS-DOS®
- LAN Manager for UNIX
- Apple Macintosh®
- IBM Warp Connect
- DEC Pathworks
- Unisys Advanced Server for UNIX
- SAMBA
- SCO UNIX

For more information about CIFS, see **http://www.microsoft.com/intdev/cifs**.

APPENDIX B

Minor Revisions to Existing Resource Kit Books

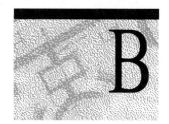

Future reprints of the four volumes in the *Microsoft Windows NT Server Resource Kit version 4.0* and the *Microsoft Windows NT Workstation Resource Kit version 4.0* will contain slightly updated information. For those customers who have the first editions of these volumes, a list of the changes that will be made when we reprint these books follows. The online Help versions of these books on the *Microsoft Windows NT Server Resource Kit Supplement 1* CD already reflect these changes.

Windows NT Server Resource Kit

The following sections contain changes made to the *Windows NT Server Resource Kit*. There is a section addressing changes for each of the three books.

Windows NT Server Resource Guide

The following changes were made to the *Windows NT Server Resource Guide*:

- Chapter 2, "Printing"
    - Page 17, next to the last paragraph, last sentence, preceding the words "printer drivers," insert the words "*x*86-based."
    - Page 34, third sentence, add the word "job" after the first instance of the word "print."
    - Page 48, last sentence, replace the word "four" with "three."

Windows NT Server Networking Guide

The following changes were made to the *Windows NT Server Networking Guide*:

- Chapter 1, "Windows NT Networking Architecture"
    - Page 9, Figure 1.1 has been changed to clarify that the Microkernel and HAL are not Windows NT Executive Services.
    - Page 58, replace the second paragraph under the heading "Remote Access Service" with the information following:

      The distinctions between RAS and remote control solutions (such as Cubix and pcANYWHERE) are important:

        - RAS is a software-based multi-protocol router; remote control solutions work by sharing screen, keyboard, and mouse over the remote link.

        - In a remote control solution, users share a CPU or multiple CPUs on the server. The RAS server's CPU is dedicated to communications, not to running applications.

    - Page 61, replace the entire section under the heading "Point-to-Point Tunneling Protocol" with the information following:

      A RAS server is usually connected to a PSTN, ISDN, or X.25 network, allowing remote users to access a server through these networks. RAS now allows remote users access through the Internet by using the new Point-to-Point Tunneling Protocol (PPTP).

      PPTP is a new networking technology that supports multiprotocol virtual private networks (VPNs), enabling remote users to access corporate networks securely across the Internet by dialing into an Internet Service Provider (ISP) or by connecting directly to the Internet. For more information, see the *Microsoft Windows NT Server Networking Supplement*, Chapter 11, "Point-to-Point Tunneling Protocol (PPTP)."

- Chapter 2, "Network Security and Domain Planning," page 109, in the first sentence under the heading "Using a RAS-connected BDC as a PDC," replace the words "dial-out-only RAS client" with the words "dial-up networking client." In the next sentence, replace the words "RAS-connected client" with the words "dial-up networking client."

- Chapter 5, "Network Services: Enterprise Level"
    - Page 283, replace the heading in the middle of the page, "Windows 95 Clients to Windows NT servers," with the heading "Windows 95 Clients Authenticating to Windows NT Servers."
    - Page 298, in the next to last paragraph, change the reference *"Windows NT Server Services for Macintosh"* to *"Windows NT Server Networking Supplement."*

- Page 335, in the first paragraph under the heading "Secure Access to Corporate Networks over the Internet," in the first line, delete the word "a" that precedes "PPTP" and the word "driver" that follows "PPTP." Also, in the first line, change the word "driver" that follows the word "WAN" to "protocol." The amended first line reads "A RAS client that has PPTP as its WAN protocol can access resources on a remote LAN by connecting to a Windows NT RAS server through the Internet." In the second line of the second paragraph, delete the word "The" that precedes the word "PPTP" and the word "driver" that follows "PPTP."

- Page 337, under the heading "Installing PPTP," replace the first sentence with "You must have the PPTP protocol installed on the RAS servers and on the client or communications servers." Change Step 4 of the procedure "To Install PPTP" to "Select Point-to-Point Protocol, and then click **Add**." Change Step 8 to "RAS setup will start and add the PPTP protocol to RAS." Also, delete "DNS" from the sentence following the procedure.

- Chapter 6, "TCP/IP Implementation Details"

  - Page 396, delete the second bulleted item "Point-Point Tunneling Protocol (PPTP)."

  - Page 397, in the first paragraph, second line, replace "RAS clients" with "dial-up networking clients." In the second paragraph, fifth line, replace "RAS client" with "dial-up networking client." Replace the heading "RAS Clients" with "Dial-Up Clients." In the paragraph before the paragraph introducing the route table, last sentence, change "Windows NT workstation" to "computer running Windows NT Workstation or Windows NT Server."

- Chapter 8, "Managing Microsoft WINS Servers," page 465, remove the two paragraphs following Table 8.10.

- Chapter 9, "Managing Microsoft DNS Servers"

  - Page 474, change the World Wide Web address for the Internet Network Information Center (InterNIC) from (**http://www.internic.com**) to (**http://www.internic.net**).

  - Page 477, add the following line to the end of the first Note: "This is done to support BIND versions earlier than BIND version 4.94."

  - Page 483, change the heading "Cache Files" to "Cache File."

  - Page 486, fifth paragraph, replace "DSN" in the next to the last line of the paragraph with "DNS."

  - Page 491, first paragraph, last sentence, delete the word "Microsoft" preceding DHCP. In Step 5 of the procedure on that page, delete the sentence "Unresolved host name queries will then be passed to a DNS server."

- Page 503, in the procedure "To clear the Microsoft DNS server statistics by using the dnsstat command," in Step 2, change "**dnstat**" to "**dnsstat**"
- Page 504, change the heading near the bottom of the page from "Zone Wizard Did Not Correctly Autocreate SOA, NS or a Record" to "Zone Wizard Did Not Correctly Autocreate SOA, NS, or A Record."

Changes at Terra Flora

Terra Flora was introduced as a fictitious corporation to provide a case study in interoperating heterogeneous networks. Chapter 4, "Terra Flora: A Fictitious Case Study," provided the history of the corporation and presented the plan for interoperability. Chapter 5, "Network Services: Enterprise Level," provided the business justification for selecting Windows NT Server services to interoperate the heterogeneous networks. It also presented specific information on the installation and configuration of Enterprise level services that support the network itself and keep the corporation-wide information synchronized.

Once the networks were interoperating, the network administrators began evaluating the potential for network failure. That evaluation process produced changes to the Terra Flora network diagram. The changes to the network diagram are as follows:

- Chapter 5, "Network Services: Enterprise Level," page 222, in the figure, remove all the Integrated Services Digital Network (ISDN) communication connections except the ISDN link from server EUNTS40DPT01. Replace the T1 communication line going into and out of the server NENTS40ENT02 with two fractional T1 communication lines. Replace the T1 communication line going into and out of server EUNTS40ENT01 with two fractional T1 communication lines. Replace the communication line going into server NENTS40DPT01 with two switched 56 communication lines.

- Appendix F, "Routers and Switches," page 826, in Figure F.3, remove all the ISDN communications connections. Add a backup router to network router CABNR10ENT02. Replace the T1 communication line, 1.54 megabits per second (Mbps), connecting the Enterprise router to Boston and on to New York with two fractional T1 communication lines, 128 kilobits per second (Kbps). Replace the switched 56 communications line, 56 Kbps, connecting the NENTS40DIV01 server to the Department with two switched 56 communication lines, 56 Kbps. Replace the T1 communication line, 1.54 Kbps, connecting the Enterprise router to Amsterdam and on to London with two fractional T1 communication lines, 64 Kbps.

- Back cover, "Terra Flora Network Diagram"
    - Remove the ISDN connections to the servers NENTS40ENT01, EUNTS40ENT01, and NENTS40DPT02. Remove the ISDN connection to the network routers CABNR10ENT01 and CABNR10ENT02.
    - Replace the ISDN communication line from the network router CABNR10ENT01 to the Disaster Recovery Site with Backup Network Link, T1.
    - Add a backup router to the network router CABNR10ENT02.
    - Replace the T3 communication line, 45 Mbps, between the routers CABNR10ENT01 and CABNR10ENT02 with two T1 communication lines, 1.45 Mbps.
    - Replace the T1 communication line, 1.54 Mbps, connecting the Enterprise router CABNR10ENT02 to Boston and on to New York with two fractional T1 communication lines, 128 Kbps. Replace the New York leased line, 128 Kbps, with two fractional T1 communication lines, 128 Kbps.
    - Replace the switched 56 communications line, 56 Kbps, connecting the NENTS40DIV01 server to the NENTS40DPT01 server with two switched 56 communication lines, 56 Kbps.
    - Replace the T1 communication line, 1.54 Kbps, connecting the Enterprise router CABNR10ENT02 to Amsterdam and on to London with two fractional T1 communication lines, 64 Kbps.

Windows NT Server Internet Guide

The following changes were made to the *Windows NT Server Internet Guide*:

- Chapter 1, "Internet Information Server Architecture," page 10, replace all references to Netmonitor with Network Monitor.
- Chapter 7, "Internet Tools," pages 147 through 154. Delete the section on Mail Server (MailSrv). The MailSrv utility no longer ships with the *Windows NT Server Resource Kit*.
- Back cover, "Terra Flora Network Diagram"
    - Remove the ISDN connections to the servers NENTS40ENT01, EUNTS40ENT01, and NENTS40DPT02. Remove the ISDN connection to the network routers CABNR10ENT01 and CABNR10ENT02.
    - Replace the ISDN communication line from the network router CABNR10ENT01 to the Disaster Recovery Site with Backup Network Link, T1.
    - Add a backup router to the network router CABNR10ENT02.

- Replace the T3 communication line, 45 Mbps, between the routers CABNR10ENT01 and CABNR10ENT02 with two T1 communication lines, 1.45 Mbps.

- Replace the T1 communication line, 1.54 Mbps, connecting the Enterprise router CABNR10ENT02 to Boston and on to New York with two fractional T1 communication lines, 128 Kbps. Replace the New York leased line, 128 Kbps, with two fractional T1 communication lines, 128 Kbps.

- Replace the switched 56 communications line, 56 Kbps, connecting the NENTS40DIV01 server to the NENTS40DPT01 server with two switched 56 communication lines, 56 Kbps.

- Replace the T1 communication line, 1.54 Kbps, connecting the Enterprise router CABNR10ENT02 to Amsterdam and on to London with two fractional T1 communication lines, 64 Kbps.

Windows NT Workstation Resource Kit

The following section contains changes made to the *Windows NT Workstation Resource Guide*.

- Chapter 5, "Windows NT 4.0 Workstation Architecture," page 103, Figure 5.3 has been changed to clarify that the Microkernel and HAL are not Windows NT Executive Services.

- Chapter 7, "Printing"
  - Page 216, second paragraph, second sentence, add the word "job" after the first instance of the word "print."
  - Page 230, under the heading "Separator Page Files," second paragraph, last sentence, change the word "four" to "three."

- Chapter 9, "The Art of Performance Monitoring"
  - Page 287, in the first paragraph, replace "Ndvdm.exe" with "Ntvdm.exe"
  - Page 288, in the first paragraph, replace "experimental" with "investigative."

- Chapter 10, "About Performance Monitor"
  - Page 293, in the first paragraph under the heading "New Counter Type," delete the phrase "but it displays a zero if the difference is negative."
  - Page 295, in the first paragraph under "Starting and Setting Up Performance Monitor," replace "boot" with "log on."
  - Page 300, in the last bulleted item, delete the sentence "If it is negative, they display a zero."
  - Page 304, delete the first bulleted item.
  - Page 305, first paragraph, delete "running Network Monitor Agent."

- Page 314, the figure has been changed to clarify that the Microkernel and HAL are not Windows NT Executive Services.

- Page 338, change the cross-reference under "All values for my disks are zero, but I know they are active" from "For information about Diskperf, see "Enabling the Disk Counters" in Chapter 6" to "For information on Diskperf, see "Enabling the Disk Counters" in Chapter 14, "Detecting Disk Bottlenecks.""

- Chapter 12, "Detecting Memory Bottlenecks," page 419, change the reference in the third bulleted item from "(as described in Chapter 7)" to "(as described in Chapter 15, "Detecting Cache Bottlenecks")."

- Chapter 14, "Detecting Disk Bottlenecks"

  - Page 474, delete the diagram on the lower half of the page.

  - Page 486, in the upper left hand corner of the figure, replace "ide.log" with "100."

  - Page 520, first paragraph of the last bulleted item, replace the word "turbulence" with "interference." In the last sentence of that paragraph, add the word "length" after the word "cable." In the second paragraph of the last bulleted item, replace all instances of "serial" with "parallel" and all instances of "parallel" with "serial."

- Back cover, the figures "Windows NT 3.51 Architecture" and "Windows NT 4.0 Architecture" have been changed to clarify that the Microkernel and HAL are not Windows NT Executive Services.

Glossary

A

access control entry (ACE) An entry in an access control list (ACL). Each access control entry defines the protection or auditing to be applied to a file or other object for a specific user or group of users. *See also* access control list (ACL).

access control list (ACL) The part of a security descriptor that enumerates both the protections to accessing and the auditing of that accessing that are applied to an object. The owner of an object has discretionary access control of the object and can change the object's ACL to allow or disallow others access to the object. Access control lists are ordered lists of access control entries (ACEs). There are two types of ACLs: discretionary (DACL) and system (SACL). *See also* access control entry (ACE); discretionary access control list (DACL); system access control list (SACL).

access permission A rule associated with an object (usually a directory, file, or printer) to regulate which users can have access to the object and in what manner. *See also* user rights.

access privileges Permissions set by Macintosh users that allow them to view and make changes to folders on a server. By setting access privileges (called *permissions* when set on the computer running Windows NT Server), you control which Macintosh can use folders in a volume. Services for Macintosh (SFM) translates access privileges set by Macintosh users to the equivalent Windows NT permissions.

access token (or security token) An object that uniquely identifies a user who has logged on. An access token is attached to all the user's processes and contains the user's security ID (SID), the SIDs of any groups to which the user belongs, any permissions that the user owns, the default owner of any objects that the user's processes create, and the default access control list (ACL) to be applied to any objects that the user's processes create. *See also* permissions.

access violation An attempt to carry out a memory operation that is not allowed by Windows NT memory management. This can include an invalid operation (such as writing to a read-only buffer); accessing memory beyond the limit of the current program's address space (a "length violation"); accessing a page to which the system forbids access; or accessing a page that is currently resident but dedicated to the use of an Executive component.

account *See* group account; user account.

account lockout A Windows NT Server security feature that locks a user account if a number of failed logon attempts occur within a specified amount of time, based on account policy lockout settings. (Locked accounts cannot log on.)

account policy Controls the way passwords must be used by all user accounts of a domain or of an individual computer. Specifics include minimum password length, how often a user must change his or her password, and how often users can reuse old passwords. Account policy can be set for all user accounts in a domain when administering a domain, and for all user accounts of a single workstation or member server when administering a computer.

ACK Short for acknowledgment. The transmission control protocol (TCP) requires that the recipient of data packets acknowledge successful receipt of data. Such acknowledgments (ACKs) generate additional network traffic, diminishing the rate at which data passes in favor of reliability. To reduce the impact on performance, most hosts send an acknowledgment for every other segment or when a specified time interval has passed.

acknowledgment *See* ACK.

active Refers to the window or icon that you are currently using or that is currently selected. Windows NT always applies the next keystroke or command you choose to the active window. If a window is active, its title bar changes color to differentiate it from other windows. If an icon is active, its label changes color. Windows or icons on the desktop that are not selected are inactive.

ActiveX™ An umbrella term for Microsoft technologies that enable developers to create interactive content for the World Wide Web.

adapter card *See* network adapter.

address Within Network Monitor, an address refers to a hexadecimal number that identifies a computer uniquely on the network.

address classes Predefined groupings of Internet addresses, with each class defining networks of a certain size. The range of numbers that can be assigned for the first octet in the IP address is based on the address class. Class A networks (values 1–126) are the largest, with over 16 million hosts per network. Class B networks (128 –191) have up to 65,534 hosts per network, and Class C networks (192–223) can have up to 254 hosts per network. *See also* octet.

address pairs Refers to the two specific computers between which you want to monitor traffic by using Network Monitor. Up to four specific address pairs can be monitored simultaneously to capture frames from particular computers on your network. *See also* frame.

Address Resolution Protocol (ARP)
A network-maintenance protocol in the TCP/IP suite that provides IP address-to-MAC address resolution for IP packets. Not directly related to data transport. *See also* IP address; media access control (MAC); packet; Transmission Control Protocol/Internet Protocol (TCP/IP).

administrative account An account that is a member of the Administrators local group of a computer or domain.

administrative alerts Administrative alerts relate to server and resource use and warn about problems in areas such as security and access, user sessions, server shutdown due to power loss (when UPS is available), directory replication, and printing. When a computer generates an administrative alert, a message is sent to a predefined list of users and computers. *See also* Alerter service; uninterruptible power supply (UPS).

administrator A person responsible for setting up and managing domain controllers or local computers and their user and group accounts, assigning passwords and permissions, and helping users with networking issues. To use administrative tools such as User Manager or User Manager for Domains, an administrator must be logged on as a member of the Administrators local group of the computer or domain, respectively.

Administrator privilege One of three privilege levels you can assign to a Windows NT user account. Every user account has one of the three privilege levels (Administrator, Guest, and User). *See also* administrator; Guest privilege; User privilege.

Advanced RISC Computing (ARC)
ARC names are a generic method of identifying devices within the ARC environment. *See also* reduced instruction set computing (RISC).

agent In SNMP, agent information consists of comments about the user, the physical location of the computer, and the types of service to report based on the computer's configuration. *See also* Simple Network Management Protocol (SNMP).

Alerter service Notifies selected users and computers of administrative alerts that occur on a computer. Used by the Server service and other services. Requires the Messenger service. *See also* administrative alerts; Messenger service.

anonymous-level security token The type of security token used when a server impersonates a client. If, when the client calls the server, the client specifies an anonymous impersonation mode, the server cannot access any of the client's identification information, such as its security identifier (SID) or privileges. The server will have to use an anonymous-level security token when representing the client in successive operations. *See also* access token.

Anonymous user A connection for which the request either did not contain a user name and password or whose user name and password were ignored because authentication is not permitted on the server.

API *See* application programming interface.

AppleShare Client software that is shipped with each Macintosh and with Apple Computer server software. With Services for Macintosh, a Macintosh use its native AppleShare client software to connect to computers running Windows NT Server that have Services for Macintosh.

AppleTalk Apple Computer network architecture and network protocols. A network that has Macintosh clients and a computer running Windows NT Server with Services for Macintosh functions as an AppleTalk network.

AppleTalk Filing Protocol The presentation layer protocol that manages access of remote files in an AppleTalk network.

AppleTalk Phase 2 The extended AppleTalk Internet model designed by Apple Computer. It supports multiple zones within a network and extended addressing capacity.

AppleTalk Protocol The set of network protocols on which AppleTalk network architecture is based. Setting up Services for Macintosh installs its AppleTalk Protocol stack on a computer running Windows NT Server so that Macintosh clients can connect to it.

AppleTalk Transport The layer of AppleTalk Phase 2 protocols that deliver data to its destination on the network.

application A computer program used for a particular kind of work, such as word processing. This term is often used interchangeably with "program."

application log The application log contains specific events logged by applications. Applications developers decide which events to monitor (for example, a database program might record a file error in the application log). Use Event Viewer to view the application log.

application programming interface (API)
A set of routines that an application program uses to request and carry out lower-level services performed by another component, such as the computer's operating system or a service running on a network computer. These maintenance chores are performed by the computer's operating system, and an API provides the program with a means of communicating with the system, telling it which system-level task to perform and when.

application window   The main window for an application, which contains the application's menu bar and work area. An application window may contain multiple document windows.

ARC   *See* Advanced RISC Computing.

archive bit   Backup programs use the archive bit to mark the files after backing them up, if a normal or incremental backup is performed. *See also* backup types.

ARP   *See* Address Resolution Protocol.

ARP reply packet   All ARP-enabled systems on the local IP network detect ARP request packets, and the system that owns the IP address in question replies by sending its physical address to the requester in an ARP reply packet. The physical/IP address is then stored in the ARP cache of the requesting system for subsequent use. *See also* Address Resolution Protocol (ARP); ARP request packet; Internet Protocol (IP); MAC address.

ARP request packet   If two systems are to communicate across a TCP/IP network, the system sending the packet must map the IP address of the final destination to the physical address of the final destination. This physical address is also referred to as a MAC address, a unique 48-bit number assigned to the network interface card by the manufacturer. IP acquires this physical address by broadcasting a special inquiry packet (an ARP request packet) containing the IP address of the destination system. *See also* Address Resolution Protocol (ARP); Internet Protocol (IP); MAC address; media access control (MAC).

AS/400   A type of IBM minicomputer.

ASCII file   Also called a text file, a text-only file, or an ASCII text file, refers to a file in the universally recognized text format called ASCII (American Standard Code for Information Interchange). An ASCII file contains characters, spaces, punctuation, carriage returns, and sometimes tabs and an end-of-file marker, but it contains no formatting information. This generic format is useful for transferring files between programs that could not otherwise understand each other's documents. *See also* text file.

associate   To identify a filename extension as "belonging" to a certain application so that when you open any file with that extension, the application starts automatically.

attributes   Information that indicates whether a file is a read-only, hidden, system, or compressed file, and whether the file has been changed since a backup copy of it was made.

A-type resource record   A line (record) in a computer's Domain Name System database that maps a computer's domain name (host name) to an IP address in a DNS zone.

auditing   Tracking activities of users by recording selected types of events in the security log of a server or a workstation.

audit policy For the servers of a domain or for an individual computer, defines the type of security events that will be logged.

authentication Validation of a user's logon information. When a user logs on to an account on a computer running Windows NT Workstation, the authentication is performed by that workstation. When a user logs on to an account on a Windows NT Server domain, authentication may be performed by any server of that domain. *See also* Basic (clear-text) authentication; challenge/response authentication; server; trust relationship.

B

backup domain controller (BDC) In a Windows NT Server domain, a computer running Windows NT Server that receives a copy of the domain's directory database, which contains all account and security policy information for the domain. The copy is synchronized periodically and automatically with the master copy on the primary domain controller (PDC). BDCs also authenticate user logons and can be promoted to function as PDCs as needed. Multiple BDCs can exist on a domain. *See also* member server; primary domain controller (PDC).

backup set A collection of files from one drive that is backed up during a single backup operation.

backup set catalog At the end of each backup set, Windows NT Backup stores a summary of file and/or directory information in a backup set catalog. Catalog information includes the number of tapes in a set of tapes as well as the date they were created and the dates of each file in the catalog. Catalogs are created for each backup set and are stored on the last tape in the set. *See also* backup set.

backup set map At the end of each tape used for backup, a backup set map maintains the exact tape location of the backup set's data and catalog.

backup types:

    copy backup Copies all selected files, but does not mark each file as having been backed up. Copying is useful if you want to back up files between normal and incremental backups, because copying will not invalidate these other backup operations.

    daily backup Copies all selected files that have been modified the day the daily backup is performed.

    differential backup Copies those files created or changed since the last normal (or incremental) backup. It does not mark files as having been backed up.

    incremental backup Backs up only those files created or changed since the last normal (or incremental) backup. It marks files as having been backed up.

    normal backup Copies all selected files and marks each as having been backed up. Normal backups give you the ability to restore files quickly because files on the last tape are the most current.

bandwidth In communications, the difference between the highest and lowest frequencies in a given range. For example, a telephone line accommodates a bandwidth of 3000 Hz, the difference between the lowest (300 Hz) and highest (3300 Hz) frequencies it can carry. In computer networks, greater bandwidth indicates faster data-transfer capability and is expressed in bits per second (bps). Also known as "throughput."

Bandwidth Throttler A feature of the IIS services that enforces a limit on the amount of bandwidth available to the IIS services. This limit applies to the sum of bandwidth used by all three IIS services. Administrators can enable the Bandwidth Throttler and set a bandwidth limit by using the Microsoft Internet Service Manager.

Basic (clear-text) authentication A method of authentication that encodes user name and password data transmissions. Basic authentication is called "clear text" because the base-64 encoding can be decoded by anyone with a freely available decoding utility. Note that encoding is not the same as encryption. *See also* challenge/response authentication; encryption.

batch program An ASCII file (unformatted text file) that contains one or more Windows NT commands. A batch program's filename has a .cmd or .bat extension. When you type the filename at the command prompt, the commands are processed sequentially.

batch queue facility A program that effects a logon without user input, used for delayed logons.

BDC *See* backup domain controller.

binary A base-2 number system, in which values are expressed as combinations of two digits, 0 and 1.

binary-file transfer A method of transferring binary files from Windows NT HyperTerminal to a remote computer. Binary files consist of ASCII characters plus the extended ASCII character set. These files are not converted or translated during the transfer process. *See also* ASCII file.

binding A process that establishes the communication channel between a protocol driver (such as TCP/IP) and a network adapter. *See also* network adapter; Transmission Control Protocol/Internet Protocol (TCP/IP).

bits per second (bps) A measure of the speed at which a device, such as a modem, can transfer data.

blue screen The screen displayed when Windows NT encounters a serious error.

bookmarks A Windows NT feature that enables you to highlight major points of interest at various points in a Performance Monitor log file and then return to them easily when you work with that log file later on during performance monitoring. Bookmarks are also used in other applications, such as Microsoft Word.

boot loader Defines the information needed for system startup, such as the location for the operating system's files. Windows NT automatically creates the correct configuration and checks this information whenever you start your system.

BOOTP *See* Bootstrap protocol.

boot partition The volume, formatted for either an NTFS or FAT file system, that contains the Windows NT operating system and its support files. The boot partition can be (but does not have to be) the same as the system partition. *See also* file allocation table (FAT); partition; Windows NT file system (NTFS).

Bootstrap protocol (BOOTP) A TCP/IP network protocol, defined by RFC 951 and RFC 1542, used to configure systems. DHCP is an extension of BOOTP. *See also* Dynamic Host Configuration Protocol (DHCP).

bps *See* bits per second.

branch A segment of the directory tree, representing a directory (or folder) and any subdirectories (or folders within folders) it contains.

bridge Connects multiple networks, subnets, or rings into one large logical network. A bridge maintains a table of node addresses and, based on this, forwards packets to a specific subnet, reducing traffic on other subnets. In a bridged network, there can be only one path to any destination (otherwise packets would circle the network, causing network storms). A bridge is more sophisticated than a repeater, but not as sophisticated as a router. *See also* packet; repeaters; router; subnet.

broadcast datagram An IP datagram sent to all hosts on the subnet. *See also* datagram; Internet Protocol (IP); subnet.

broadcast message A network message sent from a single computer that is distributed to all other devices on the same segment of the network as the sending computer.

broadcast name resolution A mechanism defined in RFC 1001/1002 that uses broadcasts to resolve names to IP addresses through a process of registration, resolution, and name release. *See also* broadcast datagram; IP address.

brouter Combines elements of the bridge and the router. Usually, a brouter acts as a router for one transport protocol (such as TCP/IP), sending packets of that format along detailed routes to their destinations. The brouter also acts as a bridge for all other types of packets (such as IPX), just passing them on, as long as they are not local to the LAN segment from which they originated. *See also* bridge; packet; router.

browse To view available network resources by looking through lists of folders, files, user accounts, groups, domains, or computers. Browsing allows users on a Windows NT network to see what domains and computers are accessible from their local computer. *See also* Windows NT browser system.

browse list A list kept by the master browser of all of the servers and domains on the network. This list is available to any workstation on the network requesting it. *See also* browse.

browse master *See* master browser; Windows NT browser system.

buffer A reserved portion of memory in which data is temporarily held pending an opportunity to complete its transfer to or from a storage device or another location in memory. Some devices, such as printers or the adapters supporting them, commonly have their own buffers. *See also* memory.

built-in groups Default groups, provided with Windows NT Workstation and Windows NT Server, that have been granted useful collections of rights and built-in abilities. In most cases, a built-in group provides all the capabilities needed by a particular user. For example, if a domain user account belongs to the built-in Administrators group, logging on with that account gives a user administrative capabilities over the domain and the servers of the domain. To provide a needed set of capabilities to a user account, assign it to the appropriate built-in group. *See also* group; User Manager; User Manager for Domains.

bulk data encryption The encryption of all data sent over a network.

C

cache A special memory subsystem that stores the contents of frequently accessed RAM locations and the addresses where these data items are stored. In Windows NT, for example, user profiles have a locally cached copy of part of the Registry.

caching In DNS name resolution, caching refers to a local cache where information about the DNS domain name space is kept. Whenever a resolver request arrives, the local name server checks both its static information and the cache for the name to IP address mapping. *See also* Domain Name System (DNS); IP address; mapping.

Callback Control Protocol (CBCP)
A protocol that negotiates callback information with a remote client.

capture The process by which Network Monitor copies frames. (A *frame* is information that has been divided into smaller pieces by the network software prior to transmission.) *See also* frame.

capture buffer A reserved, resizable storage area in memory where Network Monitor copies all frames it detects from the network. When the capture buffer overflows, each new frame replaces the oldest frame in the buffer.

capture filter Functions like a database query to single out a subset of frames to be monitored in Network Monitor. You can filter on the basis of source and destination addresses, protocols, protocol properties, or by specifying a pattern offset. *See also* capture; frame.

capture password Required to be able to capture statistics from the network and to display captured data using Network Monitor.

capture trigger Performs a specified action (such as starting an executable file) when Network Monitor detects a particular set of conditions on the network.

catalog *See* backup set catalog.

CBCP *See* Callback Control Protocol.

CCP *See* Compression Control Protocol.

centralized network administration
A centralized view of the entire network from any workstation on the network that provides the ability to track and manage information on users, groups, and resources in a distributed network.

CGI *See* Common Gateway Interface.

Challenge Handshake Authentication Protocol (CHAP)
A protocol used by Microsoft RAS to negotiate the most secure form of encrypted authentication supported by both server and client. *See also* encryption.

challenge/response authentication
A method of authentication in which a server uses challenge/response algorithms and Windows NT security to control access to resources. *See also* Basic (clear-text) authentication; encryption.

change log An inventory of the most recent changes made to the directory database such as new or changed passwords, new or changed user and group accounts, and any changes to associated group memberships and user rights. Change logs provide fault tolerance, so if your system crashes before a write completes, Windows NT can complete the write the next time you boot. This log holds only a certain number of changes, however, so when a new change is added, the oldest change is deleted. *See also* directory database; fault tolerance.

CHAP *See* Challenge Handshake Authentication Protocol.

check box A small box in a dialog box or property page that can be selected or cleared. Check boxes represent an option that you can turn on or off. When a check box is selected, an X or a check mark appears in the box.

checksum The mathematical computation used to verify the accuracy of data in TCP/IP packets. *See also* packet; Transmission Control Protocol/Internet Protocol (TCP/IP).

choose To pick an item that begins an action in Windows NT. You often click a command on a menu to perform a task, and you click an icon to start an application.

Chooser The Macintosh desk accessory with which users select the network server and printers they want to use.

Chooser Pack A collection of files, some of which contain PostScript information. When a Macintosh sends a print job to a PostScript printer, the printer uses a Chooser Pack to interpret PostScript commands in the print job. *See* PostScript printer; print processor.

circular dependency A dependency in which an action that appears later in a chain is contingent upon an earlier action. For example, three services (A, B, and C) are linked. A is dependent upon B to start. B is dependent upon C to start. A circular dependency results when C is dependent upon A to start. *See also* dependency.

clear To turn off an option by removing the X or check mark from a check box. To clear a check box, you can click it, or you can select it and then press the SPACEBAR.

clear-text authentication *See* Basic (clear-text) authentication.

clear-text passwords Passwords that are not scrambled, thus making them more susceptible to network sniffers. *See also* network sniffer.

click To press and release a mouse button quickly.

client A computer that accesses shared network resources provided by another computer, called a server. *See also* server; workstation.

client application A Windows NT application that can display and store linked or embedded objects. For distributed applications, the application that imitates a request to a server application. *See also* DCOM Configuration tool; Distributed Component Object Module (DCOM); server application.

Client Service for NetWare Included with Windows NT Workstation, enabling workstations to make direct connections to file and printer resources at NetWare servers running NetWare 2.*x* or later.

Clipboard A temporary storage area in memory, used to transfer information. You can cut or copy information onto the Clipboard and then paste it into another document or application.

close Remove a window or dialog box, or quit an application. To close a window, you can click **Close** on the **Control** menu, or you can click the close button icon in the upper right corner of the dialog box. When you close an application window, you quit the application.

collapse To hide additional directory levels below a selected directory in the directory tree.

color scheme A combination of complementary colors for screen elements.

command A word or phrase, usually found on a menu, that you click to carry out an action. You click a command on a menu or type a command at the Windows NT command prompt. You can also type a command in the **Run** dialog box, which you open by clicking **Run** on the **Start** menu.

command button A button in a dialog box that carries out or cancels the selected action. Two common command buttons are **OK** and **Cancel**. If you click a command button that contains an ellipsis (for example, **Browse...**), another dialog box appears.

Common Gateway Interface (CGI)
A standard interface for HTTP server application development. The standard was developed by the National Center for Supercomputing Applications.

common group Common groups appear in the program list on the **Start** menu for all users who log on to the computer. Only Administrators can create or change common groups.

communications settings Settings that specify how information is transferred from your computer to a device (usually a printer or modem).

community names A group of hosts to which a server belongs that is running the SNMP service. The community name is placed in the SNMP packet when the trap is sent. Typically, all hosts belong to Public, which is the standard name for the common community of all hosts. *See also* packet; Simple Network Management Protocol (SNMP); trap.

compact A command-line utility used to compress files on NTFS volumes. To see command line options, type **compact /?** at the command prompt. To access this utility, you can also right-click any file or directory on an NTFS volume in Windows NT Explorer, then click **Properties** to compress or uncompress the files.

compound device A device that plays specific media files. For example, to run a compound device such as a MIDI sequencer, you must specify a MIDI file.

Compression Control Protocol (CCP)
A protocol that negotiates compression with a remote client.

computer account Each computer running Windows NT Workstation and Windows NT Server that participates in a domain has its own account in the directory database. A computer account is created when the computer is first identified to the domain during network setup at installation time.

Computer Browser service Maintains an up-to-date list of computers, and provides the list to applications when requested. Provides the computer lists displayed in the **Network Neighborhood**, **Select Computer,** and **Select Domain** dialog boxes; and (for Windows NT Server only) in the Server Manager window.

computer name A unique name of up to 15 uppercase characters that identifies a computer to the network. The name cannot be the same as any other computer or domain name in the network.

configure To change the initial setup of a client, a Macintosh-accessible volume, a server, or a network.

connect To assign a drive letter, port, or computer name to a shared resource so that you can use it with Windows NT.

connected user A user accessing a computer or a resource across the network.

connection A software link between a client and a shared resource such as a printer or a shared directory on a server. Connections require a network adapter or modem.

connection-oriented protocol A network protocol with four important characteristics: the path for data packets is established in advance; the resources required for a connection are reserved in advance; a connection's resource reservation is enforced throughout the life of that connection; and when a connection's data transfer is completed, the connection is terminated and the allocated resources are freed.

control codes   Codes that specify terminal commands or formatting instructions (such as linefeeds or carriage returns) in a text file. Control codes are usually preceded by a caret (^).

controller   *See* backup domain controller (BDC); primary domain controller (PDC).

Control menu   *See* window menu.

control set   All Windows NT startup-related data that is not computed during startup is saved in a Registry key. This startup data is organized into control sets, each of which contains a complete set of parameters for starting up devices and services. The Registry always contains at least two control sets, each of which contains information about all the configurable options for the computer: the current control set and the LastKnownGood control set. *See also* current control set; LastKnownGood (LKG) control set.

conventional memory   Up to the first 640K of memory in your computer. MS-DOS uses this memory to run applications.

CRC   *See* cyclic redundancy check.

current control set   The control set that was used most recently to start the computer and that contains any changes made to the startup information during the current session. *See also* LastKnownGood (LKG) control set.

current directory   The directory that you are currently working in. Also called "current folder."

cyclic redundancy check (CRC)   A procedure used on disk drives to ensure that the data written to a sector is read correctly later. This procedure is also used in checking for errors in data transmission.

The procedure is known as a redundancy check because each data transmission includes not only data but extra (redundant) error-checking values. The sending device generates a number based on the data to be transmitted and sends its result along with the data to the receiving device. The receiving device repeats the same calculation after transmission. If both devices obtain the same result, it is assumed that the transmission is error-free.

D

DACL   *See* discretionary access control list; *see also* system access control list (SACL).

daemon   A networking program that runs in the background.

database query   The process of extracting data from a database and presenting it for use.

data carrier   In communications, either a specified frequency that can be modulated to convey information or a company that provides telephone and other communications services to consumers.

Data Carrier Detect (DCD)   Tracks the presence of a data carrier. *See also* data carrier.

data communications equipment (DCE)   An elaborate worldwide network of packet-forwarding nodes that participate in delivering an X.25 packet to its designated address, for example, a modem. *See also* node; packet; X.25.

Data Encryption Standard (DES) A type of encryption (the U.S. government standard) designed to protect against password discovery and playback. Microsoft RAS uses DES encryption when both the client and the server are using RAS.

data fork The part of a Macintosh file that holds most of the file's information. The data fork is the part of the file shared between Macintosh and PC clients.

datagram A packet of data and other delivery information that is routed through a packet-switched network or transmitted on a local area network. *See also* packet.

Data Source Name (DSN) The logical name used by ODBC to refer to the drive and other information required to access data. The name is use by Internet Information Server for a connection to an ODBC data source, such as a SQL Server database. To set this name, use ODBC in the Control Panel.

data stream Windows NT Network Monitor monitors the network data stream, which consists of all information transferred over a network at any given time.

Data Terminal Equipment (DTE) For example, a RAS server or client. *See also* Remote Access Service (RAS).

dbWeb Administrator The graphical user tool for Microsoft dbWeb that allows an administrator to create definition templates referred to as schemas. Schemas control how and what information from a private database is available to visitors who use the Internet to access the public Microsoft dbWeb gateway to the private database. *See also* schemas.

DCD *See* Data Carrier Detect.

DCE *See* data communications equipment.

DCOM *See* Distributed Component Object Model.

DCOM Configuration tool A Windows NT Server utility that can be used to configure 32-bit applications for DCOM communication over the network. *See also* Distributed Component Object Model (DCOM).

DDE *See* dynamic data exchange.

deadlock condition A run-time error condition that occurs when two threads of execution are blocked, each waiting to acquire a resource that the other holds, and both unable to continue running.

decision tree A geographical representation of a filter's logic used by Windows NT Network Monitor. When you include or exclude information from your capture specifications, the decision tree reflects these specifications.

default button In some dialog boxes, the command button that is selected or highlighted when the dialog box is initially displayed. The default button has a bold border, indicating that it will be chosen automatically if you press ENTER. To override a default button, you can click **Cancel** or another command button.

default gateway In TCP/IP, the intermediate network device on the local network that has knowledge of the network IDs of the other networks in the Internet, so it can forward the packets to other gateways until the packet is eventually delivered to a gateway connected to the specified destination. *See also* gateway; network ID; packet.

default network In the Macintosh environment, this refers to the physical network on which a server's processes reside as nodes and on which the server appears to users. A server's default network must be one to which that server is attached. Only servers on AppleTalk Phase 2 internets have default networks.

default owner The person assigned ownership of a folder on the server when the account of the folder or volume's previous owner expires or is deleted. Each server has one default owner; you can specify the owner.

default printer The printer that is used if you choose the **Print** command without first specifying which printer you want to use with an application. You can have only one default printer; it should be the printer you use most often.

default profile *See* system default profile; user default profile.

default user Every user profile begins as a copy of default user, a default user profile stored on each computer running Windows NT Workstation or Windows NT Server.

default zone The zone to which all Macintosh clients on the network are assigned by default.

dependency A situation in which one action must take place before another can happen. For example, if action A does not occur, then action D cannot occur. Some Windows NT drivers have dependencies on other drivers or groups of drivers. For example, driver A will not load unless some driver from the G group loads first. *See also* circular dependency.

dependent service A service that requires support of another service. For example, the Alerter service is dependent on the Messenger service. *See also* Alerter service; Messenger service.

DES *See* Data Encryption Standard.

descendent key All the subkeys that appear when a key in the Registry is expanded. A descendent key is the same thing as a subkey. *See also* key; Registry; subkey.

desired zone The zone in which Services for Macintosh appears on the network. *See also* default zone.

desktop The background of your screen, on which windows, icons, and dialog boxes appear.

desktop pattern A design that appears across your desktop. You can create your own pattern or select a pattern provided by Windows NT.

destination directory The directory to which you intend to copy or move one or more files.

destination document The document into which a package or a linked or embedded object is being inserted. For an embedded object, this is sometimes also called the container document. *See also* embedded object; linked object; package.

device Any piece of equipment that can be attached to a network—for example, a computer, a printer, or any other peripheral equipment.

device contention The way Windows NT allocates access to peripheral devices, such as modems or printers, when more than one application is trying to use the same device.

device driver A program that enables a specific piece of hardware (device) to communicate with Windows NT. Although a device may be installed on your system, Windows NT cannot recognize the device until you have installed and configured the appropriate driver. If a device is listed in the Hardware Compatibility List, a driver is usually included with Windows NT. Drivers are installed when you run the Setup program (for a manufacturer's supplied driver) or by using Devices in Control Panel. *See also* Hardware Compatibility List (HCL).

DHCP *See* Dynamic Host Configuration Protocol.

DHCP Relay Agent The component responsible for relaying DHCP and BOOTP broadcast messages between a DHCP server and a client across an IP router. *See also* Bootstrap protocol (BOOTP); Dynamic Host Configuration Protocol (DHCP).

dialog box A window that is displayed to request or supply information. Many dialog boxes have options you must select before Windows NT can carry out a command.

dial-up line A standard dial-up connection such as telephone and ISDN lines.

dial-up networking The client version of Windows NT Remote Access Service (RAS), enabling users to connect to remote networks.

directory Part of a structure for organizing your files on a disk, a directory (also called a folder) is represented by the folder icon in Windows NT, Windows 95, and on Macintosh computers. A directory can contain files and other directories, called subdirectories or folders within folders.

With Services for Macintosh, directories on the computer running Windows NT Server appear to Macintosh users as volumes and folders if they are designated as Macintosh accessible.

See also directory tree; folder.

directory database A database of security information such as user account names and passwords, and the security policy settings. For Windows NT Workstation, the directory database is managed by using User Manager. For a Windows NT Server domain, it is managed by using User Manager for Domains. (Other Windows NT documents may refer to the directory database as the "Security Accounts Manager (SAM) database.") *See also* Windows NT Server Directory Services.

directory replication The copying of a master set of directories from a server (called an export server) to specified servers or workstations (called import computers) in the same or other domains. Replication simplifies the task of maintaining identical sets of directories and files on multiple computers, because only a single master copy of the data must be maintained. Files are replicated when they are added to an exported directory and every time a change is saved to the file. *See also* Directory Replicator service.

Directory Replicator service Replicates directories, and the files in those directories, between computers. *See also* directory replication.

Directory Service Manager for NetWare (DSMN) A component of Windows NT Server. Enables network administrators to add NetWare servers to Windows NT Server domains and to manage a single set of user and group accounts that are valid at multiple servers running either Windows NT Server or NetWare.

directory services *See* Windows NT Server Directory Services.

directory tree A graphical display of a disk's directory hierarchy. The directories and folders on the disk are shown as a branching structure. The top-level directory is the root directory.

disabled user account A user account that does not permit logons. The account appears in the user account list of the User Manager or User Manager for Domains window and can be re-enabled at any time. *See also* user account.

discovery A process by which the Windows NT Net Logon service attempts to locate a domain controller running Windows NT Server in the trusted domain. Once a domain controller has been discovered, it is used for subsequent user account authentication.

discretionary access control Allows the network administrator to allow some users to connect to a resource or perform an action while preventing other users from doing so. *See also* discretionary access control list (DACL); system access control list (SACL).

discretionary access control list (DACL)
The discretionary ACL is controlled by the owner of an object and specifies the access particular users or groups can have to that object. *See also* system access control list (SACL).

disjoint networks Networks that are not connected to each other.

disk configuration information The Windows NT Registry includes the following information on the configuration of your disk(s): assigned drive letters, stripe sets, mirror sets, volume sets, and stripe sets with parity. Disk configuration can be changed by using Disk Administrator. If you choose to create an Emergency Repair disk, disk configuration information will be stored there, as well as in the Registry.

display filter Functions like a database query, allowing you to single out specific types of information. Because a display filter operates on data that has already been captured, it does not affect the contents of the Network Monitor capture buffer. *See also* capture buffer.

display password Required to be able to open previously saved capture (.cap) files in Network Monitor.

Distributed Component Object Model (DCOM)
Use the DCOM Configuration tool to integrate client/server applications across multiple computers. DCOM can also be used to integrate robust Web browser applications. *See also* DCOM Configuration tool.

distributed server system In Windows NT, a system in which individual departments or workgroups set up and maintain their own remote access domains.

DLL *See* dynamic-link library.

DNS *See* Domain Name System.

DNS name servers In the DNS client/server model, the servers containing information about a portion of the DNS database, which makes computer names available to client resolvers querying for name resolution across the Internet. *See also* Domain Name System (DNS).

DNS service The service that provides domain name resolution. *See also* DNS name servers.

document A self-contained file created with an application and, if saved on disk, given a unique filename by which it can be retrieved. A document can be a text file, a spreadsheet, or an image file, for example.

document file A file that is associated with an application. When you open a document file, the application starts and loads the file. *See also* associate.

Document file icon Represents a file that is associated with an application. When you double-click a document file icon, the application starts and loads the file. *See also* associate.

document icon Located at the left of a document window title bar, the document icon represents the open document. Clicking the document icon opens the window menu. Also known as the control menu box.

domain In Windows NT, a collection of computers, defined by the administrator of a Windows NT Server network, that share a common directory database. A domain provides access to the centralized user accounts and group accounts maintained by the domain administrator. Each domain has a unique name. *See also* directory database; user account; workgroup.

domain controller In a Windows NT Server domain, refers to the computer running Windows NT Server that manages all aspects of user-domain interactions, and uses information in the directory database to authenticate users logging on to domain accounts. One shared directory database is used to store security and user account information for the entire domain. A domain has one primary domain controller (PDC) and one or more backup domain controllers (BDCs). *See also* backup domain controller (BDC); directory database; member server; primary domain controller (PDC).

domain database *See* directory database.

domain model A grouping of one or more domains with administration and communication links between them that are arranged for the purpose of user and resource management.

domain name Part of the Domain Name System (DNS) naming structure, a domain name is the name by which a domain is known to the network. Domain names consist of a sequence of labels separated by periods. *See also* Domain Name System (DNS); fully qualified domain name (FQDN).

domain name space The database structure used by the Domain Name System (DNS). *See also* Domain Name System (DNS).

Domain Name System (DNS) Sometimes referred to as the BIND service in BSD UNIX, DNS offers a static, hierarchical name service for TCP/IP hosts. The network administrator configures the DNS with a list of host names and IP addresses, allowing users of workstations configured to query the DNS to specify remote systems by host names rather than IP addresses. For example, a workstation configured to use DNS name resolution could use the command **ping remotehost** rather than **ping 172.16.16.235** if the mapping for the system named **remotehost** was contained in the DNS database. DNS domains should not be confused with Windows NT networking domains. *See also* IP address; ping.

domain synchronization *See* synchronize.

dots per inch (DPI) The standard used to measure print device resolution. The greater the DPI, the better the resolution.

double-click To rapidly press and release a mouse button twice without moving the mouse. Double-clicking carries out an action, such as starting an application.

down level A term that refers to earlier operating systems, such as Windows for Workgroups or LAN Manager, that can still interoperate with Windows NT Workstation or Windows NT Server.

downloaded fonts Fonts that you send to your printer either before or during the printing of your documents. When you send a font to your printer, it is stored in printer memory until it is needed for printing. *See also* font; font types.

DPI *See* dots per inch.

drag To move an item on the screen by selecting the item and then pressing and holding down the mouse button while moving the mouse. For example, you can move a window to another location on the screen by dragging its title bar.

drive icon An icon in the All Folders column in Windows NT Explorer or the Names Column in My Computer that represents a disk drive on your system. Different icons depict floppy disk drives, hard disk drives, network drives, RAM drives, and CD-ROM drives.

driver *See* device driver.

drop folder In the Macintosh environment this refers to a folder for which you have the Make Changes permission but not the See Files or See Folders permission. You can copy files into a drop folder, but you cannot see what files and subfolders the drop folder contains.

DSDM Acronym for DDE share database manager. *See also* dynamic data exchange (DDE); Network DDE DSDM service.

DSMN *See* Directory Service Manager for NetWare.

DSN *See* Data Source Name.

DSR Acronym for Data Set Ready signal, used in serial communications. A DSR is sent by a modem to the computer to which it is attached to indicate that it is ready to operate. DSRs are hardware signals sent over line 6 in RS-232-C connections.

DTE *See* Data Terminal Equipment.

dual boot A computer that can boot two different operating systems. *See also* multiple boot.

DWORD A data type composed of hexadecimal data with a maximum allotted space of 4 bytes.

dynamic assignment The automatic assignment of TCP/IP properties in a changing network.

dynamic data exchange (DDE) A form of interprocess communication (IPC) implemented in the Microsoft Windows family of operating systems. Two or more programs that support dynamic data exchange (DDE) can exchange information and commands. *See also* interprocess communication (IPC).

Dynamic Host Configuration Protocol (DHCP) A protocol that offers dynamic configuration of IP addresses and related information. DHCP provides safe, reliable, and simple TCP/IP network configuration, prevents address conflicts, and helps conserve the use of IP addresses through centralized management of address allocation. *See also* IP address.

dynamic-link library (DLL) An operating system feature that allows executable routines (generally serving a specific function or set of functions) to be stored separately as files with .dll extensions and to be loaded only when needed by the program that calls them.

dynamic routing Dynamic routing automatically updates the routing tables, reducing administrative overhead (but increasing traffic in large networks). *See also* routing table.

dynamic web pages Web pages that are derived or assembled only when the client requests them. Dynamic pages are used to deliver very current information, to deliver responses to forms and queries, and to provide a customized page. They are often associated with databases, such as SQL databases. *See also* static web pages.

E

EISA *See* Extended Industry Standard Architecture.

embedded object Presents information, created in another application, which has been pasted inside your document. Information in the embedded object does not exist in another file outside your document.

EMS *See* Expanded Memory Specification.

encapsulated PostScript (EPS) file
A file that prints at the highest possible resolution for your printer. An EPS file may print faster than other graphical representations. Some Windows NT and non-Windows NT graphical applications can import EPS files. *See also* font types; PostScript printer; print processor.

encryption The process of making information indecipherable to protect it from unauthorized viewing or use, especially during transmission or when it is stored on a transportable magnetic medium.

enterprise server Refers to the server to which multiple primary domain controllers (PDCs) in a large organization will replicate. *See also* primary domain controller (PDC).

environment variable A string consisting of environment information, such as a drive, path, or filename, associated with a symbolic name that can be used by Windows NT. To define environment variables, use System in Control Panel or use the **Set** command from the Windows NT command prompt.

EPS *See* encapsulated PostScript file.

error logging The process by which errors that cannot readily be corrected by the majority of end users are written to a file instead of being displayed on the screen. System administrators, support technicians, and users can use this log file to monitor the condition of the hardware in a computer running Windows NT to tune the configuration of the computer for better performance, and to debug problems as they occur.

event Any significant occurrence in the system or an application that requires users to be notified, or an entry to be added to a log.

Event Log service Records events in the system, security, and application logs. The Event Log service is located in Event Viewer.

exception A synchronous error condition resulting from the execution of a particular computer instruction. Exceptions can be either hardware-detected errors, such as division by zero, or software-detected errors, such as a guard-page violation.

Executive The Executive is the part of the Windows NT operating system that runs in Kernel mode. *Kernel mode* is a privileged processor mode in which a thread has access to system memory and to hardware. (In contrast, *User mode* is a nonprivileged processor mode in which a thread can only access system resources by calling system services.) The Windows NT Executive provides process structure, thread scheduling, interprocess communication, memory management, object management, object security, interrupt processing, I/O capabilities, and networking. *See also* Hardware Abstraction Layer (HAL); Kernel.

Executive messages Two types of character-mode messages occur when the Windows NT Kernel detects an inconsistent condition from which it cannot recover: STOP messages and hardware-malfunction messages.

Character-mode STOP messages are always displayed on a full character-mode screen rather than in a Windows-mode message box. They are also uniquely identified by a hexadecimal number and a symbolic string.

Character-mode hardware-malfunction messages are caused by a hardware condition detected by the processor.

The Executive displays a Windows-mode STATUS message box when it detects conditions within a process (generally, an application) that you should know about.

expand To show hidden directory levels in the directory tree. With My Computer or Windows NT Explorer, directories that can expand have plus-sign icons which you click to expand.

expanded memory A type of memory, up to 8 megabytes, that can be added to an 8086 or 8088 computer, or to an 80286, 80386, 80486, or Pentium computer. The use of expanded memory is defined by the Expanded Memory Specification (EMS). Note: Windows NT requires an 80486 or higher computer.

Expanded Memory Specification (EMS)
Describes a technique for adding memory to IBM PC systems. EMS bypasses the limits on the maximum amount of usable memory in a computer system by supporting memory boards containing a number of 16K banks of RAM that can be enabled or disabled by software. *See also* memory.

Explorer *See* Windows NT Explorer.

export path In directory replication, a path from which subdirectories, and the files in those subdirectories, are automatically exported from an export server. *See also* directory replication.

export server In directory replication, a server from which a master set of directories is exported to specified servers or workstations (called import computers) in the same or other domains. *See also* directory replication.

Extended Industry Standard Architecture (EISA)
A 32-bit bus standard introduced in 1988 by a consortium of nine computer industry companies. EISA maintains compatibility with the earlier Industry Standard Architecture (ISA) but provides for additional features.

extended memory Memory beyond one megabyte in 80286, 80386, 80486, and Pentium computers. Note: Windows NT requires an 80486 or higher computer.

extended partition Created from free space on a hard disk, an extended partition can be subpartitioned into zero or more logical drives. Only one of the four partitions allowed per physical disk can be an extended partition, and no primary partition needs to be present to create an extended partition. *See also* free space; logical drive; primary partition.

extensible counters Performance Monitor counters that are not installed with Windows NT. Extensible counters typically are installed independently. Extensible counters should be monitored to make certain that they are working properly.

extension A filename extension usually indicates the type of file or directory, or the type of application associated with a file. In MS-DOS, this includes a period and up to three characters at the end of a filename. Windows NT supports long filenames, up to the filename limit of 255 characters.

extension-type association The association of an MS-DOS filename extension with a Macintosh file type and file creator. Extension-type associations allow users of the PC and Macintosh versions of the same application to share the same data files on the server. Services for Macintosh has many predefined extension-type associations. *See also* name mapping.

external command A command that is stored in its own file and loaded from disk when you use the command.

F

family set A collection of related tapes containing several backup sets. *See also* backup set.

FAT *See* file allocation table.

fault tolerance   Ensures data integrity when hardware failures occur. In Windows NT, fault tolerance is provided by the Ftdisk.sys driver. In Disk Administrator, fault tolerance is provided using mirror sets, stripe sets with parity, and volume sets. *See also* mirror set; stripe sets with parity; volume set.

FCB   *See* file control block.

Fiber Distributed Data Interface (FDDI)
A type of network media designed to be used with fiber-optic cabling. *See also* LocalTalk; Token Ring.

file   A collection of information that has been given a name and is stored on a disk. This information can be a document or an application.

file allocation table (FAT)   A table or list maintained by some operating systems to keep track of the status of various segments of disk space used for file storage. Also referred to as the FAT file system.

File and Print Services for NetWare (FPNW)
A Windows NT Server component that enables a computer running Windows NT Server to provide file and print services directly to NetWare-compatible client computers.

file control block (FCB)   A small block of memory temporarily assigned by a computer's operating system to hold information about a file that has been opened for use. An FCB typically contains such information as the file's identification, its location on disk, and a pointer that marks the user's current (or last) position in the file.

file creator   A four-character sequence that tells the Macintosh Finder the name of the application that created a file. With Services for Macintosh, you can create extension-type associations that map PC filename extensions with Macintosh file creators and file types. These associations allow both PC and Macintosh users to share the same data files on the server. *See also* extension-type association.

file fork   One of two subfiles of a Macintosh file. When Macintosh files are stored on a computer running Windows NT Server, each fork is stored as a separate file. Each fork can be independently opened by a Macintosh user.

filename   The name of a file. MS-DOS supports the 8.3 naming convention of up to eight characters followed by a period and a three-character extension. Windows NT supports the FAT and NTFS file systems with filenames up to 255 characters. Since MS-DOS cannot recognize long filenames, Windows NT Server automatically translates long names of files and folders to 8.3 names for MS-DOS users. *See also* long name; name mapping; short name.

filename extension   The characters that follow the period in a filename, following the FAT naming conventions. Filename extensions can have as many as three characters and are often used to identify the type of file and the application used to create the file (for example, spreadsheet files created by Microsoft Excel have the extension .xls). With Services for Macintosh, you can create extension-type associations that map PC filename extensions with Macintosh file creators and types.

File Replication service   A Windows NT service that allows specified file(s) to be replicated to remote systems, ensuring that copies on each system are kept in synchronization. The system that maintains the master copy is called the exporter, and the systems that receive updates are known as importers.

File Server for Macintosh service
A Services for Macintosh service that enables
Macintosh clients and PC clients to share files.
Also called MacFile.

file sharing The ability for a computer running
Windows NT to share parts (or all) of its local file
system(s) with remote computers. An
administrator creates share points by using the file
sharing command in My Computer or
Windows NT Explorer or by using the **net share**
command from the command prompt.

file system In an operating system, the overall
structure in which files are named, stored, and
organized. NTFS and FAT are types of file
systems.

file transfer protocol (FTP) A service supporting
file transfers between local and remote systems
that support this protocol. FTP supports several
commands that allow bidirectional transfer of
binary and ASCII files between systems. The FTP
Server service is part of the Internet Information
Server. The FTP client is installed with TCP/IP
connectivity utilities.

file type In the Macintosh environment, this
refers to a four-character sequence that identifies
the type of a Macintosh file. The file type and file
creator are used by the Macintosh Finder to
determine the appropriate desktop icon for that
file.

find tab Displays the words you can use to search
for related topics. Use this tab to look for topics
related to a particular word. It is located in the
Help button bar near the top of the Help window.

firewall A system or combination of systems that
enforces a boundary between two or more
networks and keeps intruders out of private
networks. Firewalls serve as virtual barriers to
passing packets from one network to another.

flat name space A naming system in which
computer names are created from a short sequence
of characters without any additional structure
superimposed.

floppy disk A disk that can be inserted in and
removed from a disk drive. Floppies are most
commonly available in a 3.5 or 5.25 inch format.

flow control An exchange of signals, over
specific wires, in which each device signals its
readiness to send or receive data.

folder A grouping of files or other folders,
graphically represented by a folder icon, in both
the Windows NT and Macintosh environments. A
folder is analogous to a PC's file system
directory, and many folders are, in fact,
directories. A folder may contain other folders as
well as file objects. *See also* directory.

font A graphic design applied to a collection of
numbers, symbols, and characters. A font
describes a certain typeface along with other
qualities such as size, spacing, and pitch. *See also*
font set; font types.

font set A collection of font sizes for one font,
customized for a particular display and printer.
Font sets determine what text looks like on the
screen and when printed. *See also* font.

font types:
   device fonts
Reside in the hardware of your print device. They
can be built into the print device itself or can be
provided by a font cartridge or font card.

   downloadable soft fonts
Fonts that are stored on disk and downloaded as
needed to the print device.

   plotter fonts A font created by a series of
dots connected by lines. Plotter fonts can be
scaled to any size and are most often printed on
plotters. Some dot-matrix printers also support
plotter fonts.

PostScript fonts Fonts that are defined in terms of the PostScript page-description language rules from Adobe Systems. When a document displayed in a screen font is sent to a PostScript printer, the printer uses the PostScript version if the font exists. If the font doesn't exist but a version is installed on the computer, that font is downloaded. If there is no PostScript font installed in either the printer or the computer, the bitmapped font is translated into PostScript and the printer prints text using the bitmapped font.

raster fonts Fonts that are stored as bitmaps. If a print device does not support raster fonts, it will not print them. Raster fonts cannot be scaled or rotated.

screen fonts Windows NT fonts that can be translated for output to the print device. Most screen fonts (including TrueType fonts) can be printed as well.

TrueType fonts Device-independent fonts that can be reproduced on all print devices. TrueType fonts are stored as outlines and can be scaled and rotated.

vector fonts Fonts that are useful on devices such as pen plotters that cannot reproduce bitmaps. They can be scaled to any size or aspect ratio. (*See also* plotter fonts, earlier in this entry.)

fork *See* data fork; file fork; resource fork.

FPNW *See* File and Print Services for NetWare.

FQDN *See* fully qualified domain name.

frame In synchronous communication, a package of information transmitted as a single unit from one device to another. *See also* capture.

Frame Relay A synchronous High-level Data Link Control (HDLC) protocol–based network that sends data in HDLC packets. *See also* High-level Data Link Control (HDLC).

framing rules Are established between a remote computer and the server, allowing continued communication (frame transfer) to occur. *See also* frame.

free space Free space is an unused and unformatted portion of a hard disk that can be partitioned or subpartitioned. Free space within an extended partition is available for the creation of logical drives. Free space that is not within an extended partition is available for the creation of a partition, with a maximum of four partitions allowed per disk. *See also* extended partition; logical drive; primary partition.

FTP *See* file transfer protocol.

full name A user's complete name, usually consisting of the last name, first name, and middle initial. The full name is information that can be maintained by User Manager and User Manager for Domains as part of the information identifying and defining a user account. *See also* user account.

full-screen application A non–Windows NT application that is displayed in the entire screen, rather than a window, when running in the Windows NT environment.

full synchronization Occurs when a copy of the entire database directory is sent to a backup domain controller (BDC). Full synchronization is performed automatically when changes have been deleted from the change log before replication takes place, and when a new BDC is added to a domain. *See also* backup domain controller (BDC); directory database.

fully qualified domain name (FQDN)
Part of the TCP/IP naming convention known as the Domain Name System, DNS computer names consist of two parts: host names with their domain names appended to them. For example, a host with host name **corp001** and DNS domain name **trey-research.com** has an FQDN of **corp001.trey-research.com**. (DNS domains should not be confused with Windows NT networking domains.) *See also* Domain Name System (DNS).

G

gateway Describes a system connected to multiple physical TCP/IP networks, capable of routing or delivering IP packets between them. A gateway translates between different transport protocols or data formats (for example IPX and IP) and is generally added to a network primarily for its translation ability. Also referred to as an IP router. *See also* IP address; IP router.

Gateway Service for NetWare Included with Windows NT Server, enables a computer running Windows NT Server to connect to NetWare servers. Creating a gateway enables computers running only Microsoft client software to access NetWare resources through the gateway. *See also* gateway.

General MIDI A MIDI specification controlled by the MIDI Manufacturers Association (MMA). The specification provides guidelines that authors of MIDI files can use to create files that sound the same across a variety of different synthesizers.

global account For Windows NT Server, a normal user account in a user's domain. Most user accounts are global accounts. If there are multiple domains in the network, it is best if each user in the network has only one user account in only one domain, and each user's access to other domains is accomplished through the establishment of domain trust relationships. *See also* local account; trust relationship.

global group For Windows NT Server, a group that can be used in its own domain, member servers and workstations of the domain, and trusting domains. In all those places it can be granted rights and permissions and can become a member of local groups. However, it can only contain user accounts from its own domain. Global groups provide a way to create handy sets of users from inside the domain, available for use both in and out of the domain.

Global groups cannot be created or maintained on computers running Windows NT Workstation. However, for Windows NT Workstation computers that participate in a domain, domain global groups can be granted rights and permissions at those workstations, and can become members of local groups at those workstations. *See also* domain; group; local group; trust relationship.

globally unique identifier (GUID) *See* universally unique identifier (UUID).

Gopher A hierarchical system for finding and retrieving information from the Internet or an intranet. Similar to FTP, Gopher uses a menu system and enables links to other servers.

group In User Manager or User Manager for Domains, an account containing other accounts that are called members. The permissions and rights granted to a group are also provided to its members, making groups a convenient way to grant common capabilities to collections of user accounts. For Windows NT Workstation, groups are managed with User Manager. For Windows NT Server, groups are managed with User Manager for Domains. *See also* built-in groups; global group; local group; user account.

group account A collection of user accounts. Giving a user account membership in a group gives that user all the rights and permissions granted to the group. *See also* local account; user account.

group category   One of three categories of users to which you can assign Macintosh permissions for a folder. The permissions assigned to the group category are available to the group associated with the folder.

group memberships   The groups to which a user account belongs. Permissions and rights granted to a group are also provided to its members. In most cases, the actions a user can perform in Windows NT are determined by the group memberships of the user account the user is logged on to. *See also* group.

group name   A unique name identifying a local group or a global group to Windows NT. A group's name cannot be identical to any other group name or user name of its own domain or computer. *See also* global group; local group.

guest   Users of Services for Macintosh who do not have a user account or who do not provide a password are logged on as a guest, using a user account with guest privileges. When a Macintosh user assigns permissions to everyone, those permissions are given to the group's guests and users.

guest account   On computers running Windows NT Workstation or Windows NT Server, a built-in account used for logons by people who do not have a user account on the computer or domain or in any of the domains trusted by the computer's domain.

Guest privilege   One of three privilege levels that you can assign to a Windows NT user account. The guest account used for Macintosh guest logons must have the Guest privilege. *See also* Administrator privilege; user account; User privilege.

GUID   Acronym for globally unique identifier. *See* universally unique identifier (UUID).

H

HAL   *See* Hardware Abstraction Layer.

handle   A handle is a value used to uniquely identify a resource so that a program can access it.

In the Registry, each of the first-level key names begins with HKEY_ to indicate to software developers that this is a handle that can be read by a program.

handshaking   Refers to flow control in serial communication, which defines a method for the print device to tell Windows NT that its buffer is full. *See also* buffer.

Hardware Abstraction Layer (HAL)

A thin layer of software provided by the hardware manufacturer that hides, or abstracts, hardware differences from higher layers of the operating system.

Through the filter provided by the HAL, different types of hardware all look alike to the rest of the operating system. This allows Windows NT to be portable from one hardware platform to another. The HAL also provides routines that allow a single device driver to support the same device on all platforms.

The HAL works closely with the Kernel.

See also Executive; Kernel.

Hardware Compatibility List (HCL)

The Windows NT Hardware Compatibility List lists the devices supported by Windows NT. The latest version of the HCL can be downloaded from the Microsoft Web Page (microsoft.com) on the Internet.

HCL   *See* Hardware Compatibility List.

HDLC   *See* High-level Data Link Control.

heterogeneous environment An internetwork with servers and workstations running different operating systems, such as Windows NT, Macintosh, or Novell NetWare, using a mix of different transport protocols.

hexadecimal A base-16 number system that consists of the digits 0 through 9 and the uppercase and lowercase letters A (equivalent to decimal 10) through F (equivalent to decimal 15).

High-level Data Link Control (HDLC)
A protocol that governs information transfer. Under the HDLC protocol, messages are transmitted in units called frames, each of which can contain a variable amount of data but which must be organized in a particular way.

high memory area (HMA) The first 64K of extended memory (often referred to as HMA). *See also* memory.

High-Performance File System (HPFS)
The file system designed for the OS/2 version 1.2 operating system.

hive A section of the Registry that appears as a file on your hard disk. The Registry subtree is divided into hives (named for their resemblance to the cellular structure of a beehive). A hive is a discrete body of keys, subkeys, and values that is rooted at the top of the Registry hierarchy. A hive is backed by a single file and a .log file, which are in the *Systemroot*\System32\Config or the *Systemroot*\Profiles*Username* folder. By default, most hive files (Default, SAM, Security, and System) are stored in the *Systemroot*\System32\Config folder.

The *Systemroot*\Profiles folder contains the user profile for each user of the computer. Because a hive is a file, it can be moved from one system to another but can only be edited by using a Registry editor.

HMA *See* high memory area.

h-node A NetBIOS implementation that uses the p-node protocol first, then the b-node protocol if the name service is unavailable. For registration, it uses the b-node protocol, then the p-node protocol. *See also* NetBIOS; p-node; registration.

home directory A directory that is accessible to the user and contains files and programs for that user. A home directory can be assigned to an individual user or can be shared by many users.

home page The initial page of information for a collection of pages. The starting point for a Web site or section of a Web site is often referred to as the home page. Individuals also post pages that are called home pages.

hop Refers to the next router. In IP routing, packets are always forwarded one router at a time. Packets often hop from router to router before reaching their destination. *See also* IP address; packet; router.

host Any device that is attached to the network and uses TCP/IP. *See also* Transmission Control Protocol/Internet Protocol (TCP/IP).

host group A set of zero or more hosts identified by a single IP destination address. *See also* host; IP address.

host ID The portion of the IP address that identifies a computer within a particular network ID. *See also* IP address; network ID.

host name The name of a device on a network. For a device on a Windows or Windows NT network, this can be the same as the computer name, but it may not be. The host name must be in the host table or be known by a DNS server for that host to be found by another computer attempting to communicate with it. *See also* Domain Name System (DNS); host table.

HOSTS file A local text file in the same format as the 4.3 Berkeley Software Distribution (BSD) UNIX \etc\hosts file. This file maps host names to IP addresses. In Windows NT, this file is stored in the *Systemroot*\System32\Drivers\Etc directory. *See also* IP address.

host table The HOSTS and LMHOSTS files, which contain mappings of known IP addresses mapped to host names.

HPFS *See* High-Performance File System.

HTML *See* Hypertext Markup Language.

HTTP *See* Hypertext Transport Protocol.

HTTP keep-alives An optimizing feature of the HTTP service. HTTP keep-alives maintain a connection even after the initial connection request is completed. This keeps the connection active and available for subsequent requests. HTTP keep-alives were implemented to avoid the substantial cost of establishing and terminating connections. Both the client and the server must support keep-alives. Keep-alives are supported by Internet Information Server version 1.0 and later and by Internet Explorer version 2.0 and later. *See also* TCP/IP keep-alives.

hue The position of a color along the color spectrum. For example, green is between yellow and blue. To set this attribute, use Desktop in Control Panel.

hyperlink A way of jumping to another place on the Internet. Hyperlinks usually appear in a different format from regular text. You initiate the jump by clicking the link.

Hypertext Markup Language (HTML)
A simple markup language used to create hypertext documents that are portable from one platform to another. HTML files are simple ASCII text files with codes embedded (indicated by markup tags) to indicate formatting and hypertext links. HTML is used for formatting documents on the World Wide Web.

Hypertext Transport Protocol (HTTP)
The underlying protocol by which WWW clients and servers communicate. HTTP is an application-level protocol for distributed, collaborative, hypermedia information systems. It is a generic, stateless, object-oriented protocol. A feature of HTTP is the typing and negotiation of data representation, allowing systems to be built independently of the data being transferred.

I

ICMP *See* Internet Control Message Protocol.

icon A graphical representation of an element in Windows NT, such as a disk drive, directory, group, application, or document. Click the icon to enlarge an application icon to a window when you want to use the application. Within applications, there are also toolbar icons for commands such as cut, copy, and paste.

IDC *See* Internet Database Connector.

IDE *See* integrated device electronics.

IETF *See* Internet Engineering Task Force.

IGMP *See* Internet Group Management Protocol.

IIS *See* Internet Information Server.

IIS object cache An area of virtual memory that the IIS process uses to store frequently used objects, such as open file handles and directory listings. The IIS object cache is part of the working set of the IIS process, Inetinfo.exe, and it can be paged to disk.

IMC *See* Internet Mail Connector.

impersonation Impersonation occurs when Windows NT Server allows one process to take on the security attributes of another.

import To create a package by inserting an existing file into Object Packager. When you import a file, the icon of the application you used to create the file appears in the Appearance window, and the name of the file appears in the Contents window. *See also* package.

import computers In directory replication, the servers or workstations that receive copies of the master set of directories from an export server. *See also* directory replication; export server.

import path In directory replication, the path to which imported subdirectories, and the files in those subdirectories, will be stored on an import computer. *See also* directory replication; import computers.

Inetinfo A process containing the FTP, Gopher, and HTTP services. This process is about 400K in size. In addition to the FTP, Gopher, and HTTP services, this process contains the shared thread pool, cache, logging, and SNMP services of Internet Information Server.

input/output activity (I/O) Read or write actions that your computer performs. Your computer performs a "read" when you type information on your keyboard or you select and choose items by using your mouse. Also, when you open a file, your computer reads the disk on which the file is located to find and open it.

Your computer performs a "write" whenever it stores, sends, prints, or displays information. For example, your computer performs a write when it stores information on a disk, displays information on your screen, or sends information through a modem or to a printer. *See also* I/O addresses.

input/output control (IOCTL) An IOCTL command enables a program to communicate directly with a device driver. This is done, for example, by sending a string of control information recognized by the driver. None of the information passed from the program to the device driver is sent to the device itself (in other words, the control string sent to a printer driver is not displayed on the printer).

insertion point The place where text will be inserted when you type. The insertion point usually appears as a flashing vertical bar in an application's window or in a dialog box.

integrated device electronics (IDE)
A type of disk-drive interface in which the controller electronics reside on the drive itself, eliminating the need for a separate adapter card.

Integrated Services Digital Network (ISDN)
A type of phone line used to enhance WAN speeds, ISDN lines can transmit at speeds of 64 or 128 kilobits per second, as opposed to standard phone lines, which typically transmit at only 9600 bits per second (bps). An ISDN line must be installed by the phone company at both the server site and the remote site. *See also* bits per second (bps).

interactive logon A network logon from a computer keyboard, when the user types information in the **Logon Information** dialog box displayed by the computer's operating system. *See also* remote logon.

intermediary devices Microsoft RAS supports various kinds of intermediary devices (security hosts and switches) between the remote access client and the remote access server. These devices include a modem-pool switch or security host. *See also* Remote Access Service (RAS).

internal command Commands that are stored in the file Cmd.exe and that reside in memory at all times.

internet In Windows NT, a collection of two or more private networks, or private inter-enterprise TCP/IP networks.

In Macintosh terminology, refers to two or more physical networks connected by routers, which maintain a map of the physical networks on the internet and forward data received from one physical network to other physical networks. Network users in an internet can share information and network devices. You can use an internet with Services for Macintosh by connecting two or more AppleTalk networks to a computer running Windows NT Server.

Internet The global network of networks. *See also* World Wide Web (WWW).

Internet Assigned Numbers Authority (IANA)
The central coordinator for the assignment of unique parameter values for Internet protocols. IANA is chartered by the Internet Society (ISOC) and the Federal Network Council (FNC) to act as the clearinghouse to assign and coordinate the use of numerous Internet protocol parameters. Contact IANA at **http://www.iana.org/iana/**.

Internet Assistant Several Internet Assistant add-on software components are available for Microsoft Office products. Each Internet Assistant adds functionality that is relevant to creating content for the Internet. For example, Internet Assistant for Microsoft Word enables Word to create HTML documents from within Microsoft Word.

Internet Control Message Protocol (ICMP)
A maintenance protocol in the TCP/IP suite, required in every TCP/IP implementation, that allows two nodes on an IP network to share IP status and error information. ICMP is used by the ping utility to determine the readability of a remote system. *See also* ping; Transmission Control Protocol/Internet Protocol (TCP/IP).

Internet Database Connector (IDC)
Provides access to databases for Internet Information Server by using ODBC. The Internet Database Connector is contained in Httpodbc.dll, which is an Internet Server API DLL.

Internet Engineering Task Force (IETF)
A consortium that introduces procedures for new technology on the Internet. IETF specifications are released in documents called Requests for Comments (RFCs). *See also* Requests for Comments (RFCs).

Internet Group Management Protocol (IGMP)
A protocol used by workgroup software products and supported by Microsoft TCP/IP.

Internet group name A name known by a DNS server that includes a list of the specific addresses of systems that have registered the name. *See also* Domain Name System (DNS).

Internet Information Server (IIS) A network file and application server that supports multiple protocols. Primarily, Internet Information Server transmits information in Hypertext Markup Language (HTML) pages by using the Hypertext Transport Protocol (HTTP).

Internet Mail Connector (IMC) The Internet Mail Connector is a component of Microsoft Exchange Server that runs as a Windows NT Server service. You can use the Internet Mail Connector to exchange information with other systems that use the Simple Mail Transfer Protocol (SMTP).

Internet Network Information Center (InterNIC)
The coordinator for DNS registration. To register domain names and obtain IP addresses, contact InterNIC at **http://internic.net**.

Internet Protocol (IP) The messenger protocol of TCP/IP, responsible for addressing and sending TCP packets over the network. IP provides a best-effort, connectionless delivery system that does not guarantee that packets arrive at their destination or that they are received in the sequence in which they were sent. *See also* packet; Transmission Control Protocol (TCP); Transmission Control Protocol/Internet Protocol (TCP/IP).

Internet Protocol Control Protocol (IPCP) Specified by RFC 1332. Responsible for configuring, enabling, and disabling the IP protocol modules on both ends of the point-to-point (PPP) link. *See also* Point-to-Point Protocol (PPP); Requests for Comments (RFCs).

Internet Relay Chat (IRC) A protocol that enables two or more people, each in remote locations, who are connected to an IRC server to hold real-time conversations. IRC is defined in RFC 1459.

Internet router A device that connects networks and directs network information to other networks, usually choosing the most efficient route through other routers. *See also* router.

Internet Server Application Programming Interface (ISAPI) An API for developing extensions to the Microsoft Internet Information Server and other HTTP servers that support ISAPI. *See also* application programming interface (API).

Internet service provider (ISP) A company or educational institution that enables remote users to access the Internet by providing dial-up connections or installing leased lines.

internetworks Networks that connect local area networks (LANs) together.

interprocess communication (IPC) The ability, provided by a multitasking operating system, of one task or process to exchange data with another. Common IPC methods include pipes, semaphores, shared memory, queues, signals, and mailboxes. *See also* named pipe; queue.

interrupt An asynchronous operating system condition that disrupts normal execution and transfers control to an interrupt handler. Interrupts can be issued by both software and hardware devices requiring service from the processor. When software issues an interrupt, it calls an interrupt service routine (ISR). When hardware issues an interrupt, it signals an interrupt request (IRQ) line.

interrupt moderation A Windows NT performance optimizing feature that diverts interrupts from the network adapters when the rate of interrupts is very high. The system accumulates the interrupts in a buffer for later processing. Standard interrupt processing is resumed when the interrupt rate returns to normal.

interrupt request line (IRQ) A hardware line over which devices can send signals to get the attention of the processor when the device is ready to accept or send information. Typically, each device connected to the computer uses a separate IRQ.

intranet A TCP/IP network that uses Internet technology. May be connected to the Internet. *See also* Internet; Transmission Control Protocol/Internet Protocol (TCP/IP).

I/O addresses Locations within the input/output address space of your computer, used by a device such as a printer or modem. *See* also input/output activity (I/O).

IOCTL *See* input/output control.

IP *See* Internet Protocol.

IP address   Used to identify a node on a network and to specify routing information. Each node on the network must be assigned a unique IP address, which is made up of the *network ID*, plus a unique *host ID* assigned by the network administrator. This address is typically represented in dotted-decimal notation, with the decimal value of each octet separated by a period (for example, 138.57.7.27).

In Windows NT, the IP address can be configured statically on the client or configured dynamically through DHCP. *See also* Dynamic Host Configuration Protocol (DHCP); node; octet.

IPC   *See* interprocess communication.

IPCP   *See* Internet Protocol Control Protocol.

IP datagrams   The basic Internet Protocol (IP) information unit. *See also* datagram; Internet Protocol (IP).

IP router   A system connected to multiple physical TCP/IP networks that can route or deliver IP packets between the networks. *See also* packet; routing; Transmission Control Protocol/Internet Protocol (TCP/IP).

IPX   *See* IPX/SPX.

IPX/SPX   Acronym for Internetwork Packet Exchange/Sequenced Packet Exchange, which is a set of transport protocols used in Novell NetWare networks. Windows NT implements IPX through NWLink.

IRC   *See* Internet Relay Chat.

IRQ   *See* interrupt request line.

ISAPI   *See* Internet Server Application Programming Interface.

ISDN   *See* Integrated Services Digital Network.

ISDN interface card   Similar in function to a modem, an ISDN card is hardware that enables a computer to connect to other computers and networks on an Integrated Services Digital Network.

ISO   Abbreviation for the International Standards Organization, an international association of member countries, each of which is represented by its leading standard-setting organization—for example ANSI (American National Standards Institute) for the United States. The ISO works to establish global standards for communications and information exchange.

ISP   *See* Internet service provider.

iteration   One of the three key concepts in DNS name resolution. A local name server keeps the burden of processing on itself and passes only iterative resolution requests to other name servers. An iterative resolution request tells the name server that the requester expects the best answer the name server can provide without help from others. If the name server has the requested data, it returns it, otherwise it returns pointers to name servers that are more likely to have the answer. *See also* Domain Name System (DNS).

In programming, iteration is the art of executing one or more statements or instructions repeatedly.

J

jump   Text, graphics, or parts of graphics that provide links to other Help topics or to more information about the current topic. The pointer changes shape whenever it is over a jump. If you click a jump that is linked to another topic, that topic appears in the Help window. If you click a jump that is linked to more information, the information appears in a pop-up window on top of the main Help window.

K

keep-alives
See HTTP keep-alives; TCP/IP keep-alives.

Kermit
Protocol for transferring binary files that is somewhat slower than XModem/CRC. However, Kermit allows you to transmit and receive either seven or eight data bits per character. *See also* XModem/CRC.

Kernel The Windows NT Kernel is the part of the Windows NT Executive that manages the processor. It performs thread scheduling and dispatching, interrupt and exception handling, and multiprocessor synchronization. The Kernel synchronizes activities among Executive-level subcomponents, such as I/O Manager and Process Manager. It also provides primitive objects to the Windows NT Executive, which uses them to create User-mode objects. The Kernel works closely with the Hardware Abstraction Layer (HAL). *See also* Executive; Hardware Abstraction Layer (HAL).

Kernel debugger
The Windows NT Kernel debugger (KD) is a 32-bit application that is used to debug the Kernel and device drivers, and to log the events leading up to a Windows NT Executive STOP, STATUS, or hardware-malfunction message.

The Kernel debugger runs on another Windows NT host computer that is connected to your Windows NT target computer. The two computers send debugging (troubleshooting) information back and forth through a communications port that must be running at the same baud rate on each computer.

Kernel driver A driver that accesses hardware. *See also* device driver.

key A folder that appears in the left pane of a Registry editor window. A key can contain subkeys and value entries. For example: Environment is a key of HKEY_CURRENT_USER. *See also* subkey.

keyboard buffer A temporary storage area in memory that keeps track of keys you typed, even if the computer did not immediately respond to the keys when you typed them.

key map A mapping assignment that translates key values on synthesizers that do not conform to General MIDI standards. Key maps ensure that the appropriate percussion instrument is played or the appropriate octave for a melodic instrument is played when a MIDI file is played. *See also* Musical Instrument Digital Interface (MIDI).

kiosk A computer, connected to the Internet, made available to users in a commonly accessible location.

L

LAN *See* local area network.

LastKnownGood (LKG) control set
The most recent control set that correctly started the system and resulted in a successful startup. The control set is saved as the LKG control set when you have a successful logon. *See also* current control set.

lease In Windows NT, the network administrator controls how long IP addresses are assigned by specifying lease durations that specify how long a computer can use an assigned IP address before having to renew the lease with the DHCP server. *See also* Dynamic Host Configuration Protocol (DHCP); IP address.

leased line A high-capacity line (most often a telephone line) dedicated to network connections.

license group License groups show a relationship (also known as a mapping) between users and computers. A license group comprises a single descriptive name for the group, a specified number of Per-Seat licenses assigned to the group, and a specific list of users who are members of the group.

line printer daemon (LPD) A line printer daemon (LPD) service on the print server receives documents (print jobs) from line printer remote (LPR) utilities running on client systems.

linked object A representation or placeholder for an object that is inserted into a destination document. The object still exists in the source file and, when it is changed, the linked object is updated to reflect these changes.

list box In a dialog box, a type of box that lists available choices—for example, a list of all files in a directory. If all the choices do not fit in the list box, there is a scroll bar.

LMHOSTS file A local text file that maps IP addresses to the computer names of Windows NT networking computers outside the local subnet. In Windows NT, this file is stored in the *Systemroot* \System32\Drivers\Etc directory. *See also* IP address; subnet.

local account For Windows NT Server, a user account provided in a domain for a user whose global account is not in a trusted domain. Not required where trust relationships exist between domains. *See also* global account; trust relationship; user account.

local area network (LAN) A group of computers and other devices dispersed over a relatively limited area and connected by a communications link that enables any device to interact with any other on the network.

local group For Windows NT Workstation, a group that can be granted permissions and rights only for its own workstation. However, it can contain user accounts from its own computer and (if the workstation participates in a domain) user accounts and global groups both from its own domain and from trusted domains.

For Windows NT Server, a group that can be granted permissions and rights only for the domain controllers of its own domain. However, it can contain user accounts and global groups both from its own domain and from trusted domains.

Local groups provide a way to create handy sets of users from both inside and outside the domain, to be used only at domain controllers of the domain. *See also* global group; group; trust relationship.

local guest logon Takes effect when a user logs on interactively at a computer running Window NT Workstation or at a member server running Windows NT Server, and specifies Guest as the user name in the **Logon Information** dialog box. *See also* interactive logon.

Local Mail Delivery Agent The component of the SMTP server that processes messages that have been received by the SMTP server and downloads the messages to the user's local computer.

local printer A printer that is directly connected to one of the ports on your computer. *See also* port.

LocalTalk The name given by Apple Computer to the Apple networking hardware built into every Macintosh. LocalTalk includes the cables and connector boxes that connect components and network devices that are part of the AppleTalk network system. LocalTalk was formerly known as the AppleTalk Personal Network.

local user profiles User profiles that are created automatically on the computer at logon the first time a user logs on to a computer running Windows NT Workstation or Windows NT Server.

lock A method used to manage certain features of subdirectory replication by the export server. You can lock a subdirectory to prevent it from being exported to any import computers, or use locks to prevent imports to subdirectories on an import computer. *See also* directory replication; export server; import computers; subtree.

log books Kept by the system administrator to record the backup methods, dates, and contents of each tape in a backup set. *See also* backup set; backup types.

log files Created by Windows NT Backup and contain a record of the date the tapes were created and the names of files and directories successfully backed up and restored. Performance Monitor also creates log files.

logical drive A subpartition of an extended partition on a hard disk. *See also* extended partition.

Logical Unit (LU) A preset unit containing all the configuration information needed for a user or a program to establish a session with a host or peer computer. *See also* host; peer.

log off To stop using the network and remove your user name from active use until you log on again.

log on To provide a user name and password that identifies you to the network.

logon hours For Windows NT Server, a definition of the days and hours during which a user account can connect to a server. When a user is connected to a server and the logon hours are exceeded, the user will either be disconnected from all server connections or allowed to remain connected but denied any new connections.

logon script A file that can be assigned to user accounts. Typically a batch program, a logon script runs automatically every time the user logs on. It can be used to configure a user's working environment at every logon, and it allows an administrator to affect a user's environment without managing all aspects of it. A logon script can be assigned to one or more user accounts. *See also* batch program.

logon script path When a user logs on, the computer authenticating the logon locates the specified logon script (if one has been assigned to that user account) by following that computer's local logon script path (usually C:\Winnt\System32\Repl\Imports\Scripts). *See also* authentication; logon script.

logon workstations In Windows NT Server, the computers from which a user is allowed to log on.

long name A folder name or filename longer than the 8.3 filename standard (up to eight characters followed by a period and a three-character extension) of the FAT file system. Windows NT Server automatically translates long names of files and folders to 8.3 names for MS-DOS users.

Macintosh users can assign long names to files and folders on the server, and by using Services for Macintosh, you can assign long names to Macintosh-accessible volumes when you create them. *See also* file allocation table (FAT); filename; name mapping; short name.

loopback address The IP address 127.0.0.1, which has been specified by the Internet Engineering Task Force as the IP address to use in conjunction with a loopback driver to route outgoing packets back to the source computer. *See also* loopback driver.

loopback driver A network driver that allows the packets to bypass the network adapter completely and be returned directly to the computer that is performing the test. *See also* loopback address.

LPD *See* line printer daemon.

LPR Acronym for line printer remote. *See also* line printer daemon.

LU *See* Logical Unit.

luminosity The brightness of a color on a scale from black to white on your monitor.

M

MAC *See* media access control.

MAC address A unique 48-bit number assigned to the network adapter by the manufacturer. MAC addresses (which are physical addresses) are used for mapping in TCP/IP network communication. *See also* Address Resolution Protocol (ARP); ARP request packet; media access control (MAC).

MacFile *See* File Server for Macintosh service.

MacFile menu The menu that appears in Windows NT Server when Services for Macintosh is set up. You can create Macintosh-accessible volumes, and set permissions and other options by using commands on this menu.

Macintosh-accessible volume Storage space on the server used for folders and files of Macintosh users. A Macintosh-accessible volume is equivalent to a shared directory for PC users. Each Macintosh-accessible volume on a computer running Windows NT Server will correspond to a directory. Both PC users and Macintosh users can be given access to files located in a directory that is designated as both a shared directory and a Macintosh-accessible volume.

Macintosh-style permissions Directory and volume permissions that are similar to the access privileges used on a Macintosh.

MacPrint *See* Print Server for Macintosh.

Mac volume *See* Macintosh-accessible volume.

Mail Server (MailSrv) The MailSrv utility no longer ships with the *Windows NT Server Resource Kit*.

Make Changes The Macintosh-style permission that gives users the right to make changes to a folder's contents; for example, modifying, renaming, moving, creating, and deleting files. When Services for Macintosh translates access privileges into Windows NT Server permissions, a user who has the Make Changes privilege is given Write and Delete permissions.

management information base (MIB)
A set of objects that represent various types of information about a device, used by SNMP to manage devices. Because different network-management services are used for different types of devices or protocols, each service has its own set of objects. The entire set of objects that any service or protocol uses is referred to as its MIB. *See also* Simple Network Management Protocol (SNMP).

mandatory user profile A profile that is downloaded to the user's desktop each time he or she logs on. A mandatory user profile is created by an administrator and assigned to one or more users to create consistent or job-specific user profiles. They cannot be changed by the user and remain the same from one logon session to the next. *See also* roaming user profile; user profile.

mapping In TCP/IP, refers to the relationship between a host or computer name and an IP address, used by DNS and NetBIOS servers on TCP/IP networks.

In Windows NT Explorer, refers to mapping a driver letter to a network drive.

In Windows NT License Manager, refers to the relationship between users and computers in license groups. *See also* Domain Name System (DNS); IP address; license group.

mapping file A file defining exactly which users and groups are to be migrated from NetWare to Windows NT Server, and what new user names and passwords are to be assigned to the migrated users.

Master Boot Record The most important area on a hard disk, the data structure that starts the process of booting the computer.

The Master Boot Record contains the partition table for the disk and a small amount of executable code. On *x*86-based computers, the executable code examines the partition table and identifies the system (or bootable) partition, finds the system partition's starting location on the disk, and loads an image of its Partition Boot Sector into memory. The Master Boot Record then transfers execution to the Partition Boot Sector. *See also* Partition Table.

master browser A kind of network name server which keeps a browse list of all the servers and domains on the network. Also referred to as browse master. *See also* browse; Windows NT browser system.

master domain In the master domain model, the domain that is trusted by all other domains on the network and acts as the central administrative unit for user and group accounts.

maximize To enlarge a window to its maximum size by using the **Maximize** button (at the right of the title bar) or the **Maximize** command on the window menu.

Maximize button The small button containing a window icon at the right of the title bar. Mouse users can click the **Maximize** button to enlarge a window to its maximum size. Keyboard users can use the **Maximize** command on the window menu.

maximum password age The period of time a password can be used before the system requires the user to change it. *See also* account policy.

MCI *See* Media Control Interface.

media access control (MAC) A layer in the network architecture that deals with network access and collision detection.

media access control (MAC) driver
See network card driver.

Media Control Interface (MCI) A standard control interface for multimedia devices and files. Using MCI, a multimedia application can control a variety of multimedia devices and files.

member server A computer that runs Windows NT Server but is not a primary domain controller (PDC) or backup domain controller (BDC) of a Windows NT domain. Member servers do not receive copies of the directory database. Also called a stand-alone server. *See also* backup domain controller (BDC); directory database; primary domain controller (PDC).

memory A temporary storage area for information and applications. *See also* expanded memory; extended memory.

menu A list of available commands in an application window. Menu names appear in the menu bar near the top of the window. The window menu, represented by the program icon at the left end of the title bar, is common to all applications for Windows NT. To open a menu, click the menu name.

menu bar The horizontal bar containing the names of all the application's menus. It appears below the title bar.

Messenger service Sends and receives messages sent by administrators or by the Alerter service. *See also* Alerter service.

MIB *See* management information base.

Microsoft dbWeb A database publishing gateway provided in the *Windows NT Server Resource Kit*. dbWeb can run under Internet Information Server to provide public access to private enterprise ODBC sources as specified by an administrator of the private enterprise.

MIDI *See* Musical Instrument Digital Interface.

MIDI setup Specifies the type of MIDI device you are using, the channel and patch settings needed to play MIDI files, and the port your device is using. *See also* Musical Instrument Digital Interface (MIDI).

Migration Tool for NetWare Included with Windows NT, it enables you to easily transfer user and group accounts, volumes, folders, and files from a NetWare server to a computer running Windows NT Server.

MIME
See Multipurpose Internet Mail Extensions.

minimize
To reduce a window to a button on the taskbar by using the **Minimize** button (at the right of the title bar) or the **Minimize** command on the **Control** menu. *See also* maximize.

Minimize button The small button containing a short line at the right of the title bar. Mouse users can click the **Minimize** button to reduce a window to a button on the taskbar. Keyboard users can use the **Minimize** command on the **Control** menu.

minimum password age The period of time a password must be used before the user can change it. *See also* account policy.

minimum password length The fewest characters a password can contain. *See also* account policy.

mirror set A fully redundant or shadow copy of data. Mirror sets provide an identical twin for a selected disk; all data written to the primary disk is also written to the shadow or mirror disk. This enables you to have instant access to another disk with a redundant copy of the information on a failed disk. Mirror sets provide fault tolerance. *See also* fault tolerance.

m-node A NetBIOS implementation that uses the b-node protocol first, then the p-node protocol if the broadcast fails to resolve a name to an IP address. *See also* IP address; network basic input/output system (NetBIOS); p-node.

modem Short for modulator/demodulator, a communications device that enables a computer to transmit information over a standard telephone line.

MPR *See* MultiProtocol Routing.

MS-DOS–based application An application that is designed to run with MS-DOS, and therefore may not be able to take full advantage of all Windows NT features.

multicast datagram IP multicasting is the transmission of an IP datagram to a host group (a set of zero or more hosts identified by a single IP destination address.) An IP datagram sent to one host is called a unicast datagram. An IP datagram sent to all hosts is called a broadcast datagram. *See also* broadcast datagram; host; IP address.

multihomed computer A system that has multiple network adapters, or that has been configured with multiple IP addresses for a single network adapter. *See also* IP address; network adapter.

multihomed system A system with multiple network adapters attached to separate physical networks.

multilink dialing Multilink combines multiple physical links into a logical "bundle." This aggregate link increases your bandwidth. *See also* bandwidth.

multiple boot A computer that runs two or more operating systems. For example, Windows 95, MS-DOS, and Windows NT operating systems can be installed on the same computer. When the computer is started, any one of the operating systems can be selected. Also known as dual boot.

multiport serial adapter A communications device that enables a computer to simultaneously transmit information over standard telephone lines to multiple computers. Similar to multiple modems contained in one device. *See also* modem.

MultiProtocol Routing (MPR) Enables routing over IP and IPX networks by connecting LANs or by connecting LANs to WANs. *See also* IPX/SPX; local area network (LAN); wide area network (WAN).

Multipurpose Internet Mail Extensions (MIME) A standard mechanism for specifying and describing the format of Internet message bodies. MIME enables the exchanging of objects, different character sets, and multimedia in e-mail on different computer systems. Defined in RFC 1521.

Musical Instrument Digital Interface (MIDI) An interface that enables several devices, instruments, or computers to send and receive messages for the purpose of creating music, sound, or lighting.

N

named pipe An interprocess communication mechanism that allows one process to communicate with another local or remote process.

name mapping Is provided by Windows NT Server and Windows NT Workstation to ensure access by MS-DOS users to NTFS and FAT volumes (which can have share names of up to 255 characters, as opposed to MS-DOS, which is restricted to eight characters followed by a period and a three-character extension). With name mapping, each file or directory with a name that does not conform to the MS-DOS 8.3 standard is automatically given a second name that does. MS-DOS users connecting the file or directory over the network see the name in the 8.3 format; Windows NT Workstation and Windows NT Server users see the long name. *See also* Domain Name System (DNS); long name; Windows Internet Name Service (WINS).

name resolution service TCP/IP internetworks require a name resolution service to convert computer names to IP addresses and IP addresses to computer names. (People use "friendly" names to connect to computers; programs use IP addresses.) *See also* IP address; Transmission Control Protocol/Internet Protocol (TCP/IP).

NDIS *See* network device interface specification.

NDS *See* NetWare Directory Services.

NetBEUI A network protocol usually used in small, department-size local area networks of 1 through 200 clients. It can use Token Ring source routing as its only method of routing. *See also* router; Token Ring.

NetBIOS *See* network basic input/output system.

NetBT Short for NetBIOS over TCP/IP. The session-layer network service that performs name-to-IP address mapping for name resolution. *See also* IP address; name resolution service; network basic input/output system (NetBIOS); Transmission Control Protocol/Internet Protocol (TCP/IP).

Net Logon service For Windows NT Server, performs authentication of domain logons, and keeps the domain's directory database synchronized between the primary domain controller (PDC) and the other backup domain controllers (BDCs) of the domain. *See also* backup domain controller (BDC); directory database; primary domain controller (PDC).

NetWare Directory Services (NDS)
A NetWare service that runs on NetWare servers. The service enables the location of resources on the network.

network adapter An expansion card or other device used to connect a computer to a local area network (LAN). Also called a network card; network adapter card; adapter card; network interface card (NIC).

network adapter card *See* network adapter.

network administrator A person responsible for planning, configuring, and managing the day-to-day operation of the network. This person may also be referred to as a system administrator.

network basic input/output system (NetBIOS)
An application programming interface (API) that can be used by applications on a local area network. NetBIOS provides applications with a uniform set of commands for requesting the lower-level services required to conduct sessions between nodes on a network and to transmit information back and forth. *See also* application programming interface (API).

network card *See* network adapter.

network card driver A network device driver that works directly with the network card, acting as an intermediary between the card and the protocol driver. With Services for Macintosh, the AppleTalk Protocol stack on the server is implemented as a protocol driver and is bound to one or more network drivers.

Network DDE DSDM service The Network DDE DSDM (DDE share database manager) service manages shared DDE conversations. It is used by the Network DDE service. *See also* dynamic data exchange (DDE).

Network DDE service The Network DDE (dynamic data exchange) service provides a network transport and security for DDE conversations. *See also* dynamic data exchange (DDE).

network device driver Software that coordinates communication between the network adapter and the computer's hardware and other software, controlling the physical function of the network adapters.

network device interface specification (NDIS)

In Windows networking, the Microsoft/3Com specification for the interface of network device drivers. All transport drivers call the NDIS interface to access network cards. With Services for Macintosh, the AppleTalk Protocol stack on the server is implemented as an NDIS-compliant protocol and is bound to an NDIS network driver. All network drivers and protocol drivers shipped with Windows NT Workstation and Windows NT Server conform to NDIS.

network directory *See* shared directory.

network driver *See* network device driver.

network driver interface specification

See network device interface specification (NDIS).

Network File System (NFS) A service for

distributed computing systems that provides a distributed file system, eliminating the need for keeping multiple copies of files on separate computers.

network ID The portion of the IP address that

identifies a group of computers and devices located on the same logical network.

Network Information Service (NIS)

A service for distributed computing systems that provides a distributed database system for common configuration files.

network interface card (NIC) *See* network adapter.

Network News Transfer Protocol (NNTP)

The protocol used to distribute network news messages to NNTP servers and to NNTP clients (news readers) on the Internet. NNTP provides for the distribution, inquiry, retrieval, and posting of news articles by using a reliable stream-based transmission of news on the Internet. NNTP is designed so that news articles are stored on a server in a central database, thus enabling a user to select specific items to read. Indexing, cross-referencing, and expiration of aged messages are also provided. Defined in RFC 977.

network number In the Macintosh environment,

the network number (also referred to as the network range) is the address or range of addresses assigned to the network, which is used by AppleTalk routers to route information to the appropriate network. Each physical network can have a range of network numbers.

network protocol Software that enables

computers to communicate over a network. TCP/IP is a network protocol, used on the Internet. *See also* Transmission Control Protocol/Internet Protocol (TCP/IP).

network range In the Macintosh environment, a

range of network numbers (routing addresses) associated with a physical network in Phase 2. Apple manuals sometimes refer to a network range as a cable range. *See also* network number; routing.

network sniffer A hardware and software

diagnostic tool that can also be used to decipher passwords, which may result in unauthorized access to network accounts. Clear-text passwords are susceptible to network sniffers.

NFS *See* Network File System.

NIC Acronym for network interface card. *See* network adapter.

NIS *See* Network Information Service.

NNTP *See* Network News Transfer Protocol.

node In the PC environment, a node is any device that is attached to the internetwork and uses TCP/IP. (A node can also be referred to as a host.) In the Macintosh environment, a node is an addressable entity on a network. Each Macintosh client is a node.

nonpaged memory Memory that cannot be paged to disk. *See also* memory; paging file.

non–Windows NT application Refers to an application that is designed to run with Windows 3.x, MS-DOS, OS/2, or POSIX, but not specifically with Windows NT, and that may not be able to take full advantage of all Windows NT features (such as memory management). *See also* POSIX.

NT *See* Windows NT Server; Windows NT Workstation.

NT file system *See* Windows NT file system.

NTFS *See* Windows NT file system.

NWLink IPX\SPX Compatible Transport A standard network protocol that supports routing, and can support NetWare client/server applications, where NetWare-aware Sockets-based applications communicate with IPX\SPX Sockets-based applications. *See also* IPX/SPX; Sockets.

O

object Any piece of information, created by using a Windows-based application, that can be linked or embedded into another document. *See also* embedded object; linked object.

object-cache scavenger A component of the IIS process that periodically flushes from the cache objects that have changed or that have not been referenced in its last timed interval. The default time interval for the object-cache scavenger is 30 seconds.

octet In programming, an octet refers to eight bits or one byte. IP addresses, for example, are typically represented in dotted-decimal notation, that is, with the decimal value of each octet of the address separated by a period. *See also* IP address.

ODBC *See* Open Database Connectivity.

offset When specifying a filter in Windows NT Network Monitor based on a pattern match (which limits the capture to only those frames containing a specific pattern of ASCII or hexadecimal data), you must specify where the pattern occurs in the frame. This number of bytes (from the beginning or end of the frame) is known as an offset. *See also* frame; hexadecimal.

OLE A way to transfer and share information between applications. *See also* ActiveX; embedded object; linked object.

one-way trust relationship One domain (the trusting domain) "trusts" the domain controllers in the other domain (the trusted domain) to authenticate user accounts from the trusted domain to use resources in the trusting domain. *See also* trust relationship; user account.

opcode Operation code; a code, usually a number, that specifies an operation to be performed. An opcode is often the first component in a contiguous block of data; it indicates how other data in the block should be interpreted.

open To display the contents of a directory, a document, or a data file in a window.

Open Database Connectivity (ODBC)
ODBC is an application programming interface that enables applications to access data from a variety of existing data sources.

Open Systems Interconnection model (OSI)
TCP/IP protocols map to a four-layered conceptual model consisting of Application, Transport, Internet, and Network Interface. Each layer in this TCP/IP model corresponds to one or more layers of the International Standards Organization (ISO) seven-layer OSI model consisting of Application, Presentation, Session, Transport, Network, Data-link, and Physical. *See also* ISO.

orphan A member of a mirror set or a stripe set with parity that has failed in a severe manner, such as in a loss of power or a complete head crash. When this happens, the fault-tolerance driver determines that it can no longer use the orphaned member and directs all new reads and writes to the remaining members of the fault-tolerance volume. *See also* fault tolerance; mirror set; stripe sets with parity.

orphaned member *See* orphan.

OSI *See* Open Systems Interconnection model.

owner In Windows NT, every file and directory on an NTFS volume has an owner, who controls how permissions are set on the file or directory and who can grant permissions to others.

In the Macintosh environment, an owner is the user responsible for setting permissions for a folder on a server. A Macintosh user who creates a folder on the server automatically becomes the owner of the folder. The owner can transfer ownership to someone else. Each Macintosh-accessible volume on the server also has an owner.

owner category In the Macintosh environment, this refers to the user category to which you assign permissions for the owner of a folder or a Macintosh volume. *See also* Macintosh-accessible volume.

P

package An icon that represents an embedded or linked object. When you choose the package, the application used to create the object either plays the object (for example, a sound file) or opens and displays the object. *See also* embedded object; linked object.

packet A transmission unit of fixed maximum size that consists of binary information representing both data and a header containing an ID number, source and destination addresses, and error-control data.

packet assembler/disassembler (PAD)
A connection used in X.25 networks. X.25 PAD boards can be used in place of modems when provided with a compatible COM driver. *See also* X.25.

packet header The part of a packet that contains an identification number, source and destination addresses, and—sometimes—error-control data. *See also* packet.

PAD *See* packet assembler/disassembler.

page fault In the processor, a page fault occurs when a process refers to a virtual memory page that is not in its working set in main memory.

A *hard page fault* occurs when data that a program needs is not found in its working set (the physical memory visible to the program) or elsewhere in physical memory, and must be retrieved from disk.

A page fault will not cause the page to be fetched from disk if that page is on the standby list, and hence already in main memory, or if it is in use by another process with which the page is shared. In this case, a *soft page fault* occurs.

paging file A special file on a PC hard disk. With virtual memory under Windows NT, some of the program code and other information is kept in RAM while other information is temporarily swapped into virtual memory. When that information is required again, Windows NT pulls it back into RAM and, if necessary, swaps other information to virtual memory. Also called a swap file.

PAP *See* Password Authentication Protocol.

parity Redundant information that is associated with a block of information. In Windows NT Server, stripe sets with parity means that there is one additional parity stripe per row. Therefore, you must use at least three, rather than two, disks to allow for this extra parity information. Parity stripes contain the XOR (the Boolean operation called exclusive OR) of the data in that stripe. Windows NT Server, when regenerating a failed disk, uses the parity information in those stripes in conjunction with the data on the good disks to recreate the data on the failed disk. *See also* fault tolerance; stripe set; stripe sets with parity.

partial synchronization The automatic, timed delivery to all domain BDCs (backup domain controllers) of only those directory database changes that have occurred since the last synchronization. *See also* backup domain controller (BDC); synchronize.

partition A partition is a portion of a physical disk that functions as though it were a physically separate unit. *See also* extended partition; system partition.

Partition Table An area of the Master Boot Record that the computer uses to determine how to access the disk. The Partition Table can contain up to four partitions for each physical disk. *See also* Master Boot Record.

pass-through authentication When the user account must be authenticated, but the computer being used for the logon is not a domain controller in the domain where the user account is defined, nor is it the computer where the user account is defined, the computer passes the logon information through to a domain controller (directly or indirectly) where the user account is defined. *See also* domain controller; user account.

password A security measure used to restrict logons to user accounts and access to computer systems and resources. A password is a unique string of characters that must be provided before a logon or an access is authorized. For Windows NT, a password for a user account can be up to 14 characters, and is case-sensitive. There are four user-defined parameters to be entered in the **Account Policy** dialog box in User Manager or User Manager for Domains: maximum password age, minimum password age, minimum password length, and password uniqueness.

With Services for Macintosh, each Macintosh user must type a user password when accessing the Windows NT Server. You can also assign each Macintosh-accessible volume a volume password if you want, which all users must type to access the volume. *See also* account policy.

Password Authentication Protocol (PAP)
A type of authentication that uses clear-text passwords and is the least sophisticated authentication protocol.

password uniqueness The number of new passwords that must be used by a user account before an old password can be reused. *See also* account policy; password.

patch map The part of a channel-map entry that translates instrument sounds, volume settings, and (optionally) key values for a channel.

path A sequence of directory (or folder) names that specifies the location of a directory, file, or folder within the directory tree. Each directory name and filename within the path (except the first) must be preceded by a backslash (\). For example, to specify the path of a file named Readme.wri located in the Windows directory on drive C, you type c:\windows\readme.wri.

PC Any personal computer (such as an IBM PC or compatible) using the MS-DOS, OS/2, Windows, Windows for Workgroups, Windows 95, Windows NT Workstation, or Windows NT Server operating systems.

PCMCIA *See* Personal Computer Memory Card International Association.

peer Any of the devices on a layered communications network that operate on the same protocol level.

Peer Web Services A collection of services that enable the user of a computer running Windows NT Workstation to publish a personal Web site from the desktop. The services include the WWW service, the FTP service, and the Gopher service.

pel Also known as a pixel, which is short for picture element, the smallest graphic unit that can be displayed on the screen.

Perl Practical Extraction and Report Language. A scripting (programming) language that is frequently used for CGI scripts.

permissions Windows NT Server settings you set on a shared resource that determine which users can use the resource and how they can use it. *See also* access permission.

Services for Macintosh automatically translates between permissions and Macintosh access privileges, so that permissions set on a directory (volume) are enforced for Macintosh users, and access privileges set by Macintosh users are enforced for PC users connected to the computer running Windows NT Server.

Personal Computer Memory Card International Association (PCMCIA)
A standard for removable peripheral devices (called PC cards) about the size of a credit card, which plug into a special 68-pin connector found most commonly in portable computers. Currently available PCMCIA cards include memory, hard disk, modem, fax, network, and wireless communication devices.

personal group In the **Start** menu on the **Programs** list, a program group you have created that contains program items. Personal groups are stored with your logon information and each time you log on, your personal groups appear. *See also* group.

Physical Unit (PU) A network-addressable unit that provides the services needed to use and manage a particular device, such as a communications link device. A PU is implemented with a combination of hardware, software, and microcode.

PIF *See* program information file.

ping A command used to verify connections to one or more remote hosts. The **ping** utility uses the ICMP echo request and echo reply packets to determine whether a particular IP system on a network is functional. The ping utility is useful for diagnosing IP network or router failures. *See also* Internet Control Message Protocol (ICMP); router.

pipe An interprocess communication mechanism. Writing to and reading from a pipe is much like writing to and reading from a file, except that the two processes are actually using a shared memory segment to communicate data. *See also* named pipe.

pixel *See* pel.

plotter font *See* font types.

p-node A NetBIOS implementation that uses point-to-point communications with a name server to resolve names as IP addresses. *See also* h-node; IP address; network basic input/output system (NetBIOS).

pointer The arrow-shaped cursor on the screen that follows the movement of a mouse (or other pointing device) and indicates which area of the screen will be affected when you press the mouse button. The pointer changes shape during certain tasks.

Point-to-Point Protocol (PPP) A set of industry-standard framing and authentication protocols that is part of Windows NT RAS to ensure interoperability with third-party remote access software. PPP negotiates configuration parameters for multiple layers of the OSI model. *See also* Open Systems Interconnection model (OSI).

Point-to-Point Tunneling Protocol (PPTP)
PPTP is a new networking technology that supports multiprotocol virtual private networks (VPNs), enabling remote users to access corporate networks securely across the Internet by dialing into an Internet service provider (ISP) or by connecting directly to the Internet. *See also* virtual private network (VPN).

POP *See* Post Office Protocol.

pop-up menu *See* window menu.

port A location used to pass data in and out of a computing device. This term can refer to an adapter card connecting a server to a network, a serial 232 port, a TCP/IP port, or a printer port.

port ID The method TCP and UDP use to specify which application running on the system is sending or receiving the data. *See also* Transmission Control Protocol (TCP); User Datagram Protocol (UDP).

POSIX Acronym for Portable Operating System Interface, an IEEE (Institute of Electrical and Electronics Engineers) standard that defines a set of operating-system services. Programs that adhere to the POSIX standard can be easily ported from one system to another.

Post Office Protocol (POP) The Post Office Protocol version 3 (POP3) is a protocol that permits a workstation to dynamically access a mail drop on a server in a useful fashion. Usually, this means that a POP3 server is used to allow a workstation to retrieve mail that an SMTP server is holding for it. POP3 is specified in RFC 1725.

PostScript printer A printer that uses the PostScript page description language to create text and graphics on the output medium, such as paper or overhead transparency. Examples of PostScript printers include the Apple LaserWriter, the NEC LC-890, and the QMS PS-810. *See also* font types.

POTS Acronym for plain-old telephone service. Also an acronym for point of termination station, which refers to where a telephone call terminates.

power conditioning A feature of an uninterruptible power supply (UPS) that removes spikes, surges, sags, and noise from the power supply. *See also* uninterruptible power supply (UPS).

PPP *See* Point-to-Point Protocol.

PPTP *See* Point-to-Point Tunneling Protocol.

predefined key The key represented by a Registry window, the name of which appears in the window's title bar. *See also* key; Registry.

primary domain controller (PDC) In a Windows NT Server domain, the computer running Windows NT Server that authenticates domain logons and maintains the directory database for a domain. The PDC tracks changes made to accounts of all computers on a domain. It is the only computer to receive these changes directly. A domain has only one PDC. *See also* directory database.

primary group The group with which a Macintosh user usually shares documents stored on a server. You specify a user's primary group in the user's account. When a user creates a folder on the server, the user's primary group is set as the folder's associated group (by default).

primary partition A partition is a portion of a physical disk that can be marked for use by an operating system. There can be up to four primary partitions (or up to three, if there is an extended partition) per physical disk. A primary partition cannot be subpartitioned. *See also* extended partition; partition.

print device Refers to the actual hardware device that produces printed output.

printer Refers to the software interface between the operating system and the print device. The printer defines where the document will go before it reaches the print device (to a local port, to a file, or to a remote print share), when it will go, and various other aspects of the printing process.

printer driver A program that converts graphics commands into a specific printer language, such as PostScript or PCL. *See also* font types.

printer fonts Fonts that are built into your printer. These fonts are usually located in the printer's read-only memory (ROM). *See also* font; font types.

printer permissions Specify the type of access a user or group has to use the printer. The printer permissions are No Access, Print, Manage Documents, and Full Control.

printer window Shows information for one of the printers that you have installed or to which you are connected. For each printer, you can see what documents are waiting to be printed, who owns them, how large they are, and other information.

printing pool Consists of two or more identical print devices associated with one printer.

print job In the Macintosh environment, a document or image sent from a client to a printer.

print processor A PostScript program that understands the format of a document's image file and how to print the file to a specific printer or class of printers. *See also* encapsulated PostScript (EPS) file.

print server Refers to the computer that receives documents from clients.

Print Server for Macintosh A Services for Macintosh service that enables Macintosh clients to send documents to printers attached to a computer running Windows NT; enables PC clients to send documents to printers anywhere on the AppleTalk network; and enables Macintosh users to spool their documents to the computer running Windows NT Server, thus freeing their clients to do other tasks. Also called MacPrint.

print sharing The ability for a computer running Windows NT Workstation or Windows NT Server to share a printer on the network. This is done by using the **Printers** folder or the **net share** command.

print spooler A collection of dynamic-link libraries (DLLs) that receive, process, schedule, and distribute documents.

private volume A Macintosh-accessible volume that is accessible by only one Macintosh user. For a volume to be a private volume, the permissions on its root directory must give the volume's owner all three permissions (Make Changes, See Files, and See Folders), while giving the primary group and everyone categories no permissions at all. When a private volume's owner uses the Chooser to view the volumes available on the server, the private volume is listed; however, no other users can see the private volume when viewing the volumes available on the server. *See also* Macintosh-accessible volume.

privilege level One of three settings (User, Administrator, or Guest) assigned to each user account. The privilege level a user account has determines the actions that the user can perform on the network. *See also* Administrator privilege; Guest privilege; user account; User privilege.

process When a program runs, a Windows NT process is created. A process is an object type which consists of an executable program, a set of virtual memory addresses, and one or more threads.

processor affinity mask A Windows NT bit mask that associates processors with network adapters. All deferred procedure calls (DPCs) originating from the network adapter are handled by its associated processor.

program file A file that starts an application or program. A program file has an .exe, .pif, .com, or .bat filename extension.

program group On the **Start** menu, a collection of applications. Grouping your applications makes them easier to find when you want to start them. *See also* common group; personal group.

program icon Located at the left of the window title bar, the program icon represents the program being run. Clicking the program icon opens the window menu.

program information file (PIF) A PIF provides information to Windows NT about how best to run MS-DOS–based applications. When you start an MS-DOS–based application, Windows NT looks for a PIF to use with the application. PIFs contain such items as the name of the file, a start-up directory, and multitasking options.

program item An application, accessory, or document represented as an icon in the **Start** menu or on the desktop.

promiscuous mode A state of a network card in which it passes on to the networking software all the frames that it detects on the network, regardless of the frames' destination address. *See also* frame; network adapter.

propagate Copy. For example, NetWare user accounts are propagated to the Windows NT primary domain controller when using Directory Service Manager for NetWare (DSMN).

property In Windows NT Network Monitor, a property refers to a field within a protocol header. A protocol's properties, collectively, indicate the purpose of the protocol.

protocol A set of rules and conventions for sending information over a network. These rules govern the content, format, timing, sequencing, and error control of messages exchanged among network devices.

protocol driver A network device driver that implements a protocol, communicating between Windows NT Server and one or more network adapter card drivers. With Services for Macintosh, the AppleTalk Protocol stack is implemented as an NDIS-protocol driver, and is bound to one or more network adapter card drivers.

protocol parser A dynamic-link library (DLL) that identifies the protocols used to send a frame onto the network. *See also* dynamic-link library (DLL); frame.

protocol properties Refers to the elements of information that define a protocol's purpose. Because the purposes of protocols vary, properties differ from one protocol to another.

protocol stack The implementation of a specific protocol family in a computer or other node on the network.

proxy A computer that listens to name query broadcasts and responds for those names not on the local subnet. The proxy communicates with the name server to resolve names and then caches them for a time period. *See also* caching; Domain Name System (DNS); subnet.

PSTN Acronym for public switched telephone network.

PU *See* Physical Unit.

public key cryptography A method of encrypting data transmissions to and from a server.

pull partner A WINS server that pulls in replicas from its push partner by requesting it and then accepting the pushed replicas. *See also* Windows Internet Name Service (WINS).

push partner A WINS server that sends replicas to its pull partner upon receiving a request from it. *See also* Windows Internet Name Service (WINS).

Q

queue In Windows NT terminology, a queue refers to a group of documents waiting to be printed. (In NetWare and OS/2 environments, queues are the primary software interface between the application and print device; users submit documents to a queue. However, with Windows NT, the printer is that interface—the document is sent to a printer, not a queue.)

quick format Deletes the file allocation table (FAT) and root directory of a disk but does not scan the disk for bad areas. This function is available in Disk Administrator or when checking disks for errors. *See also* file allocation table (FAT); root directory.

R

RAID Acronym for Redundant Array of Inexpensive Disks. A method used to standardize and categorize fault-tolerant disk systems. Six levels gauge various mixes of performance, reliability, and cost. Windows NT includes three of the RAID levels: Level 0, Level 1, and Level 5.

RAM An acronym for random-access memory. RAM can be read from or written to by the computer or other devices. Information stored in RAM is lost when you turn off the computer. *See also* memory.

RAS *See* Remote Access Service.

recursion One of the three key concepts in DNS name resolution. A resolver typically passes a recursive resolution request to its local name server, which tells the name server that the resolver expects a complete answer to the query, not just a pointer to another name server. Recursive resolution effectively puts the workload onto the name server and allows the resolver to be small and simple. *See also* Domain Name System (DNS); iteration.

reduce To minimize a window to an icon by using the **Minimize** button or the **Minimize** command. A minimized application continues running, and you can click the icon on the toolbar to make it the active application.

reduced instruction set computing (RISC)
A type of microprocessor design that focuses on rapid and efficient processing of a relatively small set of instructions. RISC architecture limits the number of instructions that are built into the microprocessor, but optimizes each so that it can be carried out very rapidly—usually within a single clock cycle.

refresh To update displayed information with current data.

registration In Windows NT NetBT name resolution, registration is the process used to register a unique name for each computer (node) on the network. A computer typically registers itself when it starts.

Registry The Windows NT Registry is a hierarchical database that provides a repository for information about a computer's configuration on Windows NT Workstation and about hardware and user accounts on Windows NT Server. It is organized in subtrees and their keys, hives, and value entries. *See also* hive; key; subtree; user account.

Registry size limit (RSL) The total amount of space that can be consumed by Registry data is restricted by the Registry size limit, which is a kind of universal maximum for Registry space that prevents an application from filling the paged pool with Registry data. *See also* hive; paging file.

Remote Access Service (RAS) A service that provides remote networking for telecommuters, mobile workers, and system administrators who monitor and manage servers at multiple branch offices. Users with RAS on a Windows NT–based computer can dial in to remotely access their networks for services such as file and printer sharing, electronic mail, scheduling, and SQL database access.

remote administration Administration of one computer by an administrator located at another computer and connected to the first computer across the network.

remote logon Occurs when a user is already logged on to a user account and makes a network connection to another computer. *See also* user account.

remote procedure call (RPC) A message-passing facility that allows a distributed application to call services available on various machines in a network. Used during remote administration of computers. *See also* remote administration.

Remote Procedure Call service *See* RPC service.

renew Client computers are periodically required to renew their NetBIOS name registrations with the WINS server. When a client computer first registers with a WINS server, the WINS server returns a message that indicates when the client will need to renew its registration. *See also* network basic input/output system (NetBIOS); Windows Internet Name Service (WINS).

repeaters The most basic LAN connection device, repeaters strengthen the physical transmission signal. A repeater simply takes the electrical signals that reach it and then regenerates them to full strength before passing them on. Repeaters generally extend a single network (rather than link two networks).

replication *See* directory replication.

replicators One of the Windows NT built-in local groups for workstations and member servers, used for directory replication functions. *See also* directory replication.

Requests for Comments (RFCs) The official documents of the IETF (Internet Engineering Task Force) that specify the details for protocols included in the TCP/IP family. *See also* Internet Engineering Task Force (IETF); Transmission Control Protocol/Internet Protocol (TCP/IP).

resolution In Windows NetBT name resolution, resolution is the process used to determine the specific address for a computer name.

resolvers DNS clients that query DNS servers for name resolution on networks. *See also* Domain Name System (DNS).

resource Any part of a computer system or a network, such as a disk drive, printer, or memory, that can be allotted to a program or a process while it is running, or shared over a local area network.

resource domain A trusting domain that establishes a one-way trust relationship with the master (account) domain, enabling users with accounts in the master domain to use resources in all the other domains. *See also* domain; trust relationship.

resource fork One of two forks that make up each Macintosh file. The resource fork holds Macintosh operating system resources, such as code, menu, font, and icon definitions. Resource forks have no relevance to PCs, so the resource forks of files on the server are never accessed by PC clients. *See also* data fork.

response In Windows NT RAS, responses are strings expected from the device, which can contain macros.

RFC *See* Requests for Comments.

right *See*; permissions; user rights.

RIP *See* routing information protocol.

RISC *See* reduced instruction set computing.

roaming user profile User profile that is enabled when an administrator enters a user profile path into the user account. The first time the user logs off, the local user profile is copied to that location. Thereafter, the server copy of the user profile is downloaded each time the user logs on (if it is more current than the local copy) and is updated each time the user logs off. *See also* user profile.

root directory The top-level directory on a computer, a partition, or Macintosh-accessible volume. *See also* directory tree.

router In the Windows NT environment, a router helps LANs and WANs achieve interoperability and connectivity and can link LANs that have different network topologies (such as Ethernet and Token Ring). Routers match packet headers to a LAN segment and choose the best path for the packet, optimizing network performance.

In the Macintosh environment, routers are necessary for computers on different physical networks to communicate with each other. Routers maintain a map of the physical networks on a Macintosh internet (network) and forward data received from one physical network to other physical networks. Computers running Windows NT Server with Services for Macintosh can act as routers, and you can also use third-party routing hardware on a network with Services for Macintosh. *See also* local area network (LAN); packet; wide area network (WAN).

routing The process of forwarding packets to other routers until the packet is eventually delivered to a router connected to the specified destination. *See also* packet; router.

routing information protocol (RIP)
Enables a router to exchange routing information with a neighboring router. *See also* routing.

routing table   Controls the routing decisions made by computers running TCP/IP. Routing tables are built automatically by Windows NT based on the IP configuration of your computer. *See also* dynamic routing; routing; static routing; Transmission Control Protocol/Internet Protocol (TCP/IP).

RPC   *See* remote procedure call.

RPC Locator service   The Remote Procedure Call Locator service allows distributed applications to use the RPC Name service. The RPC Locator service manages the RPC Name service database.

The server side of a distributed application registers its availability with the RPC Locator service. The client side of a distributed application queries the RPC Locator service to find available compatible server applications. *See also* remote procedure call (RPC).

RPC service   The Remote Procedure Call service is the RPC subsystem for Microsoft Windows NT. The RPC subsystem includes the endpoint mapper and other miscellaneous RPC services. *See also* remote procedure call (RPC).

RSL   *See* Registry size limit.

S

SACL   *See* system access control list.

SAM   Acronym for Security Accounts Manager. *See* directory database; Windows NT Server Directory Services.

SAP   In the Windows environment, SAP is an acronym for Service Advertising Protocol, a service that broadcasts shared files, directories, and printers categorized first by domain or workgroup and then by server name.

In the context of routing and IPX, SAP is also an acronym for Service Advertising Protocol, used by servers to advertise their services and addresses on a network. Clients use SAP to determine what network resources are available.

In NetBEUI, SAP is an acronym for Service Access Point, in which each link-layer program identifies itself by registering a unique service access point.

Not to be confused with SAP financial database application software for the mainframe computer.

saturation   The purity of a color's hue, moving from gray to the pure color.

scavenging   Cleaning up the WINS database. *See also* Windows Internet Name Service (WINS).

Schedule service   Supports and is required for use of the **at** command. The **at** command can schedule commands and programs to run on a computer at a specified time and date.

schemas   Schemas control how and what information from a private database is available to visitors who use the Internet to access the public Microsoft dbWeb gateway to the private database. *See also* dbWeb Administrator.

Schema Wizard   Interactive tool in dbWeb Administrator that leads a user through creation of HTML pages or through implementing an ISAPI application.

screen buffer   The size reserved in memory for the command prompt display.

screen dump   *See* snapshot.

screen elements The parts that make up a window or dialog box, such as the title bar, the **Minimize** and **Maximize** buttons, the window borders, and the scroll bars.

screen fonts Fonts displayed on your screen. Soft-font manufacturers often provide screen fonts that closely match the soft fonts for your printer. This ensures that your documents look the same on the screen as they do when printed. *See also* font; font types.

screen saver A moving picture or pattern that appears on your screen when you have not used the mouse or the keyboard for a specified period of time. To select a screen saver, either use Display in Control Panel or right-click on the desktop for properties.

scroll To move through text or graphics (up, down, left, or right) in order to see parts of the file that cannot fit on the screen.

scroll arrow An arrow on either end of a scroll bar that you use to scroll through the contents of the window or list box. Click the scroll arrow to scroll one screen at a time, or continue pressing the mouse button while pointing at the scroll arrow to scroll continuously.

scroll bar A bar that appears at the right and/or bottom edge of a window or list box whose contents are not completely visible. Each scroll bar contains two scroll arrows and a scroll box, which enable you to scroll through the contents of the window or list box.

scroll box In a scroll bar, a small box that shows the position of information currently visible in the window or list box relative to the contents of the entire window.

scroll buffer The area in memory that holds information that does not fit on the screen. You can use the scroll bars to scroll through the information.

SCSI *See* small computer system interface.

Search button *See* find tab.

section header In Windows NT RAS, a section header is a string, comprising up to 32 characters between square brackets, that identifies the specific device to which the section applies.

secure attention sequence A series of keystrokes (CTRL+ALT+DEL) that will always display the Windows NT operating system logon screen.

secure communications channel Created when computers at each end of a connection are satisfied that the computer on the other end has identified itself correctly by using its computer account. *See also* computer account.

Secure Sockets Layer (SSL) A protocol that supplies secure data communication through data encryption and decryption. SSL enables communications privacy over networks by using a combination of public key cryptography and bulk data encryption.

security A means of ensuring that shared files can be accessed only by authorized users.

Security Accounts Manager (SAM) *See* directory database; Windows NT Server Directory Services.

security database *See* directory database.

security host A third-party authentication device that verifies whether a caller from a remote client is authorized to connect to the Remote Access server. This verification supplements security already authorized to connect to the Remote-Access server.

security ID (SID) A unique name that identifies a logged-on user to the security system. Security IDs (SIDs) can identify one user or a group of users.

security identifier *See* security ID (SID).

security log Records security events. This helps track changes to the security system and identify any possible breaches of security. For example, depending on the Audit settings in User Manager or User Manager for Domains, attempts to log on to the local computer might be recorded in the security log. The security log contains both valid and invalid logon attempts as well as events related to resource use (such as creating, opening, or deleting files.) *See also* event.

security policies For Windows NT Workstation, the security policies consist of the Account, User Rights, and Audit policies, and are managed by using User Manager.

For a Windows NT Server domain, the security policies consist of the Account, User Rights, Audit, and Trust Relationships policies, and are managed by using User Manager for Domains.

security token *See* access token.

seed router In the Macintosh environment, a seed router initializes and broadcasts routing information about one or more physical networks. This information tells routers where to send each packet of data. A seed router on an AppleTalk network initially defines the network number(s) and zone(s) for a network. Services for Macintosh servers can function as seed routers, and you can also use third-party hardware routers as seed routers. *See also* packet; router.

See Files The Macintosh-style permission that give users the right to open a folder and see the files in the folder. For example, a folder that has See Files and See Folders Macintosh-style permissions is given the Windows NT-style R (Read) permission. *See also* permissions.

See Folders The Macintosh-style permission that gives users the right to open a folder and see the files contained in that folder. *See also* permissions.

select To mark an item so that a subsequent action can be carried out on that item. You usually select an item by clicking it with a mouse or pressing a key. After selecting an item, you choose the action that you want to affect the item.

selection cursor The marking device that shows where you are in a window, menu, or dialog box and what you have selected. The selection cursor can appear as a highlight or as a dotted rectangle around text.

semaphore Generally, semaphores are signaling devices or mechanisms. However, in Windows NT, system semaphores are objects used to synchronize activities on an interprocess level. For example, when two or more processes share a common resource such as a printer, video screen, or memory segment, semaphores are used to control access to those resources so that only one process can alter them at any particular time.

sequence number The identifier with which TCP marks packets before sending them. The sequence numbers allow the receiving system to properly order the packets on the receiving system. *See also* packet; Transmission Control Protocol (TCP).

Serial Line Internet Protocol (SLIP)
An older industry standard that is part of Windows NT RAS to ensure interoperability with third-party remote access software.

server In general, refers to a computer that provides shared resources to network users. *See also* member server.

server application A Windows NT application that can create objects for linking or embedding into other documents. For distributed applications, the application that responds to a client application. *See also* client application; DCOM Configuration tool; Distributed Component Object Model (DCOM); embedded object; linked object.

Server Manager   In Windows NT Server, an application used to view and administer domains, workgroups, and computers.

Server Message Block (SMB)   A file-sharing protocol designed to allow systems to transparently access files that reside on remote systems.

Server service   Provides RPC (remote procedure call) support, and file, print, and named pipe sharing. *See also* named pipe; remote procedure call (RPC).

server zone   The AppleTalk zone on which a server appears. On a Phase 2 network, a server appears in the default zone of the server's default network. *See also* default network; default zone; desired zone; zone.

service   A process that performs a specific system function and often provides an application programming interface (API) for other processes to call. Windows NT services are RPC-enabled, meaning that their API routines can be called from remote computers. *See also* application programming interface (API); remote procedure call (RPC).

Service Access Point (SAP)   *See* SAP.

Service Advertising Protocol (SAP) *See* SAP.

Services for Macintosh   *See* Windows NT Server Services for Macintosh.

session   A link between two network devices, such as a client and a server. A session between a client and server consists of one or more connections from the client to the server.

SFM   Acronym for Windows NT Services for Macintosh.

share   To make resources, such as directories and printers, available to others.

shared directory   A directory that network users can connect to.

shared network directory   *See* shared directory.

shared resource   Any device, data, or program that is used by more than one other device or program. For Windows NT, shared resources refer to any resource that is made available to network users, such as directories, files, printers, and named pipes. Also refers to a resource on a server that is available to network users. *See also* named pipe.

share name   A name that refers to a shared resource on a server. Each shared directory on a server has a share name, used by PC users to refer to the directory. Users of Macintosh use the name of the Macintosh-accessible volume that corresponds to a directory, which may be the same as the share name. *See also* Macintosh-accessible volume.

share permissions   Are used to restrict a shared resource's availability over the network to only certain users.

Shiva Password Authentication Protocol (SPAP) A two-way (reversible) encryption mechanism employed by Shiva. Windows NT Workstation, when connecting to a Shiva LAN Rover, uses SPAP, as does a Shiva client connecting to a Windows NT Server. *See also* encryption.

shortcut key   A key or key combination, available for some commands, that you can press to carry out a command without first selecting a menu. Shortcut keys are listed to the right of commands on a menu.

short name A valid 8.3 (up to eight characters followed by a period and a three-character extension) MS-DOS or OS/2 filename that the computer running Windows NT Server creates for every Macintosh folder name or filename on the server. PC users refer to files on the server by their short names; Macintosh users refer to them by their long names. *See also* long name; name mapping.

SID *See* security ID.

silent mode During IP routing in silent mode, the computer listens to RIP broadcasts and updates its route table but does not advertise its own routes. *See also* routing; routing information protocol (RIP); routing table.

simple device A device that you use without specifying a related media file. An audio compact-disc player is a simple device.

Simple Mail Transfer Protocol (SMTP) A member of the TCP/IP suite of protocols that governs the exchange of electronic mail between message transfer agents.

Simple Network Management Protocol (SNMP) A protocol used by SNMP consoles and agents to communicate. In Windows NT, the SNMP service is used to get and set status information about a host on a TCP/IP network. *See also* Transmission Control Protocol/Internet Protocol (TCP/IP).

single user logon Windows NT network users can connect to multiple servers, domains, and applications with a single network logon.

SLIP *See* Serial Line Internet Protocol.

small computer system interface (SCSI) A standard high-speed parallel interface defined by the American National Standards Institute (ANSI). A SCSI interface is used for connecting microcomputers to peripheral devices such as hard disks and printers, and to other computers and local area networks.

SMB *See* Server Message Block.

SMS *See* Systems Management Server.

SMTP *See* Simple Mail Transfer Protocol.

SNA *See* System Network Architecture.

snapshot A copy of main memory or video memory at a given instant, sent to a printer or hard disk. A graphical image of the video screen can be saved by taking a snapshot of video memory, more commonly called a screen dump.

sniffer *See* network sniffer.

Sniffer files Files saved from Network General Sniffer, a third-party protocol analyzer. *See also* network sniffer.

SNMP *See* Simple Network Management Protocol.

socket A bidirectional pipe for incoming and outgoing data between networked computers. The Windows Sockets API is a networking API used by programmers creating TCP/IP-based sockets applications. *See also* application programming interface (API); named pipe.

Sockets Windows Sockets is a Windows implementation of the widely used UC Berkeley sockets API. Microsoft TCP/IP, NWLink, and AppleTalk protocols use this interface. Sockets interfaces between programs and the transport protocol and works as a bidirectional pipe for incoming and outgoing data. *See also* application programming interface (API); named pipe; socket.

source directory The directory that contains the file or files you intend to copy or move.

source document The document where a linked or embedded object was originally created. *See also* embedded object; linked object.

SPAP *See* Shiva Password Authentication Protocol.

special access permission On NTFS volumes, a custom set of permissions. You can customize permissions on files and directories by selecting the individual components of the standard sets of permissions. *See also* access permission.

split bar Divides Windows NT Explorer into two parts: The directory tree is displayed on the left, and the contents of the current directory are on the right. *See also* directory tree.

spoofing Refers to a case where an Internet user mimics ("spoofs") the source IP address for an Internet server, proxy server, or firewall of a system to which it is trying to gain access.

spooler Software that accepts documents sent by a user to be printed, and then stores those documents and sends them, one by one, to available printer(s). *See also* spooling.

spooling A process on a server in which print documents are stored on a disk until a printing device is ready to process them. A spooler accepts each document from each client, stores it, then sends it to a printing device when it is ready.

SQL Acronym for structured query language, a database programming language used for accessing, querying, and otherwise managing information in a relational database system.

SSL *See* Secure Sockets Layer.

stabilize During subdirectory replication, when a subdirectory is stabilized, the export server waits two minutes after changes before exporting the subdirectory. The waiting period allows time for subsequent changes to take place so that all intended changes are recorded before being replicated. *See also* directory replication; export server; subtree.

stand-alone server *See* member server.

static mapping A method provided on a WINS server to assign a static (unchanging) IP address to a client.

static object Information that has been pasted into a document. Unlike embedded or linked objects, static objects cannot be changed from within the document. The only way you can change a static object is to delete it from the document, change it in the application used to create it, and paste it into the document again. *See also* embedded object; linked object.

static routing Static routing limits you to fixed routing tables, as opposed to dynamically updating the routing tables. *See also* dynamic routing; routing table.

static web pages Standard web pages that are created in advance and stored for later delivery to clients. *See also* dynamic web pages.

status bar A line of information related to the application in the window. Usually located at the bottom of a window. Not all windows have a status bar.

STATUS message A message displayed by the Executive in a Windows-mode message box when the Executive detects a condition within a process that you should know about.

STATUS messages can be divided into three types:

System-information messages. Just read the information in the message box and click **OK**. The Kernel continues running the process or thread.

Warning messages. Some advise you to take an action that will enable the Kernel to keep running the process or thread. Others warn you that, although the process or thread will continue running, the results might be incorrect.

Application-termination messages. These warn you that the Kernel is about to terminate either a process or a thread.

See also Executive messages; STOP message.

STOP message   A character-mode message that occurs when the Kernel detects an inconsistent condition from which it cannot recover. Always displayed on a full character-mode screen, uniquely identified by a hexadecimal number and a symbolic string. The content of the symbolic string can suggest, to a trained technician, the part of the Kernel that detected the condition from which there was no recourse but to stop. However, the cause may actually be in another part of the system. *See also* Executive messages; STATUS message.

string   A data structure composed of a sequence of characters, usually representing human-readable text.

stripe set   Refers to the saving of data across identical partitions on different drives. A stripe set does not provide fault tolerance; however stripe sets with parity do. *See also* fault tolerance; partition; stripe sets with parity.

stripe sets with parity   A method of data protection in which data is striped in large blocks across all the disks in an array. Data redundancy is provided by the parity information. This method provides fault tolerance. *See also* fault tolerance; stripe set.

subdirectory   A directory within a directory. Also called a folder within a folder.

subkey   A key within a key. Subkeys are analogous to subdirectories in the Registry hierarchy. Keys and subkeys are similar to the section heading in .ini files; however subkeys can carry out functions. *See also* key; Registry.

subnet   A portion of a network, which may be a physically independent network segment, that shares a network address with other portions of the network and is distinguished by a subnet number. A subnet is to a network what a network is to an internet.

subnet mask   A 32-bit value that allows the recipient of IP packets to distinguish the network ID portion of the IP address from the host ID. *See also* IP address; packet.

substitution macros   Placeholders that are replaced in command strings.

subtree   During directory replication, this refers to the export subdirectory and all of its subdirectories. *See also* directory replication.

swap file   *See* paging file.

switched circuit   *See* dial-up line.

SYN attack   SYN (synchronizing character) messages maliciously generated by an intruder in an attempt to block legitimate access to a server by proliferating half-open TCP port connections. Also called SYN flooding.

synchronize   To replicate the domain database from the primary domain controller (PDC) to one backup domain controller (BDC) of the domain, or to all the BDCs of a domain. This is usually performed automatically by the system, but can also be invoked manually by an administrator. *See also* backup domain controller (BDC); domain; primary domain controller (PDC).

syntax   The order in which you must type a command and the elements that follow the command. Windows NT commands have up to four elements: command name, parameters, switches, and values.

system access control list (SACL)
The system ACL is controlled by the system administrator, and allows system-level security to be associated with an object. SACL APIs can be used only by a process with System Administrator privileges. *See also* discretionary access control list (DACL).

system default profile   In Windows NT Server, the user profile that is loaded when Windows NT is running and no user is logged on. When the **Begin Logon** dialog box is visible, the system default profile is loaded. *See also* user default profile, user profile.

system disk   A disk that contains the MS-DOS system files necessary to start MS-DOS.

system log   The system log contains events logged by the Windows NT components. For example, the failure of a driver or other system component to load during startup is recorded in the system log. Use Event Viewer to view the system log.

System Network Architecture (SNA)
System Network Architecture is a communications framework developed by IBM. Microsoft System Network Architecture (SNA) is an optional solution that provides a gateway connection between personal computer LANs or WANs and IBM mainframe and AS/400 hosts. *See also* AS/400; gateway.

system partition   The volume that has the hardware-specific files needed to load Windows NT. *See also* partition.

system policy   A policy, created by using the System Policy Editor, to control user work environments and actions, and to enforce system configuration for Windows 95. System policy can be implemented for specific users, groups, computers, or for all users. System policy for users overwrites settings in the current user area of the Registry, and system policy for computers overwrites the current local machine area of the Registry. *See also* Registry.

systemroot   The name of the directory that contains Windows NT files. The name of this directory is specified when Windows NT is installed.

Systems Management Server   Part of the Windows NT BackOffice™ suite. Systems Management Server includes desktop management and software distribution that significantly automates the task of upgrading software on client computers.

T

T1 or T3 connection   Standard measurement of network bandwidth.

tag file   A configuration file that contains information about a corresponding file on a Gopher server or links to other servers. This information is sent to clients in response to a Gopher request.

tape set   A tape set (sometimes referred to as a tape family) in Windows NT Backup is a sequence of tapes in which each tape is a continuation of the backup on the previous tape. *See also* backup set; backup types.

TAPI   *See* Telephony API.

Task list   A window that shows all running applications and their status. View the Task list in the **Applications** tab in Task Manager.

Task Manager Task Manager enables you to start, end, or run applications, end processes (an application, application component, or system process), and view CPU and memory use data. Task Manager gives you a simple, quick view of how each process (application or service) is using CPU and memory resources. (Note: In previous versions of Windows NT, Task List handled some of these functions).

To run Task Manager, right-click the toolbar and then click Task Manager.

TCP *See* Transmission Control Protocol.

TCP/IP *See* Transmission Control Protocol/Internet Protocol.

TCP/IP keep-alives An optimizing feature of the TCP/IP service. TCP/IP periodically broadcasts messages to determine whether an idle connection is still active. *See also* HTTP keep-alives.

TDI *See* transport driver interface.

Telephony API (TAPI) An API used by programs to make data/fax/voice calls, including HyperTerminal, Dial-up Networking, Phone Dialer, and other Win32 communications applications written for Windows NT.

Telnet (VTP) A terminal emulation protocol for logging on to remote computers. Once referred to as Virtual Terminal Protocol (VTP). Defined in RFC 854, among others.

template accounts Accounts that are not actually used by real users but serve as a basis for the real accounts (for administrative purposes).

terminate-and-stay-resident program (TSR) A program running under MS-DOS that remains loaded in memory even when it is not running so that it can be quickly invoked for a specific task performed while any other application is operating.

text box In a dialog box, a box in which you type information needed to carry out a command. The text box may be blank or may contain text when the dialog box opens.

text file A file containing text characters (letters, numbers, and symbols) but no formatting information. A text file can be a "plain" ASCII file that most computers can read. Text file can also refer to a word-processing file. *See also* ASCII file.

text-file transfer A method for transferring files from HyperTerminal to a remote computer. With this method, files are transferred as ASCII files with minimal formatting characters, such as linefeeds and carriage returns. All font-formatting information is removed. *See also* ASCII file.

text-only An ASCII file that contains no formatting. *See also* ASCII file.

TFTP *See* Trivial File Transfer Protocol.

thread Threads are objects within processes that run program instructions. They allow concurrent operations within a process and enable one process to run different parts of its program on different processors simultaneously.

throughput *See* bandwidth.

time-out If a device is not performing a task, the amount of time the computer should wait before detecting it as an error.

time slice The amount of processor time allocated to an application, usually measured in milliseconds.

title bar The horizontal bar (at the top of a window) that contains the title of the window or dialog box. On many windows, the title bar also contains the program icon and the **Maximize, Minimize,** and **Close** buttons.

Token Ring A type of network media that connects clients in a closed ring and uses token passing to enable clients to use the network. *See also* Fiber Distributed Data Interface (FDDI); LocalTalk.

toolbar A series of icons or shortcut buttons providing quick access to commands. Usually located directly below the menu bar. Not all windows have a toolbar.

topic Information in the Help window. A Help topic usually begins with a title and contains information about a particular task, command, or dialog box.

transforms Rules the administrator creates to add, remove, and modify domain names appended to inbound and outbound messages.

Transmission Control Protocol (TCP)
A connection-based Internet protocol responsible for breaking data into packets, which the IP protocol sends over the network. This protocol provides a reliable, sequenced communication stream for network communication. *See also* Internet Protocol (IP); packet.

Transmission Control Protocol/Internet Protocol (TCP/IP)
A set of networking protocols that provide communications across interconnected networks made up of computers with diverse hardware architectures and various operating systems. TCP/IP includes standards for how computers communicate and conventions for connecting networks and routing traffic.

transport driver interface (TDI) In Windows networking, the common interface for network components that communicate at the Session layer.

trap In SNMP, a discrete block of data that indicates that the request failed authentication. The SNMP service can send a trap when it receives a request for information that does not contain the correct community name and that does not match an accepted host name for the service. Trap destinations are the names or IP addresses of hosts to which the SNMP service is to send traps with community names. *See also* IP address; Simple Network Management Protocol (SNMP).

trigger A set of conditions that, when met, initiate an action. For example, before using Network Monitor to capture data from the network, you can set a trigger to stop the capture or to execute a program or command file.

Trivial File Transfer Protocol (TFTP)
A file transfer protocol that transfers files to and from a remote computer running the TFTP service. TFTP was designed with less functions than FTP. Defined in RFC 1350, among others. *See also* file transfer protocol (FTP).

Trojan horse A program that masquerades as another common program in an attempt to receive information. An example of a Trojan horse is a program that masquerades as a system logon to retrieve user names and password information, which the writers of the Trojan horse can use later to break into the system.

TrueType fonts Fonts that are scalable and sometimes generated as bitmaps or soft fonts, depending on the capabilities of your printer. TrueType fonts can be sized to any height, and they print exactly as they appear on the screen.

trust *See* trust relationship.

trust relationship   A link between domains that enables pass-through authentication, in which a trusting domain honors the logon authentications of a trusted domain. With trust relationships, a user who has only one user account in one domain can potentially access the entire network. User accounts and global groups defined in a trusted domain can be given rights and resource permissions in a trusting domain, even though those accounts do not exist in the trusting domain's directory database. *See also* directory database; global group; pass-through authentication; user account.

trust relationships policy   A security policy that determines which domains are trusted and which domains are trusting domains. *See also* trust relationship.

TSR   *See* terminate-and-stay-resident program.

two-way trust relationship   Each domain trusts user accounts in the other domain to use its resources. Users can log on from computers in either domain to the domain that contains their account. *See also* trust relationship.

type   *See* file type.

Type 1 fonts   Scalable fonts designed to work with PostScript devices. *See also* font; font types; PostScript printer.

U

UAM   *See* user authentication module.

UDP   *See* User Datagram Protocol.

unavailable   An unavailable button or command is displayed in light gray instead of black, and it cannot be clicked.

UNC name   *See* universal naming convention name.

unicast datagram   An IP datagram sent to one host. *See also* broadcast datagram; Internet Protocol (IP); multicast datagram.

Unicode   A fixed-width, 16-bit character-encoding standard capable of representing the letters and characters of virtually all the world's languages. Unicode was developed by a consortium of U.S. computer companies.

Uniform Resource Locator (URL)
A naming convention that uniquely identifies the location of a computer, directory, or file on the Internet. The URL also specifies the appropriate Internet protocol, such as HTTP, FTP, IRC, or Gopher.

uninterruptible power supply (UPS)
A battery-operated power supply connected to a computer to keep the system running during a power failure.

universally unique identifier (UUID)
A unique identification string associated with the remote procedure call interface. Also known as a globally unique identifier (GUID).

universal naming convention (UNC) name
A full Windows NT name of a resource on a network. It conforms to the *\\Servername\Sharename* syntax, where *Servername* is the server's name and *Sharename* is the name of the shared resource. UNC names of directories or files can also include the directory path under the share name, with the following syntax:
\\Servername\Sharename\Directory\Filename.

UPS   *See* uninterruptible power supply.

UPS service   Manages an uninterruptible power supply connected to a computer. *See also* uninterruptible power supply (UPS).

URL   *See* Uniform Resource Locator.

user account Consists of all the information that defines a user to Windows NT. This includes such things as the user name and password required for the user to log on, the groups in which the user account has membership, and the rights and permissions the user has for using the system and accessing its resources. For Windows NT Workstation, user accounts are managed with User Manager. For Windows NT Server, user accounts are managed with User Manager for Domains. *See also* group.

user account database *See* directory database.

user authentication module Software component that prompts clients for their user names and passwords. *See also* clear-text passwords.

User Datagram Protocol (UDP) A TCP complement that offers a connectionless datagram service that guarantees neither delivery nor correct sequencing of delivered packets (much like IP). *See also* datagram; Internet Protocol (IP); packet.

user default profile In Windows NT Server, the user profile that is loaded by a server when a user's assigned profile cannot be accessed for any reason; when a user without an assigned profile logs on to the computer for the first time; or when a user logs on to the Guest account. *See also* system default profile; user profile.

User Manager A Windows NT Workstation tool used to manage the security for a workstation. User Manager administers user accounts, groups, and security policies.

User Manager for Domains A Windows NT Server tool used to manage security for a domain or an individual computer. User Manager for Domains administers user accounts, groups, and security policies.

user name A unique name identifying a user account to Windows NT. An account's user name cannot be identical to any other group name or user name of its own domain or workgroup. *See also* user account.

user password The password stored in each user's account. Each user generally has a unique user password and must type that password when logging on or accessing a server. *See also* password; volume password.

User privilege One of three privilege levels you can assign to a Windows NT user account. Every user account has one of the three privilege levels (Administrator, Guest, and User). Accounts with User privilege are regular users of the network; most accounts on your network probably have User privilege. *See also* Administrator privilege; Guest privilege; user account.

user profile Configuration information that can be retained on a user-by-user basis, and is saved in user profiles. This information includes all the per-user settings of the Windows NT environment, such as the desktop arrangement, personal program groups and the program items in those groups, screen colors, screen savers, network connections, printer connections, mouse settings, window size and position. When a user logs on, the user's profile is loaded and the user's Windows NT environment is configured according to that profile. *See also* personal group; program item.

user rights Define a user's access to a computer or domain and the actions that a user can perform on the computer or domain. User rights permit actions such as logging onto a computer or network, adding or deleting users in a workstation or domain, and so forth.

user rights policy Manages the assignment of rights to groups and user accounts. *See also* user account; user rights.

users In the Macintosh environment, a special group that contains all users who have user permissions on the server. When a Macintosh user assigns permissions to everyone, those permissions are given to the groups users and guests. *See also* guest.

UUENCODE (UNIX-to-UNIX Encode)
A utility that converts a binary file (such as a word-processing file or a program) to text so that it can be transmitted over a network. UUDECODE (UNIX-to-UNIX Decode) is the utility used to convert the file back to its original state.

UUID *See* universally unique identifier.

V

value entry The string of data that appears in the right pane of a Registry editor window and that defines the value of the currently selected key. A value entry has three parts: name, data type, and the value itself. *See also* key; subkey.

Van Jacobsen header compression
A TCP/IP network layer compression technique, VJ compression reduces the size of IP and TCP headers. *See also* Internet Protocol (IP); Transmission Control Protocol (TCP); Transmission Control Protocol/ Internet Protocol (TCP/IP).

variables In programming, a variable is a named storage location capable of containing a certain type of data that can be modified during program execution. System environment variables are defined by Windows NT Server and are the same no matter who is logged on at the computer. (Administrator group members can add new variables or change the values, however.) User environment variables can be different for each user of a particular computer. They include any environment variables you want to define of variables defined by your applications, such as the path where application files are located.

VDD *See* virtual device driver.

VDM *See* virtual DOS machine.

verify operation Occurs after all files are backed up or restored, if specified. A verify operation compares files on disk to files that have been written to tape. *See also* backup types.

virtual device driver (VDD) A driver that enables MS-DOS–based and 16-bit Windows–based applications to run on Windows NT.

virtual directory An Internet Information Server directory outside the home directory. A virtual directory appears to browsers as a subdirectory of the home directory.

virtual DOS machine (VDM) Simulates an MS-DOS environment so that MS-DOS–based and Windows-based applications can run on Windows NT.

virtual memory The space on your hard disk that Windows NT uses as if it were actually memory. Windows NT does this through the use of paging files. The benefit of using virtual memory is that you can run more applications at one time than your system's physical memory would otherwise allow. The drawbacks are the disk space required for the virtual-memory paging file and the decreased execution speed when paging is required. *See also* paging file.

virtual printer memory In a PostScript printer, a part of memory that stores font information. The memory in PostScript printers is divided into two areas: banded memory and virtual memory. The banded memory contains graphics and page-layout information needed to print your documents. The virtual memory contains any font information that is sent to your printer either when you print a document or when you download fonts. *See also* font types; PostScript printer.

virtual private network (VPN)
A remote LAN that can be accessed through the Internet by using the new PPTP. *See also* Point-to-Point Tunneling Protocol (PPTP).

virtual server
A computer with several IP addresses assigned to the network adapter card. This configuration makes the computer look like several servers to a browser.

virus A program that attempts to spread from computer to computer and either cause damage (by erasing or corrupting data) or annoy users (by printing messages or altering what is displayed on the screen).

volume A partition or collection of partitions that have been formatted for use by a file system. *See also* Macintosh-accessible volume; partition.

volume password An optional, case-sensitive password you can assign to a Macintosh-accessible volume when you configure the volume. To access the volume, a user must type the volume password. *See also* Macintosh-accessible volume; user password.

volume set A combination of partitions on a physical disk that appear as one logical drive. *See also* logical drive; partition.

VPN *See* virtual private network.

VTP Acronym for Virtual Terminal Protocol. *See* Telnet.

W

WAIS *See* wide area information server.

wallpaper A picture or drawing stored as a bitmap file (a file that has a .bmp extension).

WAN *See* wide area network.

warning beep The sound that your computer makes when you encounter an error or try to perform a task that Windows NT does not recognize.

WCAT Microsoft Web Capacity Analysis Tool. A script-driven utility that tests your client/server configuration by using a variety of predetermined, invariant workloads. WCAT can test how your server responds to different workloads or test the same workload on varying configurations of the server. WCAT is included on the *Windows NT Resource Kit Supplement 1* CD.

Web browser A software program, such as Internet Explorer, that retrieves a document from a Web server, interprets the HTML codes, and displays the document to the user with as much graphical content as the software can supply.

Web server A computer equipped with the server software to respond to HTTP requests, such as requests from a Web browser. A Web server uses the HTTP protocol to communicate with clients on a TCP/IP network.

Well Known Port Number The standard port numbers used by the Internet community for well known (commonly used) services. Ports are used in TCP to name the ends of logical connections that carry long-term conversations. Well known services are defined by RFC 1060. The relationship between the well known services and the well known ports is described in RFC 1340.

wide area information server (WAIS)
A network publishing system designed to help users find information over a computer network. WAIS software has four main components: the client, the server, the database, and the protocol. Discussed in RFC 1625.

wide area network (WAN) A communications network that connects geographically separated areas.

wildcard A character that represents one or more characters. The question mark (?) wildcard can be used to represent any single character, and the asterisk (*) wildcard can be used to represent any character or group of characters that might match that position in other filenames.

window A rectangular area on your screen in which you view an application or document. You can open, close, and move windows, and change the size of most windows. You can open several windows at a time, and you can often reduce a window to an icon or enlarge it to fill the entire desktop.

window menu A menu that contains commands you can use to manipulate a window. You click the program icon or document icon at the left of the title bar to open the window menu.

Windows Internet Name Service (WINS)
A name resolution service that resolves Windows networking computer names to IP addresses in a routed environment. A WINS server handles name registrations, queries, and releases. *See also* IP address; routing.

Windows NT–based application Used as a shorthand term to refer to an application that is designed to run with Windows NT and does not run without Windows NT. All Windows NT–based applications follow similar conventions for arrangement of menus, style of dialog boxes, and keyboard and mouse use.

Windows NT browser system Consists of a master browser, backup browser, and client systems. The master browser maintains the browse list—of all the available domains and servers—and periodically sends copies to the backup browsers. *See also* browse; master browser.

Windows NT Explorer A program that enables you to view and manage the files and folders on your computer and make network connections to other shared resources, such as a hard disk on a server. Windows NT Explorer replaces Program Manager and File Manager, which were programs available in earlier versions of Windows NT. Program Manager and File Manager are still available, and can be started in the same way you start other Windows-based programs.

Windows NT file system (NTFS) An advanced file system designed for use specifically within the Windows NT operating system. It supports file system recovery, extremely large storage media, long filenames, and various features for the POSIX subsystem. It also supports object-oriented applications by treating all files as objects with user-defined and system-defined attributes. *See also* POSIX.

Windows NT Server A superset of Windows NT Workstation, Windows NT Server provides centralized management and security, fault tolerance, and additional connectivity. *See also* fault tolerance; Windows NT Workstation.

Windows NT Server Directory Services
A Windows NT protected subsystem that maintains the directory database and provides an application programming interface (API) for accessing the database. *See also* application programming interface (API); directory database.

Windows NT Server Services for Macintosh
A software component of Windows NT Server that allows Macintosh users access to the computer running Windows NT Server. The services provided with this component allow PC and Macintosh users to share files and resources, such as printers on the AppleTalk network or those attached to the Windows NT Server. *See also* File Server for Macintosh service; Print Server for Macintosh.

Windows NT Workstation The portable, secure, 32-bit, preemptive multitasking member of the Microsoft Windows operating system family.

Windows Open Services Architecture (WOSA)
An open set of APIs for integrating Windows-based computers with back-end services on a broad range of vendor's systems. WOSA consists of an extensible set of APIs that enable Windows-based desktop applications to access available information without having to know anything about the type of network in use, the types of computers in the enterprise, or types of back-end services available. As a result, if the network computers or services change, the desktop applications built by using WOSA will not require rewriting. *See also* application programming interface (API).

Windows Sockets *See* Sockets.

WINS *See* Windows Internet Name Service.

workgroup For Windows NT, a workgroup is a collection of computers that are grouped for viewing purposes. Each workgroup is identified by a unique name. *See also* domain.

working set Every program running can use a portion of physical memory, its working set, which is the current number of physical memory bytes used by or allocated by a process.

workstation Any networked Macintosh or PC using server resources. *See also* backup domain controller (BDC); member server; primary domain controller (PDC).

Workstation service Provides network connections and communications.

World Wide Web (WWW) The software, protocols, conventions, and information that enable hypertext and multimedia publishing of resources on different computers around the world. *See also* Hypertext Markup Language (HTML); Internet.

WOSA *See* Windows Open Services Architecture.

WOW Acronym for Win16 on Win32. The translation of Windows 3.1-based application calls to standard mode for RISC-based computers and 386 enhanced mode for *x*86-based computers.

wrap To continue to the next line rather than stopping when the cursor reaches the end of the current line.

X

X.25 A recommendation published by the Comite Consultatif International de Telegraphique et Telephonique (CCITT) international communications standards organization that defines the connection between a terminal and a packet-switching network. An X.25 network is a type of packet-switching network that routes units of information (packets) as specified by X.25 and is used in public data communications networks. *See also* packet.

X.25 smart card A hardware card with a PAD (packet assembler/disassembler) embedded in it. *See also* packet assembler/disassembler (PAD); X.25.

X.400 system A messaging system that is compliant with the X.400 standards developed under the CCITT and the International Standards Organization (ISO).

XModem/CRC Protocol for transmitting binary files that uses a cyclic redundancy check (CRC) to detect any transmission errors. Both computers must be set to transmit and receive eight data bits per character.

XOR Short for exclusive OR. A Boolean operation in which the Windows NT Server stripe-sets-with-parity form of fault tolerance maintains an XOR of the total data to provide data redundancy. This enables the reconstruction of missing data (on a failed disk or sector) from the remaining disks in the stripe set with parity. *See also* fault tolerance; stripe sets with parity.

Z

zone In the Macintosh environment, a zone is a logical grouping that simplifies browsing the network for resources, such as servers and printers. It is similar to a domain in Windows NT Server networking.

In a DNS (Domain Name System) database, a zone is a subtree of the DNS database that is administered as a single separate entity, a DNS name server. This administrative unit can consist of a single domain or a domain with subdomains. A DNS zone administrator sets up one or more name servers for the zone. *See also* domain; Domain Name System (DNS).

zone data file A Domain Name System database for a zone in the DNS name space.

zone list In the Macintosh environment, a zone list includes all the zones associated with a particular network. Not to be confused with Windows NT DNS zones.

Index

Welcome to the
administrator's
survival kit *for*
Microsoft®
Office 97.

MICROSOFT® PROFESSIONAL EDITIONS

The Technical
Resource for
Installing, Compiling,
and Supporting
Microsoft Office 97

Microsoft®
Office 97
ResourceKit

Technical Information and Tools
for the Support Professional

Microsoft Press

U.S.A.	**$59.99**
U.K.	£56.49 [V.A.T. included]
Canada	$80.99
ISBN	1-57231-329-3

If you're an administrator or an IS professional, this book was written for you. Here you'll find the hands-on, in-depth information you need to roll out, support, and get the most from Microsoft Office 97 throughout your organization.

For systems running Microsoft Windows® 95 and Microsoft Windows NT® 3.51 and 4.0, this book covers it all—updating from earlier versions of Microsoft Office, switching from other applications such as Lotus 1-2-3 and WordPerfect, and coexistence among different versions of Microsoft Office. Of course, you get full information on network installation, plus the timesaving Network Installation Wizard on the companion CD-ROM. And like all the tools and utilities on the CD-ROM, this wizard is a tested, supported application designed to make your job easier.

No other volume is so packed with authoritative information, straight from the insiders who actually developed Microsoft Office 97. And you can easily update all of this information through the Microsoft Office Resource Kit site on the World Wide Web. Get the MICROSOFT OFFICE 97 RESOURCE KIT. And help your organization get the most from the newest version of the world's most popular office suite.

Microsoft Press® products are available worldwide wherever quality computer books are sold. For more information, contact your book retailer, computer reseller, or local Microsoft Sales Office.

To locate your nearest source for Microsoft Press products, reach us at www.microsoft.com/mspress/, or call 1-800-MSPRESS in the U.S. (in Canada: 1-800-667-1115 or 416-293-8464).

To order Microsoft Press products, call 1-800-MSPRESS in the U.S. (in Canada: 1-800-667-1115 or 416-293-8464).

Prices and availability dates are subject to change.

Microsoft Press

Support training for
Microsoft®
Windows NT® version 4.0.

Here's **everything** you need.

Even if you have no previous training on Windows NT, this kit provides everything you need to train yourself at your own pace. In fact, here's all the preparation you need for taking—and passing—the Microsoft Certified Professional exams. You'll learn how to install, configure, optimize, troubleshoot, and integrate networks running Microsoft Windows NT 3.51—and then supplement that material to do likewise for Microsoft Windows NT version 4.0. Wherever people want Microsoft Windows NT, they want people with these important skills. And you can get them with MICROSOFT WINDOWS NT 3.51 TRAINING PLUS VERSION 4.0 UPGRADE TRAINING.

U.S.A.	**$249.99**
Canada	$344.99

ISBN 1-57231-544-X

Microsoft Press® products are available worldwide wherever quality computer books are sold. For more information, contact your book retailer, computer reseller, or local Microsoft Sales Office.

To locate your nearest source for Microsoft Press products, reach us at www.microsoft.com/mspress/, or call 1-800-MSPRESS in the U.S. (in Canada: 1-800-667-1115 or 416-293-8464).

To order Microsoft Press products, call 1-800-MSPRESS in the U.S. (in Canada: 1-800-667-1115 or 416-293-8464).

Prices and availability dates are subject to change.

Microsoft®Press

The *ultimate* companion to
Microsoft®
BackOffice™

Microsoft
BackOffice
Resource Kit
Part One: Microsoft Exhange Server
and Microsoft Systems Management Server

Microsoft Press

U.S.A. **$79.95**
Canada $107.95
ISBN 1-55615-932-3

Written in cooperation with the Microsoft BackOffice development team, this is Part One of the MICROSOFT BACKOFFICE RESOURCE KIT—the essential resource for computer professionals working with Microsoft BackOffice. With two volumes and a CD-ROM full of useful tools, Part One covers Microsoft Exchange Server and Microsoft Systems Management Server. Part Two of the kit will update this information and cover other parts of Microsoft BackOffice. But don't wait. Build with Microsoft BackOffice and start building your resource library right now. Pick up Part One of the MICROSOFT BACKOFFICE RESOURCE KIT.

Microsoft Press® products are available worldwide wherever quality computer books are sold. For more information, contact your book retailer, computer reseller, or local Microsoft Sales Office.

To locate your nearest source for Microsoft Press products, reach us at www.microsoft.com/mspress/, or call 1-800-MSPRESS in the U.S. (in Canada: 1-800-667-1115 or 416-293-8464).

To order Microsoft Press products, call 1-800-MSPRESS in the U.S. (in Canada: 1-800-667-1115 or 416-293-8464).

Prices and availability dates are subject to change.

Microsoft Press

The *ultimate* companion to Microsoft® **Windows NT® Workstation**
version 4.0

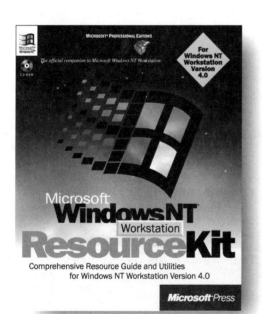

This exclusive Microsoft kit, written in cooperation with the Microsoft Windows NT Workstation development team, provides the complete technical information and tools you need to understand and get the most out of Microsoft Windows NT Workstation version 4.0. The comprehensive technical guide and a CD-ROM containing more than 100 useful tools help you take full advantage of the power of Microsoft Windows NT Workstation version 4.0. Administrators will especially like the section that describes strategies for deployment in large organizations and compatibility with other network and operating systems. Get the MICROSOFT WINDOWS NT WORKSTATION 4.0 RESOURCE KIT—and get *the* essential reference for installing, configuring, and troubleshooting Microsoft pWindows NT Workstation version 4.0.

U.S.A.   **$69.95**
U.K.   £64.99 [V.A.T. included]
Canada $94.95
ISBN 1-57231-343-9

Microsoft®*Press*

Microsoft Press® products are available worldwide wherever quality computer books are sold. For more information, contact your book retailer, computer reseller, or local Microsoft Sales Office.

To locate your nearest source for Microsoft Press products, reach us at www.microsoft.com/mspress/, or call 1-800-MSPRESS in the U.S. (in Canada: 1-800-667-1115 or 416-293-8464).

To order Microsoft Press products, call 1-800-MSPRESS in the U.S. (in Canada: 1-800-667-1115 or 416-293-8464).

Prices and availability dates are subject to change.

IMPORTANT—READ CAREFULLY BEFORE OPENING SOFTWARE PACKET(S). By opening the sealed packet(s) containing the software, you indicate your acceptance of the following Microsoft License Agreement.

MICROSOFT LICENSE AGREEMENT

(Resource Kit Companion Disks)

This is a legal agreement between you (either an individual or an entity) and Microsoft Corporation. By opening the sealed software packet(s) you are agreeing to be bound by the terms of this agreement. If you do not agree to the terms of this agreement, promptly return the unopened software packet(s) and any accompanying written materials to the place you obtained them for a full refund.

MICROSOFT SOFTWARE LICENSE

1.   GRANT OF LICENSE. Microsoft grants to you the right to install and use copies of the Microsoft software program included with this book (the "SOFTWARE") on computers you own. The SOFTWARE is in "use" on a computer when it is loaded into temporary memory (i.e., RAM) or installed into permanent memory (e.g., hard disk, CD-ROM, or other storage device) of that computer.

2.   COPYRIGHT. The SOFTWARE is owned by Microsoft or its suppliers and is protected by United States copyright laws and international treaty provisions. Therefore, you must treat the SOFTWARE like any other copyrighted material (e.g., a book or musical recording). You may not copy the written materials accompanying the SOFTWARE.

3.   OTHER RESTRICTIONS. You may not rent or lease the SOFTWARE, but you may transfer the SOFTWARE and accompanying written materials on a permanent basis provided you retain no copies and the recipient agrees to the terms of this Agreement. Except in cases of a permanent transfer, you may not redistribute any portion of the SOFTWARE without the prior written approval of Microsoft. You may not reverse engineer, decompile, or disassemble the SOFTWARE. If the software is an update or has been updated, any transfer must include the most recent update and all prior versions.

DISCLAIMER OF WARRANTY

The SOFTWARE (including instructions for its use) is provided "AS IS" WITHOUT WARRANTY OF ANY KIND. MICROSOFT FURTHER DISCLAIMS ALL IMPLIED WARRANTIES INCLUDING WITHOUT LIMITATION ANY IMPLIED WARRANTIES OF MERCHANTABILITY OR OF FITNESS FOR A PARTICULAR PURPOSE OR AGAINST INFRINGEMENT. THE ENTIRE RISK ARISING OUT OF THE USE OR PERFORMANCE OF THE SOFTWARE AND DOCUMENTATION REMAINS WITH YOU.

IN NO EVENT SHALL MICROSOFT, ITS AUTHORS, OR ANYONE ELSE INVOLVED IN THE CREATION, PRODUCTION, OR DELIVERY OF THE SOFTWARE BE LIABLE FOR ANY DAMAGES WHATSOEVER (INCLUDING, WITHOUT LIMITATION, DAMAGES FOR LOSS OF BUSINESS PROFITS, BUSINESS INTERRUPTION, LOSS OF BUSINESS INFORMATION, OR OTHER PECUNIARY LOSS) ARISING OUT OF THE USE OF OR INABILITY TO USE THE SOFTWARE OR DOCUMENTATION, EVEN IF MICROSOFT HAS BEEN ADVISED OF THE POSSIBILITY OF SUCH DAMAGES. BECAUSE SOME STATES/COUNTRIES DO NOT ALLOW THE EXCLUSION OR LIMITATION OF LIABILITY FOR CONSEQUENTIAL OR INCIDENTAL DAMAGES, THE ABOVE LIMITATION MAY NOT APPLY TO YOU.

U.S. GOVERNMENT RESTRICTED RIGHTS

The SOFTWARE and documentation are provided with RESTRICTED RIGHTS. Use, duplication, or disclosure by the Government is subject to restrictions as set forth in subparagraphs (c)(1)(ii) of The Rights in Technical Data and Computer Software clause at DFARS 252.227-7013 or subparagraphs (c)(1) and (2) of the Commercial Computer Software — Restricted Rights 48 CFR 52.227-19, as applicable. Manufacturer is Microsoft Corporation/One Microsoft Way/Redmond, WA 98052-6399.

If you acquired this product in the United States, this Agreement is governed by the laws of the State of Washington.

Should you have any questions concerning this Agreement, or if you desire to contact Microsoft Press for any reason, please write: Microsoft Press/One Microsoft Way/Redmond, WA 98052-6399.

05/06/96   32100017.DOC